DON'T QUIT
DON'T CRY

After 25,000 Weekends

DON'T QUIT
DON'T CRY

After 25,000 Weekends

JACQUES R. ROY

ARPress
ILLUMINATING IDEAS,
EMPOWERING VOICES

ARPress LLC
45 Dan Road Suite 5
Canton MA 02021
Hotline: 1(888) 821-0229
Fax: 1(508) 545-7580

Ordering Information:
Quantity sales. Special discounts are available on quantity purchases by corporations, associations, and others. For details, contact the publisher at the address above.

Printed in the United States of America.

ISBN-13:   Softcover   979-8-89330-475-6
           Hardcover   979-8-89330-477-0
           eBook   979-8-89330-476-3

Library of Congress Control Number: 2024901841

Contents

DEDICATION

This book is dedicated to the orphans of the Angola liberation struggle, and to the peasants in war-torn Angola who guided the liberation forces with food, a celestial view, knowledge of the terrain, and hope. To the MPLA, who extended an invitation to participate in the liberation struggle and to experience the political depth in a changing reality. To the ANC, in opening the unknown world of intelligence gathering.

ACKNOWLEDGMENTS

I extend my profound gratitude to the following people.

Dr. Agostinho Neto offered friendship and a life-changing experience in the struggle for the liberation of Angola. Chris Hani and Thabo Mbeki of the ANC entrusted us with two missions into apartheid- controlled South Africa.

My parents, Bernard and Cécile Roy (née Morrissette), encouraged self-determination and were there to support me in times of crisis. I saw the strain in their faces when I was very ill and their joy when Angola achieved liberation. My brother Claude and his wife Beverly gave generous financial support; my brother André joined the MPLA.

In 1968, a group of students at Simon Fraser University supported research for the liberation movements. Other West Coast friends from the 1960s include Larry Field, Jim Robson, the Kelahars, Dwight, and Liz. Professors Donald Barnett, Gerry Sperling, John O'Manique, and Rev. McDougal taught me intellectual persistence and clarity of thought. CUSO's Executive Director Frank Bogdasavich, Field Director Michael Sinclair, and Dennis and Hazel September were key supporters. SUCO's

Jean Pelletier created a support structure for the liberation movements of Southern Africa. Mike Flynn from Development and Peace, Rev. Garth Legge and Observer Editor Bob Plant at the United Church of Canada, and Rev. Tom Anthony of the Anglican Church stood out in their solidarity and hard work.

Pierre Rivard, Director of Oxfam Québec, took charge of organizing "Opération Angola" to mobilize public opinion and fundraising; support also came from Michel Blondin, Jacques Jobin, Jean Foisy-Marquis, Jean Pozatski, and Dominique Boisvert. Film support was provided by Jean Pierre Lefebvre, Michel Audi, Rock Demers, Jean-Pierre Masse, and Concordia's Dennis Murphy. Evan Godt was responsible for the daily operations of the African Relief Services Committee and political events. Clyde and Penny Sanger hosted many meetings related to Southern Africa. Special appreciation is owed to Sue Godt, Paul and Jean Godt, Peter Bunting, and Mary Jane Clark. And to Doug and Susann Anderson for their continued friendship.

Many, many Canadian citizens supported the Angola coffee boycott and the boycott of South African wine and Outspan oranges. The resulting victories demonstrated solidarity with the liberation process. The Canadian governments from 1960 onward were steadfast in their support for the independence of Southern Africa. In 1974, Dr. Neto addressed a parliamentary commission looking into support for the liberation movements.

I am grateful to John Stevens for editing this memoir, drawing from my diaries and refining and transforming previous drafts. In addition to creating a powerful electronic presentation for the 50th anniversary of the MPLA, James Austin is responsible for saving and compiling the historical paper records related to this book. I am grateful to Marvin Sheets for his friendship and an enjoyable collaboration in completing this book. Chris Broughton furnished invaluable technical support and is responsible for designing the cover and for putting this book in its final form.

Colleen provided loving care, patience, and humour. Much of my life is due to her trust.

You make a living from what you get;

you make a life from what you give.

—Winston Churchill

Hope is like a road in the country;

there was never a road, but when many people walk on it, the road comes into existence.

—Lin Yutang

PREFACE

When he left, the white man said, "Come on, Rusty, the boy is waiting to clean you."Dogs with names, men without.

—Es'kia Mpahhlele, Mrs. Ruth

had not yet voted when 1960 rolled around. I was seventeen years old, a high-school student, and a member of the student council. Pictures from Vietnam, and that memorable photo in *Time* of a US airplane circling over the hijacked Portuguese troop carrier off the coast of Angola, gave me the impression that something was wrong with the information I was being given.

This was my first taste of the contradiction in US media reporting. Something was happening in Africa to people who had suffered through slavery and colonization, and it seemed that, through a paucity of information, my hunger to know was not being fed.

Various (inspiring?) Catholic priests came to our Assumption parish church, and world events, measured against the Ten Commandments, stimulated more questions and confusion. Naturally, I attempted to synthesize all I was confronting, and I came to the unwelcome conclusion that, being white, I was part of the problem.

I learned that, in South Africa, voting was not for the majority, and marriage across "racial" lines was forbidden. There were whites-only beaches, whites-only buses, and on and on, a whole list of what I could only conclude was stupid, racist, almost incredible. Black people required a pass to move from the communities in which they slept to the communities in which they worked. How was this possible? The relationship of white and black was that of master and servant.

When I saw the opportunity to do something about this, I leapt at the chance. Somehow I found a role for myself in the liberation of

Southern Africa. Many tried to stop me, but the compelling personal stories of Nelson Mandela and Dr. Neto were not to be denied. I approached the Popular Movement for the Liberation of Angola (MPLA) and the African National Congress (ANC) wrapped in the protection of my white-Canadian identity, but it was my conviction that majority rule was essential and inevitable that gave me a chance to contribute.

The rewards were many. I learned the richness of African culture. The privilege of being an outsider, a white in nearly all-black jungle warfare, and an European intelligence officer for the ANC in South Africa gave me the opportunity to see, learn, and assist in my small way the birth of two nations. Neto, Hani, and Mbeki influenced my growing sense of myself as they saw me in what I was able and willing to contribute, whatever the personal cost. I knew the potential consequences. Mandela and his Robben Island comrades: What great men, examples of human endurance, an inspiration to all who continue the struggle for democratic rule.

What was important was how one lived, not whether one died. So many Africans, in such desperate conditions of constant hunger and disease, were great teachers; patient, humble, democratic to a fault, tenacious, and ultimately victorious.

This book tells of my political illiteracy and the education I received in friendship with those African leaders. Their personal struggles were so courageous, humble, educated, and fair, forcing me to recognize the lies of the Western media, the false arguments justifying beating up on peoples and nations who could not defend themselves, ridiculed to show the superiority of the West and justify the good fortune of the six percent of the world's population that lives in comfort, freedom, and safety.

What a unique lesson, embedded in the very process of history in the making: Do what you can; use what you have; don't quit.

This photo illustrated that I was also politically illiterate.

Time magazine—February 10, 1961

ARMALITE AR1 CAL. 7.62mm NATO issue, no. 006463, MFG. Nederlands and captured in Angola 1964.

Family Photos

Left to right: Dad, sister Huguette, brother Raymond, and Jacques at 91 Wishman, Kirkland Lake in 1948

Family photo from 1958

Legion hockey meeting at Mr. Lawless's house

At mom and dad's house; note the MPLA button.

CHAPTER ONE

To achieve greatness . . . start where you are, use what you have, do what you can.

—Arthur Ashe

Born in Kirkland Lake, a mining town in Northern Ontario, I grew up in a near-frontier environment, encountering a healthy dose of bigotry from within the support of a strong family.

My folks met in the late 1930s. My father had been asked to leave the family farm in Quebec; there were too many mouths to feed. He made his way to Willowbush, Saskatchewan, then to Northern Quebec, and finally to Kirkland Lake. My mother, the oldest of six siblings, was uprooted at the age of fifteen, moving from Buckingham, Quebec, to Kirkland Lake with her father, co-owner of Morrissette Diamond Drilling, who was doing business opening up the new mine shafts for the extraction of gold. My dad, a tall, strong, handsome man, was smart but semi-literate. Following a stint as a hard rock miner, he decided there had to be a better way, so he applied to train as an electrician. This served him well as he continued to learn and get better jobs, until his final working days as a handyman, electrician, and cook in a bunkhouse for a local lumber company. "They even pay me when I sleep," was Dad's favourite expression, as he stayed on-site during the holidays as watchman.

He was a kind man, who took care of his family, planning fishing trips and regular summer holidays to Ottawa and Quebec. We did not have a car, so for the summer holiday to Quebec, Dad rented the local taxi driver's idle vehicle. Our family doctor, Dr. LeBlanc, a native of Lévis, Quebec, knew my grandparents and in particular my grandfather's family. As a small-town doctor, he knew all our characters and medical needs. This small man spoke in clear and concise French, and was proud to be a French-speaking person. I liked that.

As for Mum, she kept the five kids—four boys and a daughter—in line, fed, and clothed. She acted as referee until Dad got home. She was a strong woman, fair, disciplined, with a great sense of humour. Mum could encourage us to go the extra distance, or she would draw the line— I think she invented "grounding." As soon as the youngest, André, was at school, she got a job at Kresge's.

Being personable, functionally bilingual, and a mother of teenagers, she was a prime candidate to manage the record department. My mother the disk jockey! Elvis, Patsy Cline—she knew 'em all.

Everyone knew Mrs. Roy, pronounced here with a Scottish accent, and therefore we not only had a popular mom, but a mom who got all the news about our "outside-the-house" behaviour.

My parents wanted to give us a Christian, French education, but none was available. The local parish paid school taxes to the public school board and the separate school board. So for the first eight years we went to school in French and perfected our English at the rinks and ball grounds.

We lived in the Federal district, at 91 Wishman Street, which was built by English-speaking builders under the supervision of my unilingual French-speaking Uncle Simon, who managed to bridge the language and cultural gap. Dad worked long hours at the Sylvanite gold mine as an electrician, and was often on call. This was okay in the summer, but in the cold, dark winter nights, it was daylight only from 7:30 a.m. to 4:00 p.m. Imagine waking at 5:30 a.m. to be dropped in the cage to the working level at 6:30 and to return to the surface at 3:00 p.m. This meant that, in the depth of the winter, from December to April, the only daylight he saw was the short hour of twilight left when he got back to the surface. And the other fathers did the same, spending most of their lives like groundhogs, taking gold out of the ground to be put in Fort Knox. To make sense of this seemed to require an adult mind.

Our neighbour, Mr. McKinnis, had working horses. Water for the house came from an outside tap up the street, shared by all the residents. We got downtown on the local bus; it was quite a distance from home. My older brother started out on the education trail two years before me, and the transportation problem was a major concern, so my parents resolved to buy a bigger house, closer to the bus route. They bought a duplex with an upper apartment on Grierson Road, and converted the bottom half into a single, large home. They rented the house on Wishman Street.

I was six when we moved and life was very happy. School, church, road hockey under the lights, and summer ball along with organized activities—fishing, the company-sponsored summer picnic, and the famous family picnic put on by the Moose Lodge. From an early age, I learned how to fix things with my dad, and enjoyed all the new techniques associated with maintenance. My father was a hard-working man, and when we got going at the Wishman apartments, he would forget about the time, and we would spend most of the day cleaning, repairing, and replacing storm windows with screens, and vice versa. These long working days were frustrating for me, as I was always hungry, and arriving at 9 a.m. and not leaving until four or five was a long haul without a break or a bite to eat. I did learn a valuable lesson—how to persevere. There was no quitting until the job was finished.

My best friend was Yvan Labonté. He did not like school, but developed talents for trapping and woodcarving, which made his life enjoyable. He lived on the other side of town, on Prince Street, a bus ride away.

In the Federal during the winter months, Mr. Benny and Danny MacDonald were responsible for making a skating rink at the Federal school. Despite the cold weather, the Federal rink provided a social setting for the English-speaking kids and their fellow hockey players. The most famous of these were the three Plager brothers, who grew into professionals, among the many who played and grew up before our eyes. They returned in the summer to play ball and work in the mines or lumberyards.

If the season ended early for the Toronto Maple Leafs, Dick Duff came home and played on the rink with the neophytes. I was impressed with his speed, skill, and incredible strength and stamina.

On Saturday mornings, we would arrive at the rink before eight and clean the ice. Some days the snowdrifts were beyond our capacity, and a snow thrower was needed. However, on normal days we were starved by one p.m. and our toes were numb. No feeling in our toes was not a good sign; as they unfroze, the whiteness turned to red, along with a burning sensation as Mom applied the folk remedy of plunging the frozen feet into cold water. In a week the frozen toes would peel like an onion, accompanied by a certain distinctive pain.

At age ten, I made the Federal bantam hockey team, and my new friends Doug Fritz, Bill Ball, and George Prime began to influence my learning. It was George's father, a WW II tank veteran, who piqued my curiosity about politics. The Nazis had been defeated, but I was learning how outrageous the repression had been under the SS, Gestapo, and other agents of the Third Reich. I could not understand the Nazi mindset. Canadians volunteered to stop this menace while, according to Mr. Prime, the USA took its time and the big battles were fought and won by the Canadians. This struck me as a little strange—the Canadians in the worst battles, before the Yankees.

So, going to George's house, especially around Christmas, ensured I would hear a new story from a vet's point of view. I was grateful for what he had done, as my family had not been directly involved. My dad had been required to work in the mine, as gold production was considered essential to a wartime economy.

In the summer, until I was twelve, I played ball. Our coaches were Ralph Backstrom of the Montreal Canadians and Dick Duff of the Toronto Maple Leafs. Summer was baseball, softball, soccer, and swimming at the supervised pool at the end of 4th Avenue, a good thirty-minute walk from home.

When I was twelve, my dad put in a word for me and I started a job at the Canada Dry soft drink plant. Mt first experience was as a helper on a truck. It was my first paid work. For five days, working from 7:30 a.m. to 6:00 p.m., I received twenty dollars minus the unemployment insurance premium, leaving $19.76 in the small envelope. I protested to the local government office that they were taking away twenty-four cents that I could never recover, because I would not qualify for unemployment benefits. Mr. Cowan, the office manager, responded that if I wanted to keep the job, I had to pay. This first lesson in inflexible government regulation was a tough one to accept.

By the second year, I was working in the plant, and I got into great physical condition lugging the heavy cases, weighing from twenty- two pounds up to fifty-five. Being a big kid, I was not harassed by many other kids, and I never went looking for trouble. If a situation did come up, then I would do what I had to, to ensure that it didn't happen again.

I finished Grade 8, and my parents sent me to a Catholic boys' school in Rouyn, fifty-five miles east of Kirkland Lake. The religious order had strict rules, and, combined with raging hormones, made for a very repressive environment. Hockey and basketball engaged me physically, and plenty of study, from French to English to Latin, kept my brain challenged as language skills developed. I learned leadership skills and organized a work crew. We were the first to get a good outside ice surface set up.

This was the first time I experienced the power of the church. Regulations were changed, imposed, and changed again during a single year. The religious brothers encouraged team sports, religious development, and critical and moral thinking. It was the year of the deadly flu. I remember being in bed with the sweats and cold symptoms for a very long period, and Brother Calvé died.

My older brother Ray had been away at a similar school in Ottawa, and our holiday reunions were joyous and full of physical challenges—wrestling, road hockey, and interminable disputes over food, hockey sticks, or whose turn it was to bring in the next pail of coal or armful of slab wood. Ray seemed to have developed a persona that made declarations of empirical data and incontrovertible truths, leaving not much room for discussion. We had long and heated debates over the role of Kennedy in world peace, especially the US involvement in Southeast Asia. We took absolutely opposing positions: I cheered for the National Liberation Front.

My sister Huguette was our hockey goalie. The cold evenings standing around with Sears catalogues for pads until the play shifted to her end depleted her interest in hockey, and soon she was off to a girls' school in Haileybury.

Claude and André were the two youngest. Both would be successful, Claude as a food and medical supplies broker, and André developing from a high school teacher of auto mechanics to a water expert in Ghana.

After one year away, my parents allowed me to return to the local high school, Kirkland Lake Collegiate and Vocational Institute. I enrolled in Grade 9 of the technical program and resumed my winter hockey and summer job at Canada Dry. I discovered girls, male friendships, and differences in relative wealth. My teammates who lived in richer areas got much better jobs in the summer. However, in the sports arena, with equivalent talent and effort, we could be equal. I was called a "frog" but that soon ended when I made it clear that those who used the "f" word would have to deal with me, physically. My favourite pastime was reading, and once a week I would purchase *Time* and read it from cover to cover. Then one day, an article described colonial conditions in Angola, in southern Africa, and the existence of "rebels" refusing to fight in colonial wars and thereby challenging Portugal's feudal regime. The photos showed a military transport ship sea-jacked by a group of Portuguese conscripts who did not want to go to war.

Time described the Angolan rebel leader Neto as a communist, poet, and troublemaker. Independence with majority rule was described as a bad thing, not a viable solution. I knew that in Canada we had elections, but in Angola they were treated like children and the living conditions were very poor. Something in this registered in me: social injustice. Illiteracy was 99 percent, infant mortality was 60 percent, and life expectancy was twenty-eight years. This struck me as a bad deal for the Angolan.

My favourite TV program was *This Hour Has Seven Days*, hosted by two young journalists who inspired discussion and thought. Hard-hitting news reportage and in-depth analysis provided material for discussion with my friends. It was so good, the CBC pulled the show. Another lesson for me in the facts of life: the news and public discussion were controlled.

High school was a great learning experience. Books, formulas, and a stint on the student council showed me a broad picture of society, its rules and deceptions. I learned how to negotiate successfully without destroying the other side. The teachers at KLCVI were patient, smart, and dedicated. Many were from local stock. Their friendly approach allowed the students to grow and invited their respect.

Principal Roger Allen was strict and funny. Mr. Preston, a neighbour in the Federal, was the gym teacher and football coach. Mr. Hamden arrived along with Mr. Orr to teach electricity and English respectively. It was Mr. Orr who dissected sentence structure and taught me how to manipulate the written word. He was an advocate of the poetry of simplicity. He would say, "Short, concise sentences get your message across."

The numerous hockey games allowed further contact with Mr. Hamilton, Mr. Puppa, and Mr. Zidar. And there was the female teaching staff. Ms. Burns was the older sister of a hockey friend. She was gorgeous, playful, and commanded respect. No student would mess with her, though I'm sure plenty dreamed of it.

In 1962, the Ontario government opened a branch of the Ryerson Institute of Technology (now Ryerson University) in Kirkland Lake, just down the street, and I enrolled in the Electronic Technology Department. I became the first president, founder of the athletic department, and captain of the hockey team. Hockey gave me a physical outlet; my skills in the classroom were lacking. I knew I would graduate, but I recognized that my real talents were in the organization and human resource fields.

Along with Brian Culhane, Gary Burke, and Ron Morely, I organized a bed on wheels to be pushed from Kirkland Lake to

Temagami, some 100 miles, to participate in the winter carnival there. I organized but did not push. I also participated in the local K club, my first experience with a service club.

In 1964, I read that a man named Nelson Mandela had been arrested and jailed under apartheid. I read of the Sharpeville massacre, where sixty-seven unarmed Africans were killed. Apartheid was a new word, a foreign word that sounded rough in my ear. I took the time to look it up, discovering a system of separate races, separate schools, buses, and beaches. Separate was a word with various intensities of meaning. Imagine setting up the Irish and French schools with a large stone wall separating the "frogs" from the "*maudits Anglais*." There were parallels, but it was not apartheid.

Blacks needed passports to travel from their "bedroom communities" to where they worked, and could be jailed if the document was not up to date, stamped, and in their possession. Dutch settlers had organized this majority into Bantustands—reserves—and governed with a white minority government backed by military power.

This seemed crazy to me. I could not understand how the white minority could have control. Mandela, a lawyer, was detained and accused of trying to overthrow an illegal government, attempting to show the rulers that majority rule was the only solution to economic disparity, violence, intimidation, and institutionalized hatred. This was the second time I had come across the domino theory (the idea that if one country came under "communist control," neighbouring countries would inevitably follow); first in Vietnam, and now in Southern Africa. I realized that I was politically illiterate, which was an uncomfortable realization: I wanted to know.

How was it possible that these human rights abuses had such low visibility? Was there a concerted effort to hide the reasons and conceal the identity of the countries implicated in creating and maintaining this inhuman treatment of so many people? My conscience was torn trying to integrate all this information. How could Mr. Prime and other Canadians fight and die to defeat Hitler while the South African apartheid system thrived? Meanwhile, Nazis hated Jews, whites hated blacks. There was a parallel, but my inability to understand led to the realization that I had much to learn. I had distinct feelings about rightness and wrongness, but no knowledge of African/world history.

The Vietnam War was raging, and a fellow from my high school thought that Vietnam was the place to take a stand for capitalism. We argued ferociously; my position supported the Vietnamese against imperial France and latterly the US presence. I challenged him that if he felt his convictions so deeply he should go and join the American troops in Vietnam. He enrolled in the Marines and went to Southeast Asia, while I cheered the National Liberation Front standing up against foreign occupation.

Why? What did he know that I did not know? The clash of values underscored my confusion: where did I fit in?

In the summers of 1962 and 1963, I worked in the gold mines of Balmertown in the extreme northwest of Ontario. I hitchhiked to Hearst and the next day made my way to Fort William-Port Arthur (now Thunder Bay). What a feeling of freedom!

I stayed at the YMCA and attended a concert by the Everly Brothers. What a thrill!

On day three, I arrived in Red Lake and made my way to the OPP station, where a high school buddy, Frank Novak, was police chief. He was very happy to drive me over to Dickenson Mines. I went to the manager's office and Mr. Gillis agreed to meet me. He explained that local kids were given priority for summer jobs. I explained that I had been on the road for three days and I really wanted to work. His patient gaze and nods of the head told me my seriousness was getting through. He asked, "Do you play ball?"

"Yes, I do."

"What position do you play?"

"Well sir, I am a catcher."

"That's terrific, since the team we sponsor needs a catcher.

You're hired."

A big break. Sports were integral to mining camp life, and Kirkland Lake boys also played hockey for Dickenson. I was so happy.

My first summer was filled with ball playing and a position on a geological crew at the mine. I was a sampler, responsible for collecting rock samples from different areas of the working mine and sending them to be assayed. I recorded the location the sample came from and transferred the data to the plans in Mr. Skully's office.

In all, six young men from out of town bunked in the hockey rink shack. It was a lesson in how to get along, in particular with John Campbell, a winter rival in Kirkland Lake, but a teammate in the summer months. It was my first experience of an all-male bunkhouse. Life in the bunkhouse was different and a good place to mature quickly. I learned to work hard and steadily, and to get along well enough with people from different backgrounds in close quarters.

Meals were announced by the ringing of the steel triangle by the chef. His kitchen delivered plenty of good food.

There was a resident teacher from Frontier College, a literacy organization, teaching ESL classes to the miners, many of whom came from Eastern Europe. He was black. One day he was taking a shower, and some white miners cut off the cold supply, and the scalding hot water immediately burned his skin. Over the next weeks I saw the scabs and peeling black skin revealing pink underneath. I was devastated by this cruel act against another human being, targeted because of his skin colour. So this was racism.

I hitchhiked back to Kirkland Lake in September with a lot of money, since there was nowhere to spend the summer paycheques. I entered the Northern Ontario Institute of Technology and began my quest for skill in electronic technology.

Time had weekly reports on the military activities in Vietnam, with body count, and the justification of the US presence. I felt manipulated by the arguments for the US intervention, the domino theory, while reading of massive bombing of a small nation so far from America, and the dehumanizing of the Vietnamese as Gooks. What had Vietnam done to America to warrant such an aggressive response? This was a long stretch from Ohm's Law and the Kirkland Lake library, and most upsetting.

I returned to Balmertown for a second summer, but this time asked for a miner's job. The work was very hard, drilling and preparing the holes for blasting, and returning the next day to clean out the broken rock and start over again. Dirty, dry rock full of gold traces meant that we earned large production bonuses. Incomes were four times the salary of a ball player. What a learning experience, though short-lived. It left a lifelong imprint. I did not want to be a hard rock miner. I wanted to be a part of changing things.

In between studies of math and electrical concepts, I continued with an active social life. In the summers of 1964 and '65, I worked with the Westinghouse Company, based in Swastika, Ontario. The most memorable incident took me out on an emergency call to the Upper Canada gold mine with Jack Wild, the manager. We were lowered to the eighth level and walked to the defective electrical panel, where my dad was waiting for us. So, in jest, I asked Mr. Wild, "So is my dad now working under my orders?" We all laughed at this one, and still do.

In February of 1966, Bell Telephone invited me and fellow classmates Boucher, Corriveau, and Nystrom to Montreal for a week in an attempt to recruit us. I had arranged our schedule over the phone in French, and I continued to speak French throughout the week, while many of my classmates floundered. This experience reinforced for me the power of a second language, and the whole week was a confidence booster. The seven days seemed like a month.

As for my spiritual side, I remained faithful to my Catholic upbringing and attended church regularly. In March of 1966, I spent many hours with a visiting priest, Father Laframboise, who ran a retreat for the French Parish of the Assumption. I liked his tone of voice, his clarity of thought, and his overall attitude towards social justice. According to my mother, he was something of a superstar on the "circuit" and influenced many young people. I skipped school and spent hours questioning him about social justice.

"If the Church is so correct in its analysis of social injustice and is apparently claiming there is a serious shortage of social activists, I can't see how joining a celibate group will help solve the problems of poverty and oppression."

He replied, "You need faith to understand." I obviously didn't have it.

However, Vietnam was eating away at me. My sense of justice could not accept it. Maybe if we created many Vietnams, we could stop the Americans from picking on one small nation at a time. With the dispersal of American troops across the globe, war would come to a halt, and independence would come to those undeveloped countries with high Catholic populations, like Angola.

In April 1966, the teachers at the Northern Ontario Institute of Technology recognized my insatiable drive and hard work by adjusting my borderline grades so that I could get on with life. My parents put on a wonderful party celebrating my graduation, and so began my self-directed journey.

On May 12, 1966, age twenty-three, I flew to Montreal and lived in the Laurentian Hotel for a week and then moved into my first apartment on Decelles Avenue in the Côte-des-Neiges area. For the next few months, Bell Telephone gave me an opportunity to earn a living and to grow into an independent and contributing adult. However, the daily reports of the brutal and senseless violence against the people of Vietnam made me question whether there was really any such thing as justice and happiness. The continued expansion in the language and prosecution of war shook up my values. World events made my daily routine as an outside engineer for Bell seem pretty insignificant. The hustle and bustle of the ongoing sexual revolution further added to my alienation. As a francophone from Ontario, I found that much of the culture of Montreal had to be learned. Going to bed at nine p.m. and getting up at midnight to go out until morning was very foreign to me. But this was the Montreal way for my age group.

I felt I was wasting my life. I needed to make a significant decision without any clear picture of the way I should go to allow my soul and spirit to expand. Critical of the way my life was drifting along, I forced myself into long walks, reading, and sheer brutal questioning of myself. I began to slow my life down. I could not discuss with my friends how the life of accumulation of goods, greed, and opulence gave me no joy. The politics of Quebec's separation seemed important, but was of no interest. During a trip to one of my worksites, which spanned Berthierville to Trois Rivières, I saw from the banks of the St. Lawrence a huge ocean liner heading to Montreal. It was enormous, so I pulled over to watch it pass. As I leaned against the car, watching it pass, a few sailors waved, and I returned the salutation. I read the ship's name: *Alexander Pushkin.* What a beauty.

My eyes scanned the ship. I was very impressed by its sleek form in the water. Then I caught sight of the red flag with the hammer and sickle floating above the funnel. My stomach went into a knot, I felt a violent tug at my heart and I caught my breath. Just blow it up, blow it up! This was my automatic reaction to the sight of a "communist" ship. It was so crazy, I really questioned my sanity.

What right did I have to wish death and destruction on those lives? I was saddened and dismayed. Was this an example of how much propaganda I had internalized? This was very depressing, but I would not let it go. Why did I react that way?

This was a turning point. I decided then and there that I must learn a better way to live and relate to people. Time for a change. Bell Telephone was history. It was time to find a way to get myself to Africa.

I searched and found that Prime Minister Lester Pearson had created an organization that gave young Canadians a chance to experience life and work in different environments. It was called CUSO, Canadian University Service Overseas. Without much hope, I put in an application. After three months, in late June, a letter came saying that, following a ten- week orientation including language training at Concordia University, I could go to Dar es Salaam to teach at Dar Technical College. This was beyond my wildest expectations. I felt humble and hopeful, all at once. Maybe, just maybe, this was the beginning of a new life.

CHAPTER TWO

I shall prepare myself and my opportunity must come.

—Abraham Lincoln

August 26, 1967, Dorval Airport, 8:00 p.m. Leaving Canada to go into a new life. This is how I saw this phase. Saying goodbye to my parents at Dorval was very difficult. Mom and Dad had always stressed independence and the doing of good deeds, but we were also a close-knit family. The reality of seeing their son off to Africa was a difficult moment. They had travelled to Montreal to visit Expo '67, and we had spent some time together. My mother's sister lived in Montreal, and with the world's fair, my parents kept busy.

Mom and Dad also met the CUSO Executive Director, Frank Bogdasavich. He was a young lawyer with a great smile and an ability to measure my parents' apprehensions. He assured my folks that the screening process and the capabilities of their son would ensure that I was safe. He was to become a great friend, a confidant, known as the Bogey Man. My mother was very steady through the final hour; however, my dad shed a tear, adding, "Take care of yourself." Although I did not know it then, these words have stayed with me all my life.

As we taxied to the takeoff area, I reflected upon how far I was going, from Kirkland Lake, my home for twenty-three years, to a teaching job in math and physics in Tanzania, a country that had self-reliance as a national objective. President Nyerere, through Tanzania African National Unity—TANU—, had focused his policies on this need.

I also reflected on my lost love and the heartbreak that this relationship had caused.

Was I running away? This was my habitual response to betrayal; I did not yet know that such painful experiences could be great teachers. Or was I setting out, without knowing it, on the road to a meaningful life?

Although my thoughts returned over and over to the anti-colonial and anti-apartheid struggles, I did not appreciate the scope of these problems or the stature of the people involved in the liberation movements.

My Air Canada flight took me to London and on to Greece after a four-hour stopover. The stop in Athens was my first direct encounter with a military government. It was about 11:00 p.m., and the dim lights at the airport created an atmosphere of mystery and foreboding. The streetlights in Athens had been reduced to a blackout, so that the great city appeared small and uninhabited. The army refused to allow us to disembark and wait in the air terminal while the plane was refuelling. The hot Mediterranean air made our confinement very uncomfortable. At 3:00 a.m., the final leg of our journey began.

I saw my first African sunrise as we flew over the Sahara, an extraordinary sight. Waveforms on the brown surface of the sand dunes evoked ocean waves, beautiful and deadly. As we entered Tanzanian air space, the pilot informed us we would soon see Mount Kilimanjaro off the left wing. The aircraft circled the highest peak in Africa to give us a better view. We could see the trail that climbers used to the eternal snows at the top. The demarcations due to elevation gave a vivid lesson in geography: from lush grasslands to sparse, stunted vegetation to bare rock and then snow. Though I have always been in awe of this mountain, I have never had a desire to climb it. Mountain climbing has always seemed to me a meaningless diversion for the rich.

Many hours later, we landed in Dar es Salaam. During the flight from Athens, I had changed into shorts, sandals, and t-shirt. When the plane doors opened, a heavy, damp rush of tropical air filled the aircraft. Welcome to East Africa.

At customs I responded to questions in Kiswahili. The hard work at language training in Montreal was paying off. The language is so logical. Telling time, for instance: to say 8:00 a.m. in Swahili, you say *saa mbele*, two, meaning it is now two hours after sunrise. You can tell what time it is by looking at the sun. At the equator, there is a twelve to twelve balance of daylight and darkness year-round. After dark the same rule applies. Eight p.m. is also two—two hours after sunset. I really needed a watch.

The customs officer asked me why I was coming to Tanzania. I responded that I was a *mwalimu*, a teacher, of math and physics, and as the words registered, I noticed the officer's eyes open a little wider and his body straighten a little, as if in respect. Later I discovered that teachers are revered in Tanzania.

Mr. Nyerere, the president of Tanzania, a former teacher and founding father of the republic, commanded great respect, and we, the new teachers, were riding on his coattails.

We met the CUSO team of Mike Sinclair and his assistant Don Barker. Sinclair was a heavyset man with a great smile, a man built for the laborious job of Field Director. Eventually he and I would cross swords.

Mike did not seem to understand the international politics of Southern Africa. He did not need to see the big picture to do his job, much of which was keeping young Canadians on the straight and narrow. For example:

A CUSO volunteer decided to open a brothel. It was very successful, though it proved to be a serious embarrassment. A field engineer, Dave R. from Hamilton, was assigned to live with another Canadian. His job as a civil engineer required extensive travel. It was during his absences that his roommate used the vacant accommodation for his house of ill repute. When Dave R. returned, he found his house was a brothel in full operation. Dave was a very religious man, and the shock drove him to attempt suicide. Mike was the man who dealt with these problems arising from immaturity and naiveté.

Another challenge for these young Canadians was the ready availability of large quantities of pot. This was of no interest to me, but others were drawn to it.

I soon learned I had little in common with most of the CUSO people. I did not frequent the field office and attended few meetings. Mike was very good to me and turned a blind eye to some of the things I got up to. Other CUSO personnel who proved more than acquaintances were Dave Beer, Barry Fleming, and Chris Brown. It was Dennis September, CUSO director in Zambia, a doer who proved to be a willing comrade in assisting the liberation movements with his political savvy and connections.

It took some two hours to get away from the airport for my first view of an open-air African market. There were fruit stands under thatched roofs, with pyramids of oranges. Lemons and coconuts, mounds of papaya, spices, and cassava were spread out on sheets of cardboard. Hanging from the rafters were pots, pans, wooden spoons, clothing, and metres of colourful *kitenge* material used to make clothing.

The red soil was very fine and seemed to colour everything. The market stretched along the road for kilometres. A large eucalyptus tree made a canopy for the Mikonde artists who carved the deepest black ebony. The local barbershop shared the same shade.

Finally we arrived at our temporary home, the Salvation Army Hostel. The African huts were gorgeous to look at. The oval thatched roofs and painted concrete walls appeared to have been set down in strategic locations by some huge crane. However, tropical, salty damp air permeated the living quarters. The room had been sealed up for some time; it needed serious ventilation. I opened the room to the sun. Later that night, I discovered the musky odour of mildew in the bed sheets and in the hammock-shaped mattress stuffed with rags, feathers, and other unidentifiable materials. It was stifling.

I was so tired from the overnight flight I went to sleep at around 1:00 p.m. It was a serious mistake.

We were summoned at around six p.m. to have dinner. I was very groggy and uncomfortable. Sleep deprivation rendered my usually alert mind slow and irritable.

My first African meal; the food was so colourful and eye-pleasing. I ate plenty of fruit. The main course was fish and chips. The whole meal was delicious. The fries were different from what I was accustomed to. I soon learned they were prepared in the English way, my first lesson in how deeply African society had been influenced by the colonizer.

I returned to my hut and tried to sleep, but my body clock was way off. I listened to the song of the dive-bombing mosquitoes while I inspected the details of the roof's construction. The structure of rafters and attachment of the thatching was very fine, gorgeous, and simple. Maybe this was the pattern of life here, simple but effective.

The next morning, at five a.m., the local roosters signalled a new day. I got out of my hammock, washed with a face cloth, and went outside. The palm trees were huge and loaded with coconuts. I was struck by the African smells, the colourful trees, the idyllic setting. I walked to the dining area and found the doors locked. It was still two hours until breakfast. This was the British way: no access to the dining room until 7:00 a.m., no coffee, and no toast. As I waited for breakfast, the incoming workers greeted me with, "*Jambo bwana.*" This is the universal greeting. In full: "*Jambo bwana, habare asabui.*" The reply: "*Nzuri sna.*" This exchange proved useful over and over again, later on even getting me free food.

At 9:00 a.m., a bus came to take us for the first time to the city centre and Dar es Salaam Technical College on Morogoro Road. We passed the Askari-soldier monument in the middle of a traffic circle. There was a clock tower at the other end of the street in the centre of another traffic circle. I got my first view of the Indian Ocean, a vision of blue-green water with whitecaps, framed by the overhanging trees, at the end of the dark tunnel of the tree trunks and the black road surface. I was to spend many an hour of quiet solitude at that ocean as my new life was taking shape.

My first day at the college was a cultural shock. It was staffed with men dressed in white shirts and baggy, well-pressed shorts with long knee socks held up by elastic garters, who spoke with a very peculiar English accent. When they opened their mouths to speak, the arrogance flowed out. They would prove to be an excellent exercise for me in listening, learning, and decoding, without reacting to their neo-colonial attitudes.

The principal, Mr. Martin, a tall, pleasant man, a womanizer, was seconded by Mr. Butchard. This huge man, 250 pounds, six feet two inches tall, was to become my best source of information on the structure, the internal politics, the education system, and the unspoken objectives for Tanzanian independence of the British community.

I soon discovered that Butchard could be manipulated. His lack of any awareness of the reality of Southern Africa's anti-colonial struggles gave me the upper hand in the upcoming events that would change my life. Like most expatriates, he thrived on sports, tennis, and socializing within the white community.

In early September, I began teaching maths and physics for a total of nine hours per week. I also took private Swahili lessons. My teacher was my best classroom student. We bartered an even hour for hour, Swahili for math, the lessons taking place in his home. His family thought this was pretty funny. They became my part-time family.

The department head was a volunteer with the Quakers, the American Friends Services Committee. The Quakers were very good with the Africans and very devoted to their religious beliefs. Many of these young Americans were conscientious objectors, volunteering overseas as a substitute for military service in Vietnam. They made valuable contributions in education and social services in Tanzania.

In particular, Eric Shiller was one of these Quaker youths who stood up to the bad behaviour of the upper echelons of our college. He was fair-haired and very articulate. I liked his attitude, and saw him as a person I could trust.

In my spare time, I explored the beaches and harbour of Dar. I read the daily English newspaper, which described the many problems of the emerging nation. No funds, few professionals, medical staff shortages, and bad infrastructure. Tanzania had received its independence in 1961, inheriting a colonial governing structure with few qualified professionals.

There was also a page dealing with events surrounding the liberation movements in Southern Africa. Mandela was in jail, and repression was reported in Angola, Mozambique, Rhodesia, and South West Africa. I attended forums about these independence movements at the University of Dar es Salaam. The Tanzanian government was supporting these movements with office space, port facilities, and other services such as training camps and radio broadcasting facilities.

The Vietnamese National Liberation Front—N.L.F.—had an embassy in Dar and offered regular screenings of newsreel footage of the ongoing war in Southeast Asia. The footage showed a completely different perspective of the war in Vietnam. The members of the N.L.F. were very articulate, calm, and determined to win. These physically small people spoke like thunder if you were willing to listen. I certainly was.

Professor Rob Martin, now at the University of Western Ontario, was the most politically astute, and we got along very well. His wife, Janet, a librarian, was a happy and also a political person. Housing was very difficult; Rob and Janet offered me their spare room until I was able to find proper lodging. This was on the top floor of the library at the Adult Education Building.

The distance from the Adult Education Building to the college was more than a mile. I required some means of transportation immediately. A friend from college drove me to the university, where a Canadian lived who was soon going home. His two-year contract had expired and he was selling his 50-cc motorcycle for sixty-five dollars. I was now mobile. At first, driving was a little scary as I got used to the left- hand drive. Developing the habit of looking to my right for oncoming traffic was a challenge.

One of the unwritten rules of the road in Tanzania was this: pedestrians are poor with little time to spare, and motorists are rich and can get where they are going more quickly; therefore, pedestrians have the right of way. In the case of a collision between vehicle and pedestrian, the driver should report immediately to a police station, with or without the vehicle, or street justice will be meted out. I saw this law applied to a bus driver who hit a pedestrian. It was not pretty.

On my third day at the college, President Nyerere came to the Adult Education Building to deliver a speech. My motorbike was parked in the lot in front of the library. It was unlicensed. The officers carrying out the security check before the president arrived spotted the infraction and started an investigation. They soon knocked on the door of the apartment and, following a brief discussion, charged me with failing to have proper ownership and with driving on a public road without insurance in an improperly licensed vehicle. Phil, an American volunteer, showed up during the discussion. He thought his knowledge of Swahili would influence the officer. This turned out to be a bad move.

I was scheduled for a court appearance the next day. Early in the morning, a large five-ton dump truck arrived at the library to bring me and the bike to court. With great effort we loaded the bike into the box of the truck. I was permitted to sit up front with the driver, as I was not considered to be a real criminal.

Just sitting in the courthouse waiting for my name to be called was a new experience. The lawyers all wore white wigs and robes, in imitation of the trappings of a British court. The guards with their batons chatted and laughed with the prisoners. When my case came up, the judge evaluated the Crown's argument and dismissed the case. After, some four wearisome hours getting the proper documentation, my *piki-piki* was now free.

Phil, the loudmouth American, had blown the whole incident out of proportion, and Mike, returning from an upcountry assignment, got the impression that I had attacked the security officer, damaging CUSO's image. A short discussion sorted out the misunderstanding. Phil was now on my list of people to avoid. He would cause more problems. How I detest these loud Americans.

During my many visits to the university, I met other Canadians who were teaching there with CIDA, the Canadian International

Development Agency. There was Paul Purritt, with the ILO (International Labour Organization) in Ottawa, and John Saul, at York University in Toronto. I particularly liked John for his refined intellect. His analysis of Southern African political events was clear and fluent. He could also be very engaging, and most of all, he could easily hold his own with Dr. Don Barnett.

It was my meeting with Dr. Barnett, author of *Mau Mau from Within*, which dramatically influenced my political education. The book was a first-hand account of guerrilla warfare in the form of a well-written biography of a freedom fighter. It opened my eyes to the hardships these men endured in their ultimately successful efforts to force the British to grant independence to Kenya. Intense, seldom smiling, Barnett was an American who thought seriously about the role of the US military in Vietnam. He had abandoned his life in Iowa, in the American Midwest, and had begun a new life with his wife and children in Dar. We spent hours discussing the situation in Southern Africa and the role of the US in its support of Portugal as a colonial power and its support of apartheid in South Africa.

Barnett and I became good friends. He was a formidable intellectual, and I had to learn quickly to keep up with him. He directed my reading and challenged me to understand a bigger picture. I had no experience debating political theory. My politics were driven by a straightforward moral sense of what was right and what was wrong. Apartheid was wrong. Colonialism, supported by aid that helped keep Africans powerless in their own homelands, was outrageously wrong. It had to be stopped. But how, and at what price?

I was opposed to the Vietnam War. I saw a bully trying to subdue the people of Indochina using the domino theory as an excuse. The USA had to be confronted and defeated militarily in order to allow the Vietnamese people to control their own destiny. Barnett saw the Vietnam War in a much larger context, as one conflict in a worldwide struggle against imperialism.

The parallels between Vietnam and Angola became clearer. Barnett and I developed a common point of view regarding what could be done to defeat US militarism. Eventually we formed a working relationship.

Another connection that I relished was with Principal Griff Cunningham of Kivukoni College. I frequently attended Sunday gatherings there with him and his wife and children. Griff was a Canadian student in England when the question of independence for Tanganyika was raised. The British did not want a repeat of the Kenya experience with the Mau Mau. The only other way seemed to be to decolonize and turn over an ill-prepared administrative structure to the locals. The civil service was totally British. Education was nearly one hundred percent British controlled.

Griff accompanied his friend Julius Nyerere on his return to his country to form the Tanganyika African National Union—TANU—to contest the upcoming election. Griff was politically skillful and the ideas he shared with Nyerere on the necessity for self-reliance led to the opening of Kivukoni College. Its mandate was to train political cadres of the TANU party with a grounding in economics, political science, agriculture, and intermediate technology (technology that uses local materials and tools).

I was very happy to get involved in many of these projects. I made use of my technical training and felt useful and appreciated. Griff became a very good friend and played an important role in my political life.

CHAPTER THREE

The need to trust and be trusted in order to feel safe, to dare,

On October 17, 1967, I took another step deeper into the political ferment of Southern Africa. I decided to visit the liberation movement for Angola, the MPLA, the Popular Movement for the Liberation of Angola, which maintained offices in the city centre. I parked my *piki-piki* on the sidewalk and climbed the long staircase leading to the second floor. When I walked through the door, a white woman of Portuguese descent asked me in broken English if she could help me. I was baffled. I couldn't understand this white woman working alongside black people—more evidence of my political illiteracy and literal black- and-white thinking. Her name was Mrs. Boavida. She offered me a newspaper and some photocopied literature from the MPLA bookshelf.

I took the documents back to the apartment at the Adult Ed library and read them with great interest. The basic message was that we must all, black and white, work together to free our [sic] country from Portuguese colonialism. The statistics were shocking: ninety-nine percent of Angolans were illiterate, infant mortality was sixty percent, and life expectancy was twenty-eight years. I could not believe my eyes. I had read these statistics in *Time* back in 1961. Nothing had changed. What was going on?

My light teaching load at the college allowed me to do a lot of reading and thinking. I got very frustrated at how little information about the liberation movements was published in the North American media. A web of deception was being woven back home, just like the misrepresentation of Vietnam.

On December 14, 1960, the United Nations General Assembly had adopted by an overwhelming majority the Declaration on the Granting of Independence to Colonial Countries and Peoples: "The subjection of peoples to alien subjugation, domination and exploitation constitutes a denial of fundamental human rights, is contrary to the Charter of the United Nations and is an impediment to the promotion of world peace and co-operation."

In 1965, the General Assembly of the United Nations called for economic measures against Portugal by appealing to UN agencies, in particular the International Monetary Fund, to refrain from granting Portugal "any financial, economical or technical assistance" as long as it failed to implement the declaration on the granting of independence.

It was an accepted policy that the United Nations Resolution on support to the population living in refugee camps and in liberated areas was a weak point. This was to be our area of focus. The African Relief Services Committee had found a mission. Existing NGOs, CUSO, Oxfam, and CARE were not interested in supporting UN resolutions. I met with nearly all NGOs and was always turned down. As for Canadian institutions such as CIDA, no success. The United Church of Canada gave support to the ARSC, but when successful projects were carried out in Angola they started to back away.

The military arm of the apartheid government in Johannesburg, though more than three thousand miles from Dar, was able to reach the freedom fighters in exile. Strafing the Tanzanian and Zambian borders, the South African air force reminded civilian populations and heads of state that they could be next.

My introduction to the reality of the war of independence was through a large explosion at the African National Congress office in the centre of Dar. It was the first of many book bombs, each one a reminder of the terrible price the Africans paid for their freedom. It was one of these cowardly book bombs that killed Dr. Eduardo Mondlane at his home in Dar. He was the founder and president of the Mozambique Liberation Front—FRELIMO. He had been educated in the United States, completing a doctorate in anthropology. I had the pleasure of meeting him on three occasions. He was very articulate and determined, a visionary like Dr. Neto. His loss was deeply felt.

Meanwhile, Barnett was making contact with all the liberation movements with the objective of lending assistance. These movements were at first suspicious of the American who claimed to speak for a group of progressive North Americans who were prepared to come to Africa to lend a technical hand. In time, Barrett wrote a paper that was published in *Ramparts* outlining his theory, which was that in order to defeat US-led imperialism, more Vietnams, more military diversions, would be needed to sap the military strength and political support required by forcing the US and its allies to fight on many fronts at once. His high profile in Dar drew public attention. However, if I were going to succeed in making a contribution to the struggle, I would need to keep a low profile, because CUSO would have a fit if they knew one of their volunteers was getting cozy with the liberation movements. I would be returned to Canada. Not an option, as far as I was concerned.

I moved out of the Adult Ed apartment and into the Agip Hotel. It was the second-best star-rated hotel in the city, second only to the Hotel Kilimanjaro. It allowed me to meet with people without the formality of invitations and appointments, which kept the risk of suspicion growing about my activities to a minimum. The Kilimanjaro had a public access teletype, and I made a daily trip to keep up on the news. One evening while I was reviewing the tickertape, I met Colin Campbell, a Canadian working on a CESO project. I appreciated his Nova Scotia humour, and it was clear that my low profile was working. Any suspicions would find their way into the gossip network very quickly.

In late October, I went with Rob Martin and a few other volunteers to Morogoro Game Park some 120 miles west of Dar es Salaam. It was my first long weekend since arriving in Africa, and the choice of a wildlife sanctuary made for a wonderful experience. It was another new experience for a kid from Kirkland Lake. I had never seen so many vultures, elephants, wildebeest and lions. On the last night, a lion attacked and killed a wildebeest in the dark nearby. We heard the growls and groans, and next morning found the wildebeest skull next to our tent. We mounted it on the front of the black station wagon we were using. It was a calculated piece of political theatre designed to show the "Ugly American"—the station wagon was painted on the side with "Gift from USAID."

The political platform of TANU prescribed self-reliance. Schools were free, and the student body in return cleaned the school and sleeping areas. They also maintained a large community garden, and the teachers who wished to lent a hand. Two of my fellow teachers, Schiller and Booth, and I volunteered. As the gardening progressed through clearing, weeding, and planting, negative comments began to emerge from the school administration. The leftover Brits would not co-operate with the project. They gave neither encouragement nor time off from the classroom to allow the students to be educated according to the Arusha Declaration, which called for encouragement and development of self- reliance in locally administered villages. As the *shamba,* the garden, grew, and student pride along with it, the students who refused to help began to feel a little heat. I found it very educational. After four successful weeks of effort by some thirty students every evening, they could see the results of their hard work and their pride was palpable. The following item is taken verbatim from my diary:

White administration, totally against this type of work, to stall this, work administrators locked the tools in an unknown shed. "This would naturally" frustrate the students and gave them a clear indication of the administration's view of their project and possibly demoralize the students. On this particular occasion, the Friday work session was held up just as the Wednesday session— cancelled—due to the lack of available tools as the key could not be located . . . a decision was taken to prove to the administration that we were serious about our legal work. A student identified the new location.

The outside door was made of solid wood . . . the inside door had a glass top.

The shed was attached to the outside part of the amphitheatre, which was occupied. After having been given permission (for a 3-minute interruption of his class by the instructor), I walked down the left-hand side of the amphitheatre towards the locked door.

As I approached the window, I removed from under the back of my back shirt and belt area a foot-long steel pipe and broke the glass. I then reached in to unlock the door, entered, and proceeded through to the outside with tools in hand. The students loved it and cheered.

The lecturer in the amphitheatre, a former colonialist, left the class in despair. The incident caused a little difficulty with the staff. I soon realized that such acts of defiance could expose my true sympathies, which could hamper my intentions. However, I was acting out my beliefs in a fundamentally concrete way for the first time, making a statement about my determination to make a worthwhile project a success.

The next morning, Principal Martin demanded an explanation and payment for the broken glass. I argued that if the administration were not hindering our self-help project, we would not have to take such actions. The sum of five shillings—one dollar—was subtracted from my pay.

My housing situation needed attention. I enquired about the possibility of house sitting for one of the expatriates who needed someone reliable and knowledgeable to take care of their home. In early December, I arranged a meeting with a Mr. Stewart, the housing secretary, a move that proved valuable in setting up the next phase of my involvement with the liberation movement. I needed to get out of the public eye, as all the liberation movements were under surveillance by both the USA and South African security.

I returned to the MPLA office six weeks later and this time came face to face with Dr. Neto, the founding father of the MPLA. He stood up to greet me and walked around the desk to shake my hand. A large photograph of him was taped to the wall, overshadowing the living, breathing Dr. Aghostino Neto.

I was so surprised that I addressed him in French, and he responded in the same language.

"Il me fais grand plaisir de faire votre connaissance," I said, to which he responded, *"Moi aussi mon chèr monsieur. Asseyez-vous."*

"Avec plaisir M. le Président."

I was flabbergasted. I was sitting with the president of the MPLA! Neto was about five feet ten inches tall, weighing about 180 pounds, with broad shoulders and large glasses. He spoke calmly and

deliberately, his thoughts focused, not smiling much.

We spoke for about thirty minutes. He addressed the question of race and friendship. This man had been brutalized by the Portuguese Secret Police—PIDE—and had been imprisoned and scheduled for execution. He was recognized as a poet. The intervention of Bertrand Russell and other men and women of conscience had saved Neto's life. He had been exiled to a Portuguese island, but in August 1962, international pressure combined with the internal pressure of progressive Portuguese families, and Neto was released. He made his way to Congo (K) and joined his country's exiles in Leopoldville, now Kinshasa.

I made it clear to Dr. Neto that I was very sympathetic to the objectives of the MPLA and added that I had skills in telecommunications to offer. We needed to talk more.

Barnett had already told Neto about a Canadian communications specialist living in Dar, but I did not know this. Barnett was not very happy about my visit to the MPLA. He wanted to control the relationship. The Angolans were to check me out as to my politics and motivations. The MPLA was in need of communications solutions, and I could help. Barnett raised questions about his own motives with his behaviour. The MPLA quickly learned how to deal with him and made it clear what their expectations of him were.

During the following week, Dr. Neto set up a meeting with Barnett and me. Daniel Chipenda, who had been a former football hero in Portugal and now was a member of the central committee of the MPLA, also attended. At five feet eight and 260 pounds, his thick chest and his low centre of gravity made him look awfully big. He seemed to have no neck, and his powerful face was hidden by a long beard. Chipenda had been educated by the United Church of Canada at their mission post at Dondi.

Our discussion set out how we could assist. First, we would conduct interviews with the leadership of the MPLA and have them published. The international information campaign needed to be stepped up because the Western countries, especially the USA, were giving more military support to the Portuguese army through NATO, an illegal act that went unchallenged in the press. The British and French were also assisting Portugal, since they had investments in the colonies.

Second, what problems could be matched with what skills as soon as possible?

A group of progressive people in Holland was supporting the MPLA. Dr. Bosgra, the director, left his teaching position at the university in Amsterdam. This tall, white-haired mathematician contributed immensely to the struggle of liberation movements in all of Southern Africa. Coffee boycotts and information campaigns launched by the *Angola Comité* were the principal European strategies that exposed the infrastructure of Portuguese colonialism and its fascist-supporting friends, namely the USA, Germany, and Britain.

In order to keep Angola in a repressed state, obligatory military service in Portugal had been extended to five years. In late 1967, the Portuguese military presence in Angola was over 150,000 soldiers, and by 1974 it was up to 200,000 men.

The Portuguese colonials numbered more than 400,000. These settlers supplied additional firepower in local militias.

On December 25, 1967, I woke up at six a.m. and went down to the Agip lobby. It was silent, vacant, and unreal. The overnight desk clerk was asleep, his head glued to the desk. A small wooden table with a ten- inch Christmas tree on top stood off in a corner. The air-conditioned comfort of a hotel on Christmas day in tropical Africa did not seem right. I needed to feel the early morning sun. From the top of the stairs of the Agip, I looked over towards the Luther House, and, in the background of this well-shaded Christian hostel, the Dar es Salaam Harbour, Harbour of Peace. It was so quiet, so cool, no wind or moving vehicles. The temperature was twenty degrees.

I was used to Christmas festivities with my family, and in this completely new setting I felt very sad. So I drove my *piki-piki* to the beach at Oyster Bay. It was five miles from Dar on the road to the university, and the wonderful beaches of white sand were deserted. I spent a few hours alone sitting under a coconut tree. I really missed my family and felt sorry for myself.

I thought a lot about what had happened in my life since August. The number of changes in my life was staggering, and now I was heading for an active political life and events which were to bring me face to face with many unknowns. I reflected on the quality of my emerging growth. It was a long day, a very sad day. Life was giving me chance to dig very deep into my soul.

How far was I prepared to travel down this road?

December 26, 1967: Rob Martin and I had planned to travel upcountry. Our trip by road took us to Morogoro, Arusha, Nairobi, and back to Dar.

We hitchhiked the first section from Dar to Morogoro. From here, the light road traffic forced us to take the local bus.

It was quite an experience. The bus was the only method of transportation for citizens as well as traders. The overhead luggage racks overflowed with wrapped bundles of foodstuffs and clothing, as well as the usual travelling live chickens.

The wide variety of odours and sounds and the constant noise were a new experience. Tanzanians were very curious as to why we were in their midst. Our Swahili was correct and fluent, and our relaxed attitude allowed us to blend in. We were on holidays. It was the white faces part that attracted more attention than we cared for.

Stops were frequent. People got off and others got on. There was a constant ducking ritual as overhead objects were lifted down and new stuffed bed sheets with new travelers settled in.

At one stop, the driver left his seat and walked over to a ten-hut village. He greeted everyone and soon disappeared. The disappearing act caused quite a commotion.

After much chit-chat, we deciphered that the reason for this four-hour stop was that the driver's girlfriend lived in the village. He was just doing his family duty. We soon continued on to Arusha, an idyllic setting where the TANU leadership had created and formalized the constitution—the birthplace of the Arusha Declaration.

We visited the base camp of Mount Kilimanjaro. It is from here that the aspiring climbers of Africa's tallest mountain take their first steps. Though it was a pretty sight, the thought of climbing the monster hill still did not appeal to me.

We visited the Ngorongoro crater and the Serengeti Plains. The beauty of this crater was awesome. We hooked up with a travel group that was going into the crater. From the ridge of the crater, we could see the winding roadway that we would follow. Lush vegetation overhung the steep and narrow roadway. Some two hours later, we reached the crater floor, a vast, flat surface where large aircraft carrying European tourists could land. This was the top tourist area in East Africa

We stayed in a small cabin about 200 metres from the main lodges and dining area. Dinner was served at seven p.m., so the walk to the dining room was at sunset. However, the return trip at around ten

p.m. was a little scary, as there was wildlife out there somewhere. The dark, unlit trail made us a little apprehensive. No wonder the faraway cabin was so cheap.

So New Year's Eve of 1968 turned out to be a very good time.

January 1, 1968: We made our way to Nairobi by bus. On entering Kenya, the language became aggressive, while the tone and harshness of speech was a distinct contrast to the Tanzanians' softness of the language. I suspect that the rule of terror by the Kenya government under Kenyatta had something to do with this. This government allowed tribalism to flourish and exploited it to maintain control, so aggressive behaviour was taken for granted.

We were constantly being hit upon for money and other favours. This was very different from Dar and other areas in Tanzania. Corruption was rampant and extortion scams ever so creative.

We needed to find a sleeping area and decided the city hall grounds would be adequate and safe.

We approached the *askari* and got permission to put our sleeping bags under the large tree at the back of city hall. He demanded fifteen shillings, and we obliged. We slept very well, but before daylight the armed guard began shouting at us to get up and get out of the area. We did not argue. We packed our bags and headed to the city centre. We took a room in the well-known hotel were Ayn Rand, Richard Leakey, and Ernest Hemingway had stayed. After a two-day visit, we made our way back to Dar es Salaam; lovely landscape, excellent foods, and natural beauty. Once in Dar, I headed back to the Agip while Rob returned to the arms of a waiting Janet.

On January 5, 1968, the housing secretary, Mr. Stewart, called me at school and offered me an expatriate's house for three months. It was situated in the eastern core of the city. It was very large with a large, screened front porch. The living area was very spacious and the large windows allowed the daylight to fill the space. The lot was well treed and therefore there was plenty of shade. Air circulation was provided by ceiling fans, the best possible arrangement.

I installed a mattress in the middle of the floor in the living area and hung a double-sized mosquito net from a ceiling hook. It was a comfortable bed and kept the malaria-bearing bugs at a safe distance.

I ate most of my meals outside my home. I frequented a small Indian restaurant where the food was plentiful and nutritious, and for five shillings I ate as much as I wished.

Mike Sinclair had a new assistant, Barry Fleming. One evening, I invited him out to a meal at this same restaurant. He was totally disgusted with the surroundings. I still remember his comment about the quality of the food: "A million flies can't be wrong."

This former professional hockey player (in the Italian league) needed to be watched closely. His politics and his arrogance did not sit well with me. Given his status within CUSO, the eventual departure of Mike Sinclair would make Barry the big cheese. We would talk a lot about hockey and other non-political interests.

My ongoing secret relationship with the MPLA gave me an opportunity to meet with Angolans and test the political waters. Every meeting lowered my apprehensions and insecurities about the liberation movement. I realized I could make myself useful, and our mutual friendship became very comfortable.

I received a request for mechanic's tools from the head of MPLA logistics, Camarade Petroff. He gave me a list of hand tools and different types of measuring instruments, so I approached Barry about using discretionary funds from CUSO to purchase these important items. The Angolan freedom fighters were getting their supplies, guns, and food via the ports of Dar es Salaam, to be transported across the continent more than 2,000 miles to Angola. They used the Dar–Lusaka Highway, known as the Highway of Death because no other word can adequately describe this road.

Barry was unsure. "Can I trust the Angolans to purchase these items, or will they squander the money?"

I was absolutely livid. I lost my cool and told him off: "Barry, you arrogant jerk! You are completely off-base. Where is your sense of decency?"

Barry realized that he had overstepped and revealed his limited ideological development. I backed off and offered to do the purchases for the Angolans and give him the receipts. He set a limit of 10,000 shillings.

The list was quite long, but I convinced the Indian trader that it was for a new religious group and he should give the best price possible and a little more.

I told the merchant to make sure that the bill would not go over the limit. In fact I said, "Make the bill for 9,990 shillings." He was puzzled, but complied.

I turned the tools over to a grateful and very pleased Petroff. We spoke for some time, and I could not get enough of the warmth and friendship. To me, this kind of project was so simple and necessary. Just help the movements. The United Nations had established it as a moral imperative that these movements were to be helped.

So, armed with the receipt, I drove over to the CUSO office above the ice cream parlour. I spotted Barry sitting and eating a cone. I said, "Barry, I have the receipt." He looked at it and seemed puzzled by the amount. "By the way, Barry, here is your change, ten shillings. I would not want you to accuse me or the Angolans of shortchanging you."

Barry was really pissed off. I let him vent.

I finally said, "Listen, Barry, you talk a pretty good game, but where the liberation movement is concerned, your tangible actions are few."

This would not be the last time we spoke. I had to make sure he could not find out what I was doing or thinking about. So I stayed clear.

Barry was friends with Dave Beer, the assistant country director for Zambia. It seemed Dave had been a CUSO man forever. He was married to a Zambian woman, Irene, but this did not seem to give him a nuanced insight into the politics of liberation. He was considered by serious political people to be unreliable. When obliged to deal with Beer because of CUSO business, I knew how to lie around him and I always had a story, a viable story. He had "loose lips."

His presence gave the CUSO a legitimate role in Zambia, satisfying Zambian authorities by supplying Canadian volunteers.

It was Dennis September and his wife, Hazel, who supported the liberation movements. He not only carried out the day-to-day CUSO tasks with Dave Beer, Dennis worked in a clandestine fashion with the freedom fighters' leadership in Angola, Mozambique, South Africa, Rhodesia, and South West Africa. He was trusted, respected, and a valuable ally.

In his role as CUSO director, he met with Zambian officials and was able to take their political pulse and attitudes towards the liberation movements. Zambia was obliged to help the movements but it was not a heartfelt generosity. The internal political problems of Zambia and the lack of political ideological fervour made for a difficult time.

Tribalism flourished in Zambia. In western Zambia, for example, the Angola/Zambia border was historically unsupervised and fluid. The geographical boundaries established by the colonial powers were irrelevant and the flow of persons was not controlled by the states. Now, with the anti-colonial struggle in Angola, the MPLA also saw the need to address the tribal factor. Tribalism was traditionally used by the colonizer to divide the Angolans, and with the urgent need to build a nation, tribalism had to be addressed.

Tribalism was similarly exploited by the neo-colonial settlers to prop up the UNITA, a tribal liberation movement born out of a split with the CIA-backed FNLA. Its masochistic, petulant leader, Savimbi, became the darling of the USA and apartheid. But here in Zambia, because of his tribal connections, the Zambian government was assured a favourite cousin status, which meant that Zambia would help UNITA and hinder the MPLA.

While defining the volunteer needs of Zambia, Dennis tried to work the liberation movement's needs into his volunteer requests. Requesting a doctor in Mongu or Kalabo for Zambia would generate a similar request for MPLA. Therefore, the recruiting of a doctor had a medical and political dimension.

This kind of piggybacking was very important to the liberation movements. Total discretion was required. Dennis was the only trusted person.

These movements officially sanctioned by the United Nations were the only groups to receive help. The USA had set up its own liberation groups. The battle lines were drawn, and Zambia was a big political theatre. Lusaka, the Zambian capital, was one of the homes for the liberation movements. As the immediate neighbour to Rhodesia, it played an important role in the propaganda war. The military was also present. At the radio station of the Zambian Broadcasting Corporation— ZBC—, the anti-colonial movements used their air time to keep their people, living in liberated areas or not, informed about military developments. This also involved the passing of secret messages to guerrilla units in the field.

The ongoing wars of liberation in five southern African nations had a devastating impact on Zambia. Cross-border raids by the Rhodesian Armed Forces killed many Zambians. The South African Army travelled from their military bases all the way to Lusaka and bombed the liberation centre movement offices some ten miles south of Lusaka. Zambian Armed Forces did not have the military hardware and the Zambian government did not have the will to back up the inevitable independence of their neighbours. Each country was different. For one it was apartheid, for two others Portuguese colonialism, for another South African occupation of South West Africa and the other, Rhodesia, a group of whites who had declared unilateral independence.

All were minority-ruled and illegal in the view of the United Nations.

Mid-January 1968: I continued to teach but without much enthusiasm. The rude and paternalistic attitudes of the school administrators made me very uncomfortable.

The good thing in my life was the ongoing relationship with the MPLA. My first working relationship with the MPLA took place in the Dar office. Dr. Neto, Petroff, and Daniel Chipenda attended.

Barnett did not attend this meeting. It was held on a need-to-know basis.

I was finally putting distance between myself and Barnett while increasing my own confidence.

Dr. Neto focused on radio communications needs. We studied the map of Angola and searched for the best areas to set up the new communications network. Angola is one big country with mountains in the north, a large plateau in the central part, and desert in the south. There are large rivers and plenty of roads.

I was assigned the task of coming up with a communication system that would link eastern Angola to the Cabinda region, including secondary radio units and walkie-talkies. With no electricity in the liberated regions, the power requirements presented quite a challenge. I took these problems back to my secluded residence and did the analysis. Dr. Neto stipulated that visits to the MPLA must cease and telephone contacts only were permitted.

As a college student, I had put little effort into electronics. I really preferred economics, English, and writing. But now the responsibility was real, the demands were concrete, and every plan required a beginning, a middle, an end, a budget, and a training course. The training language could be English or French.

I spent hours and hours going over details and details of the plan, poring over catalogues that had been sent by a friend in Ottawa. I drew plans and specs of an equipment list for an overall plan with a budget. Another issue was the place of purchase. The choices were Ottawa or New York.

Two weeks later, a second meeting was called for 2:00 p.m. My afternoons were always free, as school hours were from 7:30 a.m. to 12:30 p.m.

Dr. Neto and Chipenda came to my new home. I watched them arrive in a small car and park at the rear of the house, hidden from the road. They were both big men and as they exited the vehicle, the car rose dramatically on its springs.

During the next three hours, I answered questions related to the radio set-up and equipment list, and also a number of non-technical questions.

The questions related exclusively to security matters in Dar among the expatriates.

Dr. Neto asked, "How did you meet Barnett?" Then they asked about my views, my real views, on racism, Vietnam, and the war in Angola. Dr. Neto was very satisfied with my answers, unsophisticated but clear. It was clear I was going to do what the MPLA was asking.

The project was approved, and then came the big question, the method of payment—cash, in US dollars, and the equipment was to be purchased in North America. This purchase *must not* be traced.

We needed to create a credible front, a fictional organization to import the goods into Dar. False documentation was necessary. Dr. Neto called for a third meeting in two weeks.

With a lot of soul-searching and thought, I came up with a religious front—The African Relief Services Committee—and a cover story of religious books, with a p.o. box address belonging to the MPLA. This meant no customs check and duty, as the MPLA had the proper documents to get the goods.

The cash problem proved to be a tough one. Cash was the only possible way, because the banking system in Tanzania was very bureaucratic and demanded a full paper trail. The equipment could be perceived as anti-Tanzanian; at worst, something could tip off the anti-independence elements so very present in Dar.

But most of all, the MPLA needed complete secrecy, as the Portuguese and their friends would dearly love to know of this new support for the anti-colonial and anti-apartheid movements. This new phase of radio capability developed in collaboration with non-Africans in the Southern Africa wars promised a new strategic advantage for the liberation movements.

At the end of January, I was invited by some new acquaintances of the MPLA to spend a few days in Morogoro. We had packed a tent and food. Our site was situated about one kilometre into the mountains, north of the traffic circle. The camping area overlooked a natural water slide that ended in series of deep, cold-water pools. The surroundings were lush and green, and Tanzanians lived on the side of the mountain. The altitude of the region was conducive to a variety of agricultural crops, banana trees, sisal plantations, and palm trees. A large jail facility in Morogoro transformed the jute fibres used in the fabrication of cloth, bags, and rope.

The purpose of this weekend, as it turned out, was to check my political credentials and character.

The daily routine of teaching was punctuated with personal development in economics, political science, and African history. I attended political functions at the Vietnamese embassy. Public platforms at the university gave the citizens of Dar an opportunity to hear about the aspirations of freedom from the movement leaders.

I met Oliver Tambo, one of Nelson Mandela's co-defendants, at an ANC gathering in Dar. The ANC had quite a different struggle. Fighting a fascist government without a common border with a free African nation presented a formidable military challenge. It was the first time I considered the question of intelligence: At this distance, how does the ANC organize actions to confront apartheid?

The time-tested journalist's "W5" formula was the answer. Why, where, who, when, what.

How do you organize such an important department? There is lots of room for creative input. How can I help?

World opinion was still very dormant. Mandela was in jail and all blacks who wanted independence were considered communists or terrorists. It was at an ANC-sponsored event that I received a lesson in opportunism and racism.

Ben Turok, a leading ANC leader, had been condemned to jail time for his anti-apartheid activities. On his release, he immediately fled to Dar. If he had not, he would have been placed under house arrest. This was the way the apartheid movement controlled persons whom they deemed dangerous: put them under house arrest and forbid them to work. Also forbid them to see more than one person at a time.

The press interviewed Turok while the ANC arranged a public forum at the university. Senior liberation representatives were present along with Tanzanian government officials.

Each liberation movement gave a brief update of their struggle, with the ANC presenting Mr. Turok as the guest speaker. Ben began by thanking the Tanzanian government for their unfaltering support to the freedom movement in all of colonized Africa.

Some five minutes into Ben's presentation, Stokely Carmichael, the American student leader who was on an official visit to Tanzania, jumped on top of a table in the audience, shouting slurs and verbally attacking Turok. A tirade.

"White man, what right do you have to speak to us black men?" His words inflamed the audience, mainly university students, and they cheered wildly. I felt very uncomfortable. Carmichael had thoughtlessly launched a terrible disruption of the evening. He finally ran out of breath, and had made his point. In my view, Carmichael had shown that American blacks are very different from African-born blacks; the evolution of independence was a very different path. This was the last time that the liberation movements would have anything to do with the black student groups from the USA. The Tanzanian students had bought into the racist argument and the elite position of being a student. Soon President Nyerere would close the university and send the students back home to their parents' *shamba*. The new black student elite was not to have its way.

This incident made me realize that my race could be held against me. The racism question was continually present in the media. Angolans found it very tiring while in exile. The MPLA addressed this issue in its political platform. The battle cry of the MPLA was: Down with Colonialism, Down with Racism, Down with Tribalism.

A Lutta Continua, A Victoria e Certa: The Struggle Continues, Victory Is Certain.

I liked the MPLA because they addressed the three main problems. The MPLA continually fought for justice based on majority rule with elections to build a multi-racial nation. MPLA saw the mess of tribalism in Zaire and Kenya and took political measures to eradicate it at home.

My political maturation accelerated. At times, the leaps seemed enormous and complex, my thirst for knowledge insatiable.

Did I have the right stuff to handle these complex issues?

I had found a group of friends determined to change their terrible state while building an alternative based on the UN's *Universal Declaration of Human Rights*.

February 4, 1968: The MPLA put on a public evening to celebrate the beginning of the war of independence. They started with two minutes of silence for fallen comrades. It was very silent. This day in 1961, Dr. Neto had been arrested and flown to Portugal and told that he would never see Angola again. Tonight, Dr. Neto was giving life to the dream of independence. Dr. Neto spoke about the difficulties facing the MPLA. A brutal colonial regime was causing major hardship for his people. Portuguese military tactics now included lessons from Vietnam, the use of strategic hamlets and napalm. (Strategic hamlets were enclosed villages created to prevent the rural people from supporting guerrillas in the field.) The political pressures by the USA on Tanzania and Zambia became more overt as support for the liberation movements was being discouraged.

The evening was filled with Angolan music and testimonials to

the courage of the Angolans.

Meanwhile, the challenging reality of getting soldiers and equipment out of Dar and on the road to Angola continued. During the rainy season, the red soil turned to a greasy morass, highly dangerous and often impassable. With the war in Angola escalating, the normally reliable Benguela Railway was attacked and the secure export route for Zambian copper was cut off. Tanzania and Zambia needed to unite their efforts to create a rail line from Lusaka to Dar, avoiding the route through enemy territory, Rhodesia and South Africa. Tanzanian and

Zambian officials put out public tenders for the construction of this 2,500-kilometre rail line. Canada turned it down on the grounds that it was not technically feasible, and the USA chimed in with a similar answer.

This was preposterous. These two great Western nations, capable of so many feats of engineering, were playing mind games, attempting to prevent African development according to African needs: Neo-colonialism laid bare in the newspaper. Nyerere and Kaunda were outraged at this blatant insult to self-determination. Nyerere flew to China and signed an agreement for a rail link that would take five years to build. Within a month of the signing, Chinese agricultural experts arrived with civil engineers to lay out the route. Agronomists planned large food- producing areas to feed the Chinese crews as they made their way towards Lusaka, so that they would not tax the local food supply. They would also help the Tanzanians expand their *shambas,* and, after the crews finished the rail link, the former Chinese gardens were turned over to local co- operatives.

The USA was angered by this Chinese contract, so, through USAID, decided to improve a section of road. As the rail line grew, it came across the road and the Americans were there. It did not take very long for the Chinese to figure out that the imperialists were intending to slow down the development of the rail line. Soon the shovels and fists were flying. The Americans were getting their butts kicked. The Chinese were going to finish their intended lifeline for Africa. Using hand-operated cement mixers and local materials, the project was finished in three and half years. Independent Africa had prevailed, Canada and the USA humiliated and still arrogant. A similar scenario developed regarding the processing of sisal into cloth and other merchandise. Tanzania wanted to create employment. The USA proposed massive use of electrical motors and minimal manpower. China proposed 30,000 jobs for the capital city. Tanzania got what it wanted, while the West again showed its nature in fostering underdevelopment. It was clearly racist and paternalistic. My views were taking shape: The West wants to control the Third World, and I will work for the liberation movements towards self- determination.

Border crossing from Tanzania to Zambia was slow and open to multiple inspections. Corruption made the journey very costly for the MPLA. Important sums of money were used up to "smooth" the transit of Angolan goods and recently trained soldiers through Zambia.

But as Neto had said so many times, "The Portuguese colonial regime refuses to negotiate an end to their 500-year occupation, therefore forcing us to open an eastern front . . . this gives us more problems. Problems, yes, but an incredible opportunity to develop the infrastructure that will be required after independence."

Logistics along with the infrastructure to support it was the first hurdle, followed by the unloading of military hardware in Tanzania. The diplomatic staff and the information department honed their skills in many languages: Swahili for Tanzania, English for the world, French in the Congo, Portuguese for Angola. *The Voice of Angola Combatant* produced daily radio broadcasts in Portuguese and five Angolan languages.

February 20, 1968: MPLA made Dr. Boavida available for an interview. It was my first interview in French.

Boavida shook my hand and gave me a big hug. The warmth of the man settled me down. I asked about his family. His wife worked in the Dar office and they had a four-year-old son, Munduman. Life in the war zones was very difficult for the family. He told of his life under Portuguese colonial rule. For educated black men, the Portuguese had created a special classification, *assimilado*.

He was not to be considered *preto*, black, he was to be a person espousing Portuguese morals and values, a model of Portugal's mission tocivilize.

In Luanda, he had practised medicine, but he was still put down and ostracized by the colonizers. He could treat Portuguese as patients during the day, but would always be a second-class citizen everywhere else. After the bloody events of 1961,[1] he left his lucrative practice and went to Kinshasa to work for the Volunteer Corps, caring for the Angolan refugees fleeing the military repression of Salazar's army.

He spoke of the famine in the war zones as the Portuguese established their free fire zones. All vegetation, wildlife and people were to be exterminated. Defoliation agents were used extensively, a lesson learned from Vietnam. Boavida had just returned from the eastern front of Angola and showed me how many notches he had added to his belt. He was very thin.

This interminable war and the suffering it generated were weighing on him. His demeanour was pensive, but there was no lack of vision and determination.

Dr. Americo Boavida had authored a book called *500 Years of Portuguese Colonialism*. It is an economic analysis of Angola describing clearly how it was being raped. Colonial authorities, with the help of the occupying army, organized "labour pools" and sold services to the mining interests in South Africa for two-year terms. Horrific stories about the working conditions in the mines and camps have been well documented. His book outlined the political-military structure that tied Portuguese colonial policy to apartheid. This mixture of ideologies was rationalized by the need for continued economic development to sustain the minority ruling elite. This rich land mass had diamonds, oil, iron ore, and more to be discovered; and vast food production capabilities with multiple yearly crops and large cattle herds capable of feeding more than 250 million people, according to CIA statistics. Angola was also the world's third- largest coffee producer.

Boavida was responsible for the medical services in the eastern region of Angola and faced an immense task—the legacy left by five centuries of Portuguese colonialism. He described the situation as follows: "Angolans suffer from diseases unheard of in developed countries: malaria, scurvy, polio, leprosy, filariasis, parasitism, dysentery, kwashiorkor; they die from ills such as measles and bronchitis, which are no more than a nuisance to people with modern medical care. As

---

1   Following the arrest of Neto on February 4, 1961, Angolans attacked the Luanda prison and some 1,500 were killed and over 3,000 injured.

a result, infant mortality rates are as high as sixty percent in the rural areas, while the life expectancy of a black Angolan is only twenty-eight years . . .

"I've had fifteen years' experience and have practised in several African countries, but I've run across cases in Angola which I would not have thought possible. The Portuguese provided absolutely nothing for these people in the way of medical services."

During our interview, he spoke of the problems faced by S.A.M. (Service Assistance Medical): "Our major needs are very basic: vaccines and serums to inoculate against endemic diseases and locally trained medical cadres to administer our programs.

"Transportation and storage of medicines have also been a problem, as supplies must be carried long distances. The lack of electricity has been a barrier to setting up refrigerated facilities."

In 1967, under Boavida's leadership, S.A.M. began a program to train medical personnel in Angola. Intensive medical and nurses' aide courses lasting from three to six months were given at the medical centres in the liberated areas in Angola.

He went on: "Outside Angola, medical personnel are receiving advanced training as doctors, surgeons, lab technicians in African countries and socialist countries."

Dr. Boavida concluded with these words: "This is the sad heritage of 500 years of Portugal's rule. Malnutrition, disease, and death have accompanied Portugal's destruction of African economic and social structures and the continued use of slavery under the guise of 'contract labour.'"

According to the United Nations, ". . . medical services are . . . practically non-existent, there is one doctor for every 114,000 persons—Canada has one doctor per 890 persons—. . . most Africans have never seen a doctor, much less an infirmary." (*Afrique Asie Magazine*, book review by B.J. Quidado.)

As we parted, Boavida added, "You must come and see our living conditions. Though very poor, the population in the liberated areas is free. No oppression, no forced labour."

I accepted the invitation eagerly. Our two-hour face-to-face interview was a wonderful experience. We hugged and wished each other good luck.

I was worn out. What a difficult life for the Angolans. What appalling conditions! Could it really be that bad?

Within a few days, I had transcribed and translated the interview. I showed it to Barnett. He was pleased. He also, without my knowledge, began to publish my material under his name.

Everyone knew Barnett spoke no French. It was intellectual theft. I needed to watch out!

Boavida's story kept turning over in my head. I did not sleep well. I needed to find corroborating stories. I thought seriously about the living conditions. If the MPLA did invite me into Angola, how would I hold up? Malaria and yellow fever were the only two diseases Boavida had mentioned that I recognized and against which I had been inoculated. The thought of dying haunted me.

I needed to find a copy of *Angola Awake* by Rev. Dr. Sid Gilchrist, a Canadian missionary who had served thirty-eight years as a medical doctor in the central highlands, appointed by the United Church in 1928, serving first at Camundongo, then at the Dondi mission, some 450 miles east of Luanda, near Huambo, and finally at Bailundo. I was back in Canada in early 1969 before I got a copy. What struck me were the medical descriptions and details of the results of colonialism, which corroborated what Dr. Boavida had told me in the 1968 interview.

Boavida graphically described the agonies of his daily work: "We do the clinical examination, and as we examine the child, our minds picture the pathology inside the sad body under our fingers. The fatty degeneration of the liver and pancreas, the extreme deficiency of essential enzymes due to the damaged vital cells that should produce them, the blood serum so pitifully poor in proteins and all the other things that happen as a result of denial to a growing child of eggs, meat, fish, milk, peanuts, soybeans—any one of these or simply a good mixed diet.

". . . Rather, they—diseases—are manifestations of an intricate complex of interwoven and interrelated problems of disease, ignorance, economic evil and error, exploitation of subjected peoples."

This book, a real gem, published by Ryerson, confirmed the horrific conditions in Angola. Following the publishing of *Angola Awake,* the Portuguese would not issue him another working visa. The mission's work continued with Rev. Murray McInnis and other Canadian medical and religious staff, but now under constant surveillance. These Canadians were just another group of "terrorists," agents of international communism. These labels would not stick to the truth that Dr. Gilchrist had witnessed and now put down on paper.

Dr. Gilchrist writes:

It is easy to argue that all the good we missionaries have beenable to do in Angola . . . would never have been possible had we spoken clearly against the denial of human rights to Africans. It is much more difficult, however, to convince oneself that we should have waited so long to declare to the world the enormity of the evils of colonialism.

I have felt for a long time that the churches were the vehicle to population control by colonials and neo-colonials to the benefit of the West—the argument that if we were not here to save their souls, they would go to hell, founded on the belief that a better life will be had in heaven. As kids, we used to "purchase" Chinese people with collections of stamps. It was similar to sponsoring a Third-World child today, but that was the language the Church used: "Jacques has bought three Chinese" . . . the racist attitudes of the church were then translated into Western society terms: we are superior and the little niggers and yellows need to be saved.

The MPLA seemed very pleased with my efforts and demeanour. I met another leader of the MPLA, Pascal Luvale, head of the Trade Union for Angola, UNTA, who granted me an interview.

Pedro Van Dunen was introduced as "Loy," another top person of MPLA's youth.

In order to protect the identity of the families in the occupied areas of Angola, the Angolans adopted guerrilla names. Loy, Monimambu, Kimba, Toka, Quidado were all names that would become familiar. The *noms de guerre* were cities, events, or personalities.

These men and women were the builders of a new Angola.

In early March, Dr. Neto invited me to have dinner at his Kurassini home, and a small car came to pick me up.

The driver, known as Katumbela, spoke only Portuguese, so the greetings were brief and the ride fairly silent. Upon arriving at Dr. Neto's home, I was ushered into the parlour and waited. My eyes scanned the walls of the modest home, posters, photographs of Angola. There was a large photograph of the Luanda harbor. It was a vast area. And the small finger-shaped island to the left, with large palm trees. It was beautiful, as beautiful as Dar.

Dr. Neto's family entered, the kids first, followed by Mrs. Neto and Dr. Neto. The presentations were formal and very relaxed. I felt right at home. The Netos inquired about my family back in Canada. We talked about Angola, and its status and aspirations. The concerns were genuine. A cold beer called Tusker was served. It was brewed locally and quite tasty.

About an hour later, we moved to the dining room and sat down at a well laid-out table. A large fruit bowl centred the ten-plate settings. The driver and four other Angolans joined us.

It was my first meal of *funge*—a paste substance with a cassava base having a rubbery consistency. Neto explained the importance of this food. "Even if the rains don't come, the peasants can still get a crop. It is our national food. The Portuguese do not like this, but we can plant it everywhere and it grows. We have many different ways of preparing it. Just cut a piece of it with a knife and add a little fish sauce to your plate."

At this point he showed me how to eat the *funge* with my fingers. It was very chalky. Not so good. Neto offered me some *pili-pili*—Swahili for "spice."

I took a mouthful. The molten spice hit my palate, teeth, and

gums with an unannounced burst of fire. It felt like a hot iron. Water seemed to make it worse. I suppose that the beer made it better but the ensuing heartburn and associated pain were most uncomfortable. I suppose I gasped and went red, sweat bursting out on my forehead. The kids laughed. Neto said to the cook, "Please get him another cold beer."

So my first Angolan meal, though very good, gave me a little heartburn. After the dessert, Neto, President Dr. Neto, that is, suggested that we move back to the sitting room. As he rose, he put his dishes in the main plate, gathered a safely balanced load and brought it to the kitchen. We all followed his lead. This really impressed me. Most homes in Dar relied on servants to get things done. The new Angolan history was to be formed in a new way. I guess Neto had seen enough slavery and humiliation to make the effort to break the cycle.

We spoke about work that I had done and about the Boavida interview. The MPLA were very happy with the collaboration. Dr. Neto told me that an invitation to go and see Angola was being extended.

This was good news. This was great news. It was exactly what I had been hoping for, and yet it came as a shock. It was time to act; no more theory and idle talk.

Over the next four weeks, in numerous meetings, a plan of action was set out. MPLA agreed to bring a filmmaker into Tanzania, Roy Harvey from the Barnett group in California, and I was to join Barnett and travel to the eastern region of Angola.

By April 1968, I needed to find a new home. My house-sitting in Dar had come to an end. Mr. Stewart and the owners of the house were very pleased with the upkeep and condition of the house. Stewart immediately found me another house to sit.

It was on Zambia Avenue in the Oyster Bay area. This secluded house was an ideal place for my continued work with the MPLA. It was very difficult to find, due to bad signage and lots of trees and hedges. My new political friends visited in relative comfort and security. I met an Ethiopian man, Berhan Teckle. He had escaped the war-torn area of Asmara and was a Christian refugee living at the Luther House. I inquired about him, and his credentials from the managers of Luther House proved legitimate. I invited him to share the house. It was a very wise move, as he could pass for a house servant, keeping prospective walk-ins away. He was very involved with the Eritrean Liberation Front and understood the necessity of the "need-to-know" policy, so he exercised the required discretion. I learned how cruel Haile Selassie and his regime were and added to my global knowledge of repressive states.

April 9, 1968: The college administration, with the complicity of CUSO, called me into the principal's office and announced that I was being transferred immediately to the Iringa secondary school, 250 miles away on the Dar to Lusaka road. The activities of CUSO workers, demonstrating that Westerners could offer education and training and also show respect for the aspiring nation, were an affront to the neo-colonialist attitudes of the outgoing Brits. They were convinced they knew "how to control these Africans," and did not enjoy the contradictory evidence. CUSO was too accommodating of this attitude. Mike Sinclair, to his credit, did not challenge me, but neither did he come to my defence when I was removed from my teaching post.

For the first time in living memory, I did not react. I kept my cool. I took deep breaths and waited for the silence to be broken by the other side. Somehow, I seemed to have acquired some of the patience so well demonstrated by my MPLA friends.

I needed time to sort out my affairs in Dar. The following morning, I met with the administration and won a two-week delay. During the next fifteen days, I met a teacher returning from Iringa. He indicated that the school was closing from May 17 to July 2. Bingo. Just what I needed to know.

I immediately drove to the ferry and crossed Dar Harbour to see my friend Griff Cunningham. I explained the big picture and asked for his help. I needed a letter saying that my work at Kivikoni College had not been terminated and that Griff "needed" my services. The secondary schools were closing in a few weeks, and I could be of greater value in Dar than in an empty school. With his letter in pocket, I met with Mike Sinclair, the CUSO big cheese in the region, and explained my dilemma.

He bought my version of the story.

CUSO broke the news to Principal Martin. However, the college brass had given the approval that allowed me to stay for a few more weeks. I did not have to use the letter.

The new development was taken in by MPLA and set in motion the departure date for Barnett, Harvey, and me.

However, getting the visas for Zambia proved a far greater challenge than expected. In my case, as a Canadian passport holder, there was no need for a visa, as Zambia was a Commonwealth member. I could get an air ticket if the Tanzanian tax department issued a release form. I could go on to Zambia as a tourist. Barnett and Harvey had to wait in Dar till they got their documents.

The MPLA now wanted to get the communications project under way. Another meeting. This time it was about the money. I signed a receipt for the cash. The MPLA trusted that I would deliver.

This was another big step into new territory for me. I felt the responsibility keenly. I had never moved money, imported stuff, purchased offshore equipment. They had a need and they were willing to let me try. It was a great morale booster and another step to becoming a revolutionary in a just cause. MPLA was now expanding its operations to include comrades who could walk the walk. The MPLA gave me a chance to grow politically. Being close to a liberation movement is different from being part of it. I was now part of it. Being separate and having to invent a continuing persona in order to be useful to the movement added further sleepless nights. I had to become a chameleon on my own. It was very hard. Often alone, I continually had to reassure myself that my actions were helping the MPLA.

The next hurdle presented itself: How do we get this cash out of Tanzania?

The answer was looking at us: Carol and the three kids. Barnett had to send his family back to the USA, as he was running out of money. The appearance that the whole family had gone Stateside was necessary. Barnett had burned his bridges here. It was time for him to drop out of sight. Any problems created by outsiders could harm the interests of the newly independent state. The Africans were becoming their own spokespersons.

Within seven days, Carol had a flight. So the task was to hide the money in the clothing the kids and Carol wore for the flight. It was a chore requiring lots of safety pins. The kids were briefed, and, as they were already very political, their co-operation was assured. Carol carried my plans and specs to New York. She now held the success of our plan to help the MPLA in her hands.

She purchased the radio equipment and sent the parcels labelled "Religious Material" to the Rev. J. Roy c/o MPLA Dar es Salaam.

Another difficulty to overcome was keeping my parents from worrying. I was going to go underground for some time, perhaps up to a year. I did not want my parents to worry. So the only way to head off their concern was to write a number of letters in advance. Using different ink and pencil combinations, the letters were to be mailed off regularly by my roommate, Berhan. When CUSO called, for they were sure to, my mom could say that her son was okay and that she had just received a letter postmarked Dar es Salaam.

Then there was the matter of getting into good physical shape. MPLA told us that the eastern region was all savannah and lots of sand. Barnett and I walked the beaches in our work shoes. Walking in the sand was very tiring. I also walked back and forth to school. I followed the same route every day. However, one day I crossed the path of bees, African bees. The first stung my left eye, another the left knee and more bees stung the left eye. They were vicious. As the stings pierced the skin, I felt a deep burning sensation. I took off running and waving my arms and using my hands to push away the bees as they homed in on my eyes. Within one minute I reached the nearest house and the lady saw me coming and opened the small porch off to the right so I could hide. The bees did not follow me into the room. They disappeared. My eyes began to swell and my sight was failing. The lady called the hospital and within another minute she wheeled her car to the side door and I got in. I was in serious trouble. The African bee, known for its deadly venom, had killed horses, mules, and people.

On arrival, the medical team gave me two injections and I was out. The woman stayed by my side and some four hours later drove me home. The effect of the medication and the poison put me out of commission for three days. That was enough excitement for now.

As to the main project, time seemed to drag, there was no sign of a visa, and my time was running out. The original plan was that Barnett and Harvey and I would all travel together, but the deadline according to the CUSO agreement for my stay in Dar was coming up. I was expected to be on the train to Iringa the same day. A double plan was put in motion.

I arranged for a taxi to pick me up at the Oyster Bay house at 9:00 a.m. I had made train reservations, so it was only a case of picking up my ticket. I also had the tax release document, so I could make a reservation on Air Tanzania. The flight to Lusaka, Zambia, was scheduled for 11:00 a.m. MPLA made arrangements to have me picked up at the Lusaka airport.

June 28: Here is how it played out. The taxi arrived on time. Berhan came to the train station with me. I purchased the train ticket and said goodbye to Berhan. He left in the same taxi that had brought us.

With backpack in hand, I walked through the station to Barnett waiting in his Volkswagen Kombi. He drove me to the Dar airport. I did not see anyone I recognized, and boarding went very smoothly. I was on my way to Lusaka, as a Canadian volunteer on holiday, a tourist, and, according to the government, soon to be a "terrorist." It was 10:30 a.m.

During the flight, I concentrated on remembering the description of the two Angolans coming to pick me up. One was a man of forty with a grey mustache and a red hat, the other a young man my age.

We landed, and I was the first out, as I had only hand luggage. I walked into the airport lobby and saw the red hat and the grey mustache of a man of about forty and at his side a young black man.

He asked, "Are you Roy from Canada?" A connection: mission accomplished.

The older man was Anibal de Mello, one of the original founders of the MPLA, and the younger, Afonso M'binda, a promising cadre.

The trip to the Ridgeway Hotel in a blue Fiat station wagon took about twenty minutes. M'binda and de Mello stayed with me for half an hour and assured me that I was secure here.

They left. My head was spinning from the day's events. I had no dinner, just a shower and off to bed, after a little shortwave radio listening. One of my small but hugely important tasks was listening to Radio Canada International, France Inter, and the propaganda of the Voice of America and Radio Moscow.

CHAPTER FOUR

Problems are only opportunities in work clothes.

—Henry J. Kaiser

June 29, 1968.

I woke up very early and made my way down to the reception area. The usual continental breakfast of toast and coffee was available; the dining room would open at 7:30. I sat in the garden with a copy of the *Times of Zambia.* There were lots of trees, walking paths, and well-trimmed grass. Trees were the main feature at the front of the hotel, along with some colourful red and pink flowers in large terracotta pots on the top step of the entranceway.

This hotel was a typical remnant of British colonialism. Situated on a hillside, two massive white concrete pillars supporting a massive decorative beam with an imbedded emblem formed the entryway. I walked through to the parking lot to get a better view of the surroundings. The sun came up slowly and revealed a very different scene outside the colonial comfort of the hotel. The air was very dry and sound seemed to travel differently. The traffic of large lorries and buses and a few cars threw up red dust clouds.

The shoulders of the roadway were a brick red, and dropped off sharply into large ditches. The surrounding fields had a few sparse grasses sticking up. The parched expanses indicated that this was the dry season. I walked for more than an hour just to get oriented. It certainly was a shock, a stark contrast to Dar es Salaam. For one thing, I did not speak the two local languages. They sounded harsh and I had a feeling tribalism was endemic here. The atmosphere on the street was aggressive and unfriendly. All the shops were enclosed in wire mesh with a sleeping guard at the door. The city shut down after working hours. The lack of fruit and vegetables was a stark contrast to the plenty of Dar.

By 7:30, I was back at the Ridgeway and went for breakfast. I recognized the fried tomatoes, badly cooked bacon, eggs, and dry, cold toast. Served by the roving waiters, coffee certainly helped to mask the flavour of my first breakfast in Zambia.

Within twenty minutes, I returned to my room and awaited the scheduled 8:30 telephone call. Sure enough, the phone rang at the half hour. De Melo and M'binda were in the lobby. I walked down to the lobby with my little packsack and we drove to the city centre in the blue Fiat. The large central avenue was a boulevard; we had to overshoot the left turnoff we wanted and double back at the traffic circle.

Commercial shops lined both sides of the street. It looked as if a movie of Harlem was being filmed. Windows and doors had steel mesh coverings. Security guards were omnipresent. It was not a pretty sight. We turned right at the bank and drove past the Lusaka Hotel on the right. After the stop sign, I noticed the public library on the right. After another stop sign, we turned left and proceeded a few metres to the Annex Hotel. We parked and walked through the opened glass door to the front desk. The strong odours of urine and sweat, along with poor lighting and ventilation, welcomed the three of us to my new home. For the next weeks, this was my arena for personal and political struggle.

The Annex was a hotel for Africans travelling through or on short working assignments in Lusaka.

Registration was complicated. Identification papers, passport, and reason for staying in Zambia were a few of the obligatory items on the registration form. Plus who was to pay and how. De Mello had to spell out it was the MPLA paying, with cash. This triggered a reaction from the desk clerk. For him MPLA meant war, immeasurable risk. Explanations followed. Finally, the clerk gave up on the detailed registration requirements. He trusted the Angolans. I would be an okay guest. Daily cost was $4.50—in real terms, my daily wages as a college teacher.

The Annex was a two-storey building with the kitchen, dining room, and reading room at the street level. Sleeping quarters were on the top level. We made our way up the creaky stairs. All the walls were light green. We reached the landing and I could see, in the dim light, dirty floors and long shiny "pucky" green hallways. Pretty grim.

The key, attached to a large piece of flat wood, indicated Room

Midway along the hall to the right was the common shared bath and toilet. To the left, a wooden door, and at eye level, in pencil, the room number, 19. We entered and found three single beds separated by three small wooden tables with drawers and a small clothes closet. Three upright wooden chairs completed the basic room furniture. The walls and ceiling were the same lime green as the hallways.

A large window with three separate pieces of glass overlooked the street. I took the bed closest to the window.

The room clerk, who had given us the tour, announced that this room, the last available, was to be shared with other travellers. This was very upsetting news. However, the MPLA gave it their okay, as they felt that I would be safe and secure. De Mello gave me Zambian currency, ten *kwatcha*, and took my passport. The MPLA needed to inform the Zambia security officials that I was their guest and their responsibility. As ID, I had my volunteer card with photograph and describing me as a teacher in the Republic of Tanzania.

I was very tired. The last three days in Dar es Salaam had been hectic and nerve-racking.

This cheap hotel was acceptable for a short stay, and the green room provided for my immediate and minimal needs. My two newfound friends from the MPLA said goodbye, promising to return the next day.

Two problems required immediate attention. Iringa school authorities and CUSO needed to be informed. I prepared a telegram for the Iringa principal and a letter for CUSO and found my way to the post office. These two transactions cost eight *kwatcha*. My money was fast disappearing; Zambia seemed very expensive. I walked the streets and window shopped between the hotel and post office and saw dress shirts for the equivalent of sixty-five dollars, shoes at fifty dollars. Upon my return to the Annex, I had a shower and observed the street activity as the daylight faded to darkness, and retired by ten p.m.

I was another step deeper in. I felt acutely aware of my surroundings. The reality of warfare, of the hostile surroundings of Zambia— Rhodesia, Angola, Mozambique, and Zaire—made for constant unease. Knowing that Zambia gave vocal and political support to UNITA it was understandable that the Zambian authorities and the population near the Zambia-Angola border were very afraid of the MPLA. MPLA draws Portuguese planes to Zambia to "kill our people and destroy our crops". The *Times of Zambia* supported the tribalist policies of UNITA—the "only true movement"—created by the Portuguese colonials who did not want to leave Angola. This pleased the Portuguese, the Smith UDI government, the Apartheid government in Johannesburg, and of course the USA. It was all quite overwhelming. My conviction that I was doing the right thing did not waver, but my spirit was at a low ebb.

The next day, de Mello and M'binda returned. Hotel rules, no doubt left over from colonial days, forbade residents at the Annex having guests in their room. So the hotel staff came to fetch me and brought me to the reading room, where my two MPLA friends were waiting. They wanted to know how I was holding up in my new quarters. It was the first time MPLA had put someone at the Annex. I told them the story of my first day and night. Within ten minutes they were gone, apparently satisfied I was going to be okay. They had a revolution to sustain and they were the two main players for Angola in the Zambian office. As the only white person in the hotel, *mzungu*, a *Mwandele*, a foreigner, I had no colour to hide behind. I felt very vulnerable in Lusaka, forced to improvise my behaviour because I could not say why I was there. A journalist is a suspicious figure, maybe a spy. I was always looking over my shoulder.

The breakfast on offer was dry toast and a thermos of coffee. With two *kwatcha* in my pockets, I began exploring the capital of Zambia. The city had long paved streets with few trees and still fewer flowering trees. It was very so different from Tanzania.

My first stop was at the public library. It offered a slim selection of daily newspapers, while the book section showed that independence had not had a large impact on collection. There were not many volumes, and many of them were from another era. Though Zambia had been independent since 1964, I could not detect any improvements. The library offered four or five hours of welcome solitude and minimal visibility. This period could be understood as serious research with a low risk of security attention. Zambians were constantly reminded of the presence of foreigners on their soil, in particular South African and Rhodesian. Wars were being conducted on five fronts, and Zambia was the launching area for four of them.

I purchased a bag of apples from the small store one block east of the library. That left me with fifty *ngwee*.

So for the next two days, it was apples for lunch and dinner. I also kept my face clean-shaven. Beards were synonymous with rebels and guerrillas and a magnet for suspicious questions.

I had never in my life been without good food and water. Now I wanted to be part of the movement to change the extreme poverty of Angolans, which has its counterpoint in Canada's wealth. Think of coffee plantation slavery for the sake of cheap coffee on our breakfast table. I was prepared to live on bad water and poor food, sometimes very little of either, in order to help change the system. It was a challenging adjustment.

I had located the CUSO offices late on the first night and stayed away from the Lusaka city centre and high traffic areas during business hours. However, on day three, I faced the first crisis. As I was finishing my daily diary entries, there was a loud knock at my door. I hesitated and the knock was repeated, louder. So I got up and opened the door. There stood a short white guy. He identified himself as Chris Brown from the CUSO Lusaka office. He stated that CUSO Tanzania had ordered me back to Dar. I said that I was on holidays and asked him to leave. He did so.

How did he know I was here? I thought long and hard. I retraced my steps and looked at the two documents that I had sent. It came to me. I had reversed the method of delivery, mail and telegram. The school had gotten the information that I was not coming before CUSO knew that I had disappeared. The trace came via the telegram, as I had been obliged to put a return address and had been truthful. Big mistake. Something had to be done if these CUSO people were not to add to our difficulties. I called Afonso and the MPLA transferred me to a motel south of Lusaka on the road to Rhodesia. It was more expensive than the Annex, but offered greater privacy and security.

This was a place where personal and political contradictions arose. MPLA kept contact, although they had a political office to run in Lusaka. I was an important distraction, but a distraction nonetheless. MPLA was learning how difficult it was to keep a friendly foreign comrade happy, not realizing how much I had to absorb in this new situation. I had no one to rely on as I went through this personal revolution. They in their modest surroundings had their language, customs, focused purpose, and shared poverty. I had isolation, little food, and the constant awareness that I did not fit in Zambian society. In fact, I stood out, since growing a beard due to having no shaving equipment or funds to buy any fed the stereotype of beard means guerrilla, communist, and subversive. Being aware of my shortcomings was a constant reminder that wanting to help the Angolans required depth of soul and spirit.

The road in front of the motel was unpaved. The dry season meant strong winds, and dust blew into the room through the unsealed bottom of the door. Red dust was everywhere. This made breathing so difficult that I could not sleep. I improvised by blocking the bottom of the door with a wet towel. The winter season continued cold and very windy.

These new conditions were very uncomfortable and required strenuous adjustment. Breakfast was again toast and coffee in a thermos. Within a few days, I got my bearings and planned new activities.

My second serious physical conditioning period began. The motel was eight kilometres south of Lusaka, and this distance gave me an opportunity to improve my walking endurance. I left my room at six a.m. and force-marched to the library. The winding trail from the motel to Lusaka was used by the Zambians as a major walking and bike thoroughfare. In Africa, one is expected to greet everyone within a certain distance. I had learned the Zambian greeting, *muli bwanji*— hello—and the response, *teelee bwino*—good day. On arriving in Lusaka, I walked the secondary and transverse streets and meandered my way to the library for nine o'clock. I read extensively on the history of Southern Africa. Living conditions for the disenfranchised majority indicated dire poverty. Wealth was for the whites, and the descending degrees of have to have-not corresponded to the spectrum of shades between white and black.

Alongside the steady consumption of daily newspapers and

monthly magazines, the hunger pains seemed secondary. Before sunset, I walked back to the motel. While in Dar, I maintained a high intake of fresh fruit and protein, but Zambia presented problems. Fruit was virtually nonexistent and very expensive if I could find it. Now my lack of money imposed hunger. This period, as it turned out, was very beneficial. Hunger changed my perspective. To follow my dream, I needed strength, tenacity, and a sense of humour. Constant effort was needed to keep to a satisfying work schedule.

Next to the motel was a drive-in theatre. As soon as the movie started, I would leave my room with my sleeping bag tucked under my arm and find a hiding spot in the surrounding long bushes and watched the "silent" movie. The starry nights were cold and beautiful. This southern sky gave me an unexpected lesson in the planets and stars of the southern hemisphere. These nights out gave me a few hours' respite from the monotony of personal survival and an escape from boredom and isolation.

During this period, MPLA kept frequent contact, and I met many Angolan leaders. Our meetings were mutually satisfactory.

In June of 1968, M'binda requested that I move back to the Annex. It was a safer place, and he visited more often. But it was still Room 19. M'binda was a little older than I and stuttered seriously. He seemed over his head with multiple responsibilities; or were his health problems related to some trauma inflicted by the forces of colonialism? It was too early to ask, but most important to me. He was a gentle and kind man. He listened to my descriptions of my new reality, and he'd answer, "That's our struggle."

One of the tough political struggles I had to undergo began when De Mello made arrangements for visas to be cleared in Dar for the two Americans. Due to disastrous inefficiency, they did not get them. Being alone for nearly two weeks with no mail made me scared, angry, and irritable. I swore at them, "They must know I am broke, since I sent them the only currency I had. They must know I am broke." I felt very sorry for myself. It took two days of struggle to overcome this false sense of persecution. When I resolved this conflict, I could see how ridiculous it was that I let the lack of a letter become the central issue in my life. Being unproductive was also an important contributor to my evil mood. Another lesson: learning to accept a situation over which I had no control. The narcissistic individualism so cultivated in our North American society has to be brought under control and attenuated.

So I broke through my self-pity. I had no restrictions on my movements, I had my books, and I was not in jail. Though I had no food, it seemed a pretty good deal.

I remembered how Ben Turok had been jailed for two and a half years, six months of it in solitary confinement. Along with the continuing imprisonment of Nelson Mandela, this reminded me of the contract between the MPLA and its friends. If you want to survive, you have got to be tough, resilient and creative. Becoming a new person seemed to be the only way; reality was not going to change.

Another difficult experience, and a totally unexpected benefit, was my being forced to wait. It's a necessary, a very necessary exercise. A person going from North America directly into the war zones of

Angola without having had some tough lessons in patience would find it extraordinarily difficult. Their presence, unschooled in this discipline, would be a grave danger for their companions.

A high political consciousness is required and could be obtained only through physical and psychological adaptations. Once I crossed the line from observer to actor, all speech and action had to be purposeful. This included tasks that we do not like to do, willingly taking on responsibilities and language training, and adapting to new cultures.

During this Lusaka period, the lack of money created a difficult situation. On one occasion, the MPLA gave me another ten *kwatcha*. With food so expensive, this amount fed me for two days. This first incident occurred five days following my arrival in Zambia. I had only sixty *ngwee* and this was to last three days. I needed some library books for the weekend. A library card costing fifty *ngwee,* and ten *ngwee* for tea later in the day, meant no lunch or dinner. With eight apples to eat, versus one meal today with tea tomorrow, no library card meant no books for "home." I needed books to survive.

The library card won out.

My hunger-stimulated creativity soon had me hoarding energy supplies. Coffee was served before breakfast in the room, so I poured out the water from the thermos and stored the coffee and loaded up on the available sugar. This assured me of a coffee break with an apple. This combo counted as lunch and was served sometime after 12:30. Lack of funds also had a positive value. The absence of money taught me how to reduce my diet from three meals a day to one apple "meal" and a tea break. Reducing my appetite and continuing to function at a near-normal level was certainly an important lesson. However, following a three-day period of only coffee and sugar, I decided to get creative about food. Good food. With no money.

I went to the Lusaka hotel before lunchtime. It was a security risk, and from the comfortable sofas in the lobby, I observed the ins and outs of the dining room staff. There did not seem to be a control mechanism on who entered the eating area. As a white person, my presence was judged normal. So, taking a deep breath, I walked into the dining area and told the African maître'd that I was waiting for someone. I took my time during this exploratory walk-through. I sat down and retold my story of waiting for someone while enjoying the cold glass of water while evaluating the flow of food and the dining room protocol.

It took me a few minutes to size up the situation and returned to the lobby for ten minutes. Gathering my courage, I walked to a table near the kitchen and stood by, observing that one waiter had the traditional face markings of a Northern Tanzanian African. I greeted him with "*Shikamo mzee.*" This greeting means, "I am below your dignity," a traditional child's greeting of an adult, to which the adult responds "*Maharaba*"—"You may rise, be of equal status." This greeting from a white man speaking kiswahili caught him off-guard. I quickly followed up with "*Nianja,*"—"I'm hungry"— "*na kasi yangu iko uhuru ya Angola,*" "my work is independence for Angola." His facial expression changed with a jerk of his head as he said, "*Kaa hapa, ngoja kidogo*"— "Sit and wait a little."

Somehow, I knew how to do this. He returned and pointed to a specific table. I walked over and sat down. The usual formalities of a detailed billing were being overlooked. "Bingo," I said under my breath, with my heart pounding away. He brought a basket of warm brown rolls with butter. I had to hold myself back. The urge to wolf it down was almost overwhelming. I was so very hungry and it would hurt later if I loaded up now.

He continued to serve other patrons on his table watch, while observing my demeanour. In a very discreet way he took away the first basket and replenished it with another. On his following pass he placed a bowl of hot soup on my table. When he saw this dish empty, he picked it up and returned with a plate of fish, potato, and carrots. I gulped it down and finished off the rolls and the cold water. I sensed that my mission wasover, it was time to leave. "*Assante sana mze,*" —"Thank you very much, old man." With this, I got up and headed for the washroom situated in the lobby. I washed my hands and walked through the lobby, turning right and finding freedom as my shoes touched the sidewalk. It was library time. This time on a full stomach.

The "senior Tanzanian citizen" had helped me out at some risk to his livelihood, and I really appreciated his gesture. I did not ask it of him again. Back at the Annex, the front desk had a rotating shift and one of the "fab four" was very sticky on hotel rules. No guests in the rooms. When pressed to relax the rule, he threatened to call the police. On one occasion M'binda, accompanied by Commander Monimambu, came to visit. They had made it to my room without consequences. I was very pleased to see Monimambu. There was a definite purpose to their presence. Following greetings and some news, M'binda pulled an invoice from his appointment book. "*Camarade* Jacques Roy, we have received in Dar the radio equipment. Could you tell us why the information in the box relating to method of payment has the initials CIA?"

I was taken back by the question and even more by the political implications of the acronym. "We will come back tomorrow," M'binda added.

I was really shocked. What could this mean? The MPLA had paid for the equipment with cash. I spent the next hours thinking about it and finally came up with an answer. Carol and the kids had carried the funds to America and had paid up front for the radio equipment.

The next day, Dr. Neto, de Mello, and M'binda showed up at the Annex and were escorted to Room 19, where I greeted them and offered them a seat. Dr. Neto enquired about the living conditions at the hotel and added, "Now, *Camarade* Jacques, you are beginning to see the types of problems we face in our march towards independence." I could only nod in agreement.

"*Nous voulons savoir que veut dire CIA sur le document qui accompagne leséquipements de radio.*" (We would like to know why the letters CIA appear in the method of payment box.)

"*Et bien, Dr. Neto, la facture a été payé en avance de la livraison et en anglais, ceci explique le CIA.*" (Well, Dr. Neto, the method of payment was cash in advance, therefore CIA.) Dr. Neto accepted the explanation, and I felt a whole lot better. So they left and I resumed my life of isolation and waiting for the day that we would be heading for Angola.

The sharing of Room 19 caused many problems. During an evening while absent on a walking session, an Egyptian man rented a bed. He stole a camera, film, and a munitions belt that I had converted to a film carrier. Before he was picked up by the CID—criminal investigation department—he had been to three hotels with these goods. According to the police, he claimed that he had caught a spy in Room 19 of the Annex Hotel. I returned at ten p.m. and found the lobby occupied by police officers and plainclothes white detectives. As I entered the lobby, the desk clerk pointed me out to the police as the guy living in Room 19. My surprised look must have said it all. The police took me into the reading room and started with the questions.

"What are you doing here?"

I answered, "I am a journalist visiting Zambia."

"Why do you have so much film in a military ammunition belt and two cameras?"

I took a deep breath and repeated that I was a photojournalist.

They accepted the photojournalist story. It was the military belt that made them uncomfortable.

They would not allow me to call my friend M'binda. I was caught out. The multitude of questions kept coming, and the answers were judged inadequate but plausible. They finally stopped the flow of questions. The police now wanted to deal with the thief.

Most of all, I did not want to press charges. I was happy to get my stuff back without charging him. This did not persuade the police to go away. The police asked to see my passport. Since the MPLA had it, I presented my CUSO volunteer card. It was a nice try, but I was forced to declare my connection with the MPLA. As I told my story, I registered that they didn't have a clue about my statement. To sum up one white detective's view, "You are a white Canadian, living at this hotel as a guest of the 'terrorists' from Angola, waiting to go to Angola to take photos of the war."

"That's freedom fighters, sir, not terrorists."

"In our books, these are guys running around with guns and probably communists." No further comment from JR. The interview are over.

As we left the reading room, my eyes focused on the hotel doorway. The presence of police jeeps and CID cars created a hell of a commotion at the hotel entrance. A crowd had gathered. They wanted to see the spy in Room 19.

What a mess. It culminated with the police saying they knew the mentally deranged man. I went to my room with a heavy heart and sagging shoulders. I was burned out.

So the next morning, M'binda showed up and, as I told him the story of the theft, he really stuttered. He was stunned. "I, I, I, got, got, to go to the authorities to explain what, what is going on." I reassured M'binda that everything seemed to be okay. He accepted that. He then took away all of my equipment. I had only my diary and I kept it on my body. The MPLA now knew that the set-up was precarious, filled with unknowns and vulnerable to potential danger.

August 1, 1968: Dr. Neto and de Mello came to the hotel and the co-operating clerk was on duty. They came to the room and told me of the difficulties with the visas for our two friends. They were also upset about the theft, just another difficulty due to a lack of funds and co-operation from the Zambian authorities. A truck would be leaving within a few days for Angola.

I should get ready to leave. Finally, all the waiting, boredom, and hunger focused on the *raison d'être*.

CHAPTER FIVE

*Credibility is a perceived phenomenon, conviction, character, care,
courage, composure.*

I was really excited, and the remaining hours dragged by. On the
following Friday, at six p.m., M'binda came to inform me, "You will
be leaving tonight. Here is ten *kwatcha* to purchase a little food."

I went to the little store near the hotel and purchased five cans of
condensed milk. I remembered from my camping and fishing days in
Kirkland Lake that this was instant energy. I had learned in my many
conversations with MPLA comrades in French or Portuguese that the
"guerrilla" did a lot of walking, running to hide from enemy aircraft and
required lots of patience. Also, food was to be supplied by the peasants
living in the liberated regions, and if peasants had to flee due to military
activity, then there would be little or no food.

At ten p.m., de Mello and M'binda arrived, and we left the Annex
in a Land Rover and headed for the outskirts of Lusaka. A large five-ton
truck was waiting with the back covered with a tied-down tarp. M'binda
introduced Toka as commander of the mission, and his assistant Joao.
This short man had the task of getting us to the Angola border.

I hugged my hosts M'binda and de Mello and thanked them for
their patience and all they had done for me.

Toka indicated in Portuguese that I would be sitting up front in
the middle seat.

"*Vamos camarade,*" he added. M'binda and de Mello in unison
replied, "*A Lutta Continua.*" Commander Toka and Joao responded,

"*A Victoria e Certa.*" Toka climbed aboard and started up the big diesel unit. Joao got in and sat to my left. We were on our way. I was in the middle position and on a slippery leather seat with little foot room to steady myself.

We drove due west for about two hours. Our first stop was obligatory: the left rear outside tire was flat. We got out and undid the tied-down tarp to get at the jack and replacement tire. Voices came from under the tarp and everyone got out. They had been sitting on bags of food and cases of ammunition next to the drums of fuel. There were ten blacks and an Indian Asian. I stood aside, watching the tire operation proceed. A tall African approached, and through the dim light came a voice: "You must be the Canadian journalist who is accompanying us." The speaker came closer, and to my great surprise it was Dr. Boavida. He was also very surprised. We threw out our arms and hugged each other warmly. From this moment, we would be together. He took my hand and we walked over to the watching "Angolan inspectors" who were assessing the work to be done.

The first introduction, in French, was to the journalist Aquino

Braganza from Goa. He was an old friend of Dr. Neto's and a freelance journalist for *Afrique-Asie*, the Paris-based monthly magazine. Boavida told Braganza that during our interview back in February in the Dar office, he had stated that, "A white man could not survive six months in Angola." I added, "I am not going to commit suicide. I trust the MPLA *camarades*."

Switching to Portuguese, Boavida introduced Dilolwa, Quidado, and Lingatti. These three young men smiled, and two responded in French and the other in Swahili. I shook hands with the other Angolans and they greeted me in Lingala and Chokwe. These Angolan peasants also used their left hand to hold their right elbow when shaking with the right hand. I asked Boavida why. "It is to show you that they have disarmed the left arm, proof that they will not harm you." This handshake is particular to the Kwando Kubango region. These fellow travellers were to be my ears and eyes. I had read up on the basics of guerrilla warfare, and trust was the one element I gave willingly to my friends. Quidado was twenty-eight years old, a veteran of the First and Second Regions, and a military commander with an excellent reputation. Lingatti was twenty-two years old, a six-foot-four- inch Angolan and a two-year veteran of the eastern region military campaign. We spoke a compatible Swahili, as his Portuguese was weak and mine non-existent. *Camarada* Dilolwa, a mulatto schoolteacher, spoke an impeccable French. He was very bright and responsible for the Department of Education and Culture (DEC) for the Third Region.

The tire change was done, and we resumed our trip. Every bit of road was washboard. The first night, we drove untill three a.m.

Following a thirty-minute rest and a fuel transfer, we resumed the journey. It was very cold, five degrees Celsius, and sitting between commander Toka and Joao the sous-chef co-driver was very uncomfortable. We kept on going. We travelled through the Kafue Game Reserve. At one point a lion was caught in the headlights of the truck. It ran and followed the road, so we had a view of a running lion for a good fifteen minutes. The reason for travelling at night through Kafue was to escape the deadly tsetse fly, which transmits sleeping sickness.

At the end of day two, disaster struck. We were miles off- course because all the people on this convoy were from another region of Angola or had never travelled this route. We had lost time and exposed ourselves to Zambian curiosity.

While we were stopped to change another flat tire, seven police officers in a Land Rover stopped to investigate why so many Wazungu (plural of Mzungu, white person) were in this truck. In fact, I was the only white. However, the many shades of the travellers, combined with the historical illiteracy of the Zambian authorities, made this question relevant. Language barriers and the madness of dealing with political illiteracy required immense patience and repeated shoulder shrugs.

We were detained for twelve hours, and all the high-level bureaucrats with security powers in the region had a crack at us. They could not understand why I was risking my life with these unarmed freedom fighters. Zambian officials kept saying the Portuguese have guns and planes and they shoot even our Zambian people. MPLA knew this very well but to try and explain the history and the struggle to correct the damage of colonialism was futile. I just listened and shook my head, thinking that this would make a great movie.

Zambian authorities did not search the truck. They used me to translate their English questions into French for Toka and Boavida.

This experience was typical of the external problems that the MPLA faced every time it moved. We had to be prepared to meet such problems, which meant having a passport, press card, and a credible story.

From my diary:

Our trip to this point was very revealing. The *camarades* were always happy, satisfied that it was not as tough as it might be. They were disciplined, non-inquisitive as to why they were picked to do certain tasks . . . deep and warm, warm relationships developed even though (verbal) communications are minimal. I learned to respect their courage and simplicity (when facing new problems); not being able to trust their Zambian neighbours . . . their non-racist attitude toward the Portuguese exemplified by such statements as, "we want to destroy the Portuguese, not because they are Portuguese or white but because they are colonizers and have oppressed the people of Angola for 500 years."

They were absolutely convinced they could win, even though it might take another 5 to 10 years, but if we must fight for 20 years, we will.

The sous-chef in our group, Joao, had never driven but when Commandant Toka got tired, Joao took over. At one point his unskillful driving—not knowing how to shift gears—stalled the engine repeatedly, and drained the battery. Every time the truck stalled, it had to be pushed to get it going. This was the first time that I noticed Quidado. The road was covered with eight inches of dry, loose sand and pushing a truck, loaded with eight to ten tons of goods, to a start, was very difficult and energy consuming. This is how we did it: The eight inches of sand on top had to be removed in order to get down to the moist sand, a hard, compacted subsurface. This meant all four wheels had to touch the hard surface and a twenty-metre path in front of each tire had to be cleared. Then we could push it to a jumpstart. Driving could no longer be done at night after the battery failure.

The incident that brought us to near demoralization was when we stalled the truck on an upgrade. We chugged along in the incorrect gear to the eventual stall. Commander Toka and Quidado were of the same political military rank. As Toka was in charge of this mission, he controlled the group. Toka chose Quidado to walk to Mongu, some 100 kilometres away, and send an MPLA jeep or mechanic to get us going. The Zambians could not be trusted, therefore asking the local police to pull us to a start was out of the question. *Camarada* Quidado covered the distance in two days, supplied only with water. It was waiting time again. We slept in the bush out of sight of the truck. During this wait, Boavida taught me Portuguese words. The Latin base of French helped me with pronunciation. My weakness was the vocabulary. So I learned as much as my mind could absorb. The lack of food began to affect my mind and my ability to retain information. Boavida spoke of his book, *500 Years of Exploitation.* The sheer volume of human indignities against the Angolans staggered the mind. The profitability of colonial exploitation meant that the exploiters had no reason to welcome Angola as an independent member of the free world. They would fight, and fight they did.

Diary entry:

Sleeping in the forest with millions of mosquitoes kissing my skin left a lot to be desired. No sooner had the sun risen than wild bush flies accompanied every move. I covered my mouth, nose, ears with a piece of bed sheet. This was held in place with my tight-fitting hat. The tenacity of the peasants and guerrillas in these difficult conditions was moving. The lack of food, water and comfort is second to the will of wanting Angola to struggle against Portuguese colonial forces.

Zambian vehicles used this road, and the MPLA could not afford contact. Our food supply was cassava, Russian tinned sardines, and *funge,* called *foo foo* here, but still the paste substance that Dr. Neto had introduced to my palate back in Dar. Getting to know my travelling companions was an education in history, sociology, political science, economics, and international politics with its own political and military agenda. And finally guerrilla warfare, the ten-to-one ratio of mobile forces used to tie down, demoralize, and defeat a traditional army. I needed time to process and absorb this information.

Extracts from my diary:

Finally the Land Rover arrived and pulled us to a start. A shout of joy belted from everyone's lungs when the big Bedford moved under its own power. Boavida's smile filled his face. "*C'est notre realité*," it's our reality. We still had toget to Mongu.

fter travelling for 12 hours, stopping once only for the transfer of gasoline from the drum . . . to the gas tank we came across a shallow creek. My mind raced to the possibility that we could wash our faces and feel the cool water. No such chance. We did not stop and it was really difficult to understand why we didn't. So I asked Commandant Toka, "Why hadn't we stopped even for 5 minutes so that we could wash and recover our legs?" After all, we have been exposed to the dust and dry air. Toka said, "We must avoid at all cost any contact with the peasants of this area, especially since you are white. The local people ask many questions so we must create as few problems as possible. You saw the difficulties we had at that small village with the police officers who wanted to detain you." Enough said. We arrived at the Mongu MPLA staging area.

By the time we arrived at the Zambezi River, it was 1800 hours and night was falling. The ferry crossing was feasible only in daylight. We had to stop the engine. Fortunately, we were the first vehicle for the next trip in the morning, and the road to the riverbank had a decent downward slope, a natural launching pad for the Bedford. We got out of this hot box and regrouped to plan the "overnight motel" and accompanying activities. Human activity on both sides of this huge and fast-moving river made an incredible scene. A permanent group of vendors of food and spices, medicine men pitching their cures, charcoal sellers, cloth sellers, and families from babies to toothless elders gathered to carry on commerce with the passing traffic. The Zambezi's crocodiles and hippos were very active, their grunts and bellowing mingling with the noise of the crowds on either shore. Small cooking fires also provide heat in the chill night air, cooled by a constant wind off the racing river current, the flickering light casting fantastic larger-then-life shadows.

I could not take pictures; no activity to attract the curious could be risked. The large ferry was attached by a pulley system to a heavy-duty cable that was strung from opposite shores in order to give the tugboat the required direction needed for a safe landing. The Zambezi at this point is very fast flowing, and the ferry could not cross, maintain direction, and unload the vehicles safely on its own. The evening turned from burning a thirty-five degrees Celsius to a cool five degrees celsius. It was very cold. We huddled near the truck and had no contact with the Zambians. They also kept their distance, due to the language difference. Following our meagre food intake— cassava sticks called *bon bon-*candy, tasting like school chalk—we returned to our regular position. Sleeping in the sitting position on a worn leather seat between two others was very uncomfortable. The Zambezi shores and waters were very noisy. The hippos, the crocodiles, and monkeys added a dimension of unbelievably surreal nightlife. It was a long, long, cold night. I woke up often, still taking in this African reality: Hardship, with so many problems to solve in order to achieve the sacred goal of independence. These MPLA guerrillas had seen enough of colonialism, and this motivated them with the necessary strength and drive to carry on. It was up to me to muster the energy and fortitude to go the distance. I must add to the effort, not be a distraction.

At the first light of day, the river ferry workers, who slept on

the opposite shore, loaded and crossed with the first two vehicles. Toka explained our starting method in his best English. A small Land Rover was driven on first and with a little push our truck was started and loaded onto the ferry.

On crossing the Zambezi River, one of the *camarades* accidentally shut off the Bedford engine . . . unbelievable. Now what? After the Land Rover got off the ferry, we agreed that this would the one push we could not miss. So we pushed, I mean really pushed, all together with heads down. The Bedford started to move and Toka let out a shout,

"Push harder," and we did. The short takeoff distance of some ten metres offered a good foot grip and the combined effort gave us enough momentum for a push to start. It is as if our lives depended on it.

Hearing the engine turn over was a great relief, and Toka just floored the engine and bounced off the river raft and to shore. Not a pretty sight as the truck bounced up on hitting the downgrade of the river bank and bounced again when the rear wheels rolled off the ferry and hit the sandy shores. We all cheered loudly. How many more bounces did we need before getting to our destination? We made it to Mongu.

Next stop, Kalabo.

The journey from Lusaka to Kalabo took five days. It was the first time that a day meant something. We lived many long, continuous hours and engaged in so many struggles. We stopped for a few hours for *funge* accompanied by a mildly flavoured chicken sauce and a chance to wash and relax. This MPLA base had a large central house, a small hospital, a garage maintenance area, and a few large tents. It was clean, and the few trees offered some relief from the equatorial sun.

The next leg of the trip was beyond Kalabo. Toka, Boavida, Braganza, and Lingatti with two Angolan soldiers fitted tightly into the newly acquired Land Rover. I remembered the names of these towns and rivers from planning the radio communications project. Kalabo was fifty miles as the crow flies from the Zambezi; however, the Southern Lueti River had no bridge and was too deep to cross with the jeep at this point. We found a shallow spot downstream and crossed with ease, but the trip had required a 150-kilometre trek, many hours, and much fuel. I saw how useful the new radio equipment would be. No more hand-delivered notes by road, by dugout canoe, to the final location of the MPLA base camp. We arrived and enjoyed a four-hour rest.

Beyond Kalabo, and out of reach of the Barotse Flood Plains, in Sikongo, the MPLA had set up their final staging area before entering Angola. The mood here was serene, serious, and focused; the radio was on continuously and tuned to Radio Luanda. The English service broadcast opened with the byline "You are tuned to the National Radio

Station of Portugal in Africa, a daily feature of Portuguese activities in the overseas provinces of Angola." I really preferred the French version "*Ici le Portugal en Afrique,*" this is Portugal in Africa. I could not believe my ears. This was the dictionary definition of colonialism in action, though it had a positive psychological effect on the MPLA. This propaganda by the Portuguese colonials—abbreviated to Tugas—gave the news of events in Angola as well as coded messages for the some 180,000 soldiers stationed throughout Angola. Military confrontations were ignored or played down, but the ongoing news from the MPLA ensured that MPLA successes were announced, creating further problems for the Tugas. The most important military defeat of the Tugas had taken place at Karipanda. Not only had the most important post of the colonial military presence been blown up, but the accompanying settlers had abandoned the region. The influx of these settlers into the next military base created insecurity in the settler community and doubt about the ability of the military to "control Angola."

In the evening, the MPLA broadcast, at 8:00 p.m., called *Angola Combatent*, gave a summary of military events in Portuguese and Angola's five national languages. MPLA underground activities and events in the major centres of Luanda, Huambo, Luso, Cabinda, and Malange as examples gave the liberation movement an opportunity to focus on the whole territory. The words of political encouragement were daily reminders that progress was being made.

News on activities in Mozambique, South Africa, South West Africa, Rhodesia, and Guinea Bissau gave an overview to political and military and dimensions of the struggle in Southern Africa.

August 8, 1968:

Commander Toka told us to rest. "We're leaving tonight . . . prepare for the long walk."

2330 hours. Twelve guerrillas, armed, carrying large backpacks gather in front of the hut. Commander Toka got all of the people who are leaving now in a semi-circle for final instruction and walking order. The order: four guerrillas, Toka, Boavida, myself, Braganza, four more guerrillas, fifteen Angolan peasants, and on the rear guard the last four armed guerrillas.

I had a sleeping bag, packsack with two cameras, film, tape recorder, my shortwave radio, an extra shirt, and a twenty-four by eighteen-inch bed sheet. This homemade towel was part of my personal effects for the whole trip. We did not have scented soap, as this would indicate a foreign presence to the animals, causing noise and greatly increasing the risk of being discovered. The Tugas would have the advantage. As soon as we left the camp, we crossed a small creek. Our feet and boots were now wet. For the next hours it was sand, sand, and more sand. Walk, walk, and more walk. I stared at Boavida's heels, up, down, up, down, hypnotized.

The first stretch of our walk lasted till about 0800. We felt the cool night air disappear, saw the sun rise, and soon began to sweat.

Diary: "Any notion of romanticism had by now been utterly destroyed."

Following a twenty-minute rest, we resumed walking at a good pace. I slowly consumed my first can of condensed milk.

Two hours later, the word *aviaõ*, 'plane, was added to my vocabulary. The leading guerrilla shouted, "*Aviaõ, aviaõ!*"

We ran towards the wooded area on our right, and three minutes later a Portuguese DC-4 reconnaissance plane came from Angola and penetrated the Zambian airspace. Ten minutes later, it flew over our hideaway on a northwest bearing back to Angola. Along the trail in the open areas, large underground bunkers dug out by the MPLA became our refuge.

Diary: "Continue trip but now with greater awareness of reality." Within the hour, we arrived at the stone marking the Zambia– Angola border. Boavida was so proud. He turned to me and whispered, "*Camarade Jacques, nous sommes chez nous,*" "*Camarade* Jacques, we are home." The other Angolans also expressed their pride at being home. We had crossed into the semi-liberated regions of Angola. Within three hours, we came to a river where three comrades with their dugout canoe were waiting. I was the first to get a ride up the river, with a second canoe following behind.

They took me for a twenty-minute ride and then we came to a landing spot. Once out of the canoe, I was told to follow the trail. I had some uncomfortable thoughts about a white man leading. Sure enough, an armed guerrilla jumped out of the tall grass and ordered me to stop. I found myself looking down the barrel of a gun. The accompanying comrades quickly identified me as a friend and got permission to pass and enter the Semi-Liberated Region—SLR. The SLR designation meant giving up the territory when challenged by the Tugas army, but otherwise occupying it to stage their own actions. We walked for another three hours and rested. By late afternoon, under a low sun, we resumed our journey, another forced march. Time awareness was by now slipping from my numbed brain . . . sand in my damp Hush Puppies, grinding into my heels and toes; forced marching from sunset to sunrise, interspaced with short rests; the new morning sun turning up the heat, demanding more energy, more condensed milk. Just after the noon sun, we stopped at a small base camp.

Diary:

The kind comrades show me to a hut. I lay down and slept till 4 pm. Boavida wakes me up [with] a cup of super sugared hot tea. My right knee is very tight. By late afternoon we are accompanied by a detachment of guerrillas . . .

At 11 pm the marching column, led by Commandant Toka, stopped for the night in a forested area which sheltered some 35 peasants. As soon as I arrived at the camping area I laid out my bag, unzipped it and crawled in it with all my clothes on and fell asleep. Next morning, I found a cold bowl of rice, which I should have eaten before sleeping. That gives some indication of how tired I was . . .

Starting out about 0930, I became aware of the simple elements which I had been used to: time and distance. The guerrillas taught me another lesson in this warfare, don't ask time or how far to go. Answer was always, soon.

After some three hours, only a guess, we arrived at another detachment. We were met by peasants singing and clapping their hands to the rhythm of revolutionary songs in Portuguese and Lingala. Here I met Commandant Janguinda, whose bearded face resembled that of Che Guevara. The detachment had many people—fifty of them well armed. We rested for two hours, then back to marching. Daylight to darkness. We arrived at a new camp at 8:00 p.m., in time to listen to the Angolan news over *Angola Combatent*.

A military parade was held, followed by the singing of the national anthem. We were treated to a large bowl of rice. This is home till further notice. We met an Italian filmmaker, Stefano de Stefani, and a print journalist, Augusta Conchilia, who have been in this base camp for a month. They worked as a team putting together a film and photo album for Italian television and print media.

Dr. Neto and the Central Committee were to arrive soon to conduct the first eastern regional conference. This established the political-military front called Third Region. We had passed many burned-out former Portuguese houses, and our location inside Angola was close to the Ninda-to-Lumbala road. This expanding political front was another blow to the colonial army and a slap in the face for the political leaders in Portugal who continued to tell the world that the war was coming to an end, that they were winning.

Aquino Braganza and I were assigned a thatched hut. It measured six feet by four feet, open at both ends, and contained two small beds made of one-inch by fourteen-inch pieces of branches located next to the wall. This gave a common area of twenty inches, just enough to have a small fire to combat the cold nights. The sleeping bag was both mattress and blanket. Two additional blankets were assigned to us. These sleeping quarters, for security reasons, were some distance from the central camp. A 10 p.m. curfew was in effect.

The sleeping period was terminated at 4:45, a full hour before daylight. Enough time to hide the blankets in the bush and be ready to move, as the Portuguese normally attacked between 5:00 and 5:30.

We had military jackets, scarves, shoes, and sweaters. The guerrillas wore light shirts, and many had short pants and no shoes in the same weather conditions. They slept outdoors, with only one blanket, near the fire in the main camp area. I found this a little strange, as light from the flames could be seen far away. I was assured that our comrades had set up a perimeter beyond the visibility range of the fire. More learning for my semi-dormant brain.

Breakfast was around 7:30, and by 8:00, when possible, Aquino and I shared a radio to listen to *Radio France International, RFI,* from Paris.

My two Angolan colleagues, from the communications department, were away on a mission. Without colleagues, I had no direction. On the first morning following the military parade and task assignments, I asked Lingatti where *Camarada* Quidado was. "*Twendani rafiki,*" "Follow me, friend." Lingatti pointed to an area away from the campsite, and I followed. As he walked through the dense, wooded area some 300 metres from the main camp, we came to another MPLA area. We entered the main hut, and there lying on a bed was Quidado. He was lying down, while his legs were raised about ten inches above the bed level and secured in two V-shaped branches. This was to take the pressure off his swollen and bandaged legs. I was so pleased to see him. "*Camarada Jacques, les Camarades disent que vousavez bien marché et que vous avez de la difficulté avec votre genou droit,*" ". . . you walked well but had difficulty with your right knee," said Quidado. I responded, "*C'est vrai,*" "It's true." He wanted to know all that was happening to me, as he knew that our time together was intense and purposeful. I could add to the struggle for Angolan independence, and, most of all, Quidado felt a real kinship with me and it was quite noticeable. I was very happy to be there and with a purpose. My returning to Canada with what I had seen could be valuable if I could get the Canadian government and NGOs to offer support for the MPLA with real deeds, with concrete action.

Quidado was only twenty-eight years old and a veteran of the Cabinda military front in the Second Region. Opened in 1963, the

Cabinda enclave was the first oil production facility in Angola. Cada Quidado was the military commander in Zone B of the Third Region. He was in Zone C to attend the scheduled conference.

Diary entry about Quidado:

Story-teller, energetic, and the first to volunteer. One thing for sure—once you met him you could not forget him. Whenever we got stuck in sand he and Lingatti were the first to begin working. Quidado supplied the vocal force and encouragement when we were all pushing the truck out of its sandy hole . . .

I really liked Quidado. His soft voice and smile drew respect from all ranks. He often hummed the Angolan song "Revolution Revolution" as a sign of happiness and commitment.

The relationship that he had with all Angolan visitors and other leaders was a testament to how the revolution had transformed this man into a great human being.

Quidado asked, "Is there anything I can help you with?" I replied, "How about a bath?" "Leave it with me," he said. Lingatti and I returned to the main area.

Here is Lingatti's profile. At sixteen, apprentice in Luanda carpenter shop. His boss used to beat him often, so he "decided" to go and work in the South Africa mines under the contract labour laws. Because of his size, six feet four inches, 200 pounds, the mining authorities treated him like a horse, harnessed him to pull ore cars underground. After two years, he returned to Angola and heard of MPLA and its war to get rid of Tugas. Got permission to go meet MPLA in Zambia, joined and received military training. Asked why he joined the MPLA, he replied, "My father is dead, I don't know where my mother is, the same for my brothers and sisters. I don't even know if they are alive. The MPLA is my family." Now he is *chef de section*— group leader of twelve guerrillas.

Diary:

In the daytime there were thousands of wild bush flies, everywhere you go they follow, penetrating nose, eyes and ears. The best protection against them was the inside of a small hut. The flies would not enter this cooler than outside temperature. Or you could sleep under a tree and cover your face, head with an eighteen-by-thirty-inch material from an old bed sheet with little or no activity, no tasks to do, all the previous waiting and learning how to wait became very relevant. I was tormented with trying to find something to do . . . one would make big issues out of small ones . . . best time . . . planning a little trip to go and take a bath.

Day two, Quidado sent a message: *avant lever du soleil, nous allons au rio . . . preparez*, before sunrise, we go to river . . . prepare.

Early the next day, Quidado led a small group to the river some three kilometres from camp. We followed, stepping in exactly the same places, because the Tugas had planted land mines in gardens and on the well-travelled trails. A perimeter guard was set up to listen for distant aircraft while the rest of us stripped to enjoy the water and rinse our clothing. It was here, when he removed his bandages, that I saw the badly damaged legs of *Camarade* Quidado. When I asked about them, Quidado explained that, some four years ago, a group of guerrillas had been caught in an ambush. He survived and escaped with bullet wounds to his legs.

Diary: Third day a small safari to a river, 40 min. away. Must go early in the am so as to return before the sun rose too high. While one comrade stood guard, the others washed body and clothing. Water is cold and very clean.

Knowing how warm, sweaty and dry we got during the day appreciated this as a very special privilege.

Diary: Four days following my arrival at the [*Poste de Contrôle*], political meeting was held between the MPLA cadre and the adjacent village peasantry. At this meeting they introduced me as *Camarade* Jacques from a faraway country. I was then hustled out like a prisoner. I was very angry and asked *Camarade* Janginda for permission to explain my feelingson how I interpreted the fast exit.

He agreed to discuss the matter but only after the meeting. During the meeting and question period, the president of the village criticized the MPLA cadres for their action vis-à-vis *Camarade* Jacques. As told by Janginda later that day, "The President (of the village) said that if *Camarade* Jacques is our friend then why can't we know where he comes from and why can't we meet him." The very next day a special meeting was held with the villagers.

Diary: The MPLA made a public self-criticism and introduced me as *Camarade* Jacques Roy coming from Montreal, Canada: a progressive North American who is a friend of our *Camarade* President Neto. He has come to see our struggle and will be helping us with some of our radio problems. I was asked to speak, expressed support for the MPLA, and encouraged them to continue. Following the meeting, I met by shaking hands all of the villagers who seemed very pleased with the outcome. The meeting had been translated from Portuguese to Balovale and back when necessary.

Diary: Dr. Boavida invited me to observe a clinic he was conducting. The main purpose of this class was to show the peasants to use soap to elevate the hygienic level so that infectious disease control could be started. It was practically fruitless because there was not enough soap for everyone to practise simultaneously, let alone enough for each one to take home and practise what had just been taught. Their skinny, sick bodies are carried around often by sheer willpower. They are very sick; most have some form or types of worms and they suffer from bronchitis, leprosy, asthma, TB, polio, not to mention malaria and sleeping sickness. The conditions as Dr. Neto had so many times told me are as they were in the 12th century . . . I just shake my head.

Two weeks preceding the eastern regional conference, all comrades were very busy. I kept up my diary and observed the workings of a revolution. The food was our old friend *foo-foo* with a spicy sauce of chicken or fish. The small nearby river provided some fish.

The best time of day was from 5 to 11 p.m.

Diary: Now the flies had gone and our warm clothes were adequate untill late in the night. We made our way to the sleeping area a half hour away. Fires were lit at 19:00 and a supply of wood was put inside the hut

. . . Braganza and I chatted till 19:45 . . . the night watch guard came by to identify himself and to give instructions of what to do in case of military activity.

He then gave us the nightly password required for security reasons. One night, I had to go to the bathroom and got turned around on my way back. A voice said, "*Que passé*," "Who passes"; the code word was "Tanzania," and I spoke it very clearly, as I knew that the consequences of getting it wrong were fatal.

My hut mate, Aquino Braganza, in his early forties, was born in Goa, another Portuguese possession on the western coast of India. He knew the MPLA leadership personally and politically, because most of the intellectuals from these Portuguese territories had met during their studies in Lisbon or other cities in the mother country. His front-line articles in *Afrique-Asie* made this French monthly a primary source of inside information on the liberation struggles for the "Portuguese Overseas Provinces."

Aquino spoke of the enormous difficulties faced by the MPLA, especially the logistics associated with the Third Region.

Having to go through Tanzania and then Zambia required courage, diplomacy, and lots of street smarts.

Angola's potential wealth made the war effort by those opposing independence for Angola a priority. The slave-labour conditions on coffee plantations, for example, meant that the coffee buyers had a cheap and lucrative bean. We talked about Vietnam and speculated on the next American debacle. Would it be Angola?

And how—through surrogates, like the Vietnamization of the Southeast Asia conflict? All of southern Africa was in step towards independence, an independence gained through armed struggle. As the white minority governments were incapable of accepting majority rule, wars of national liberation were inevitable. American foreign policy was apologizing for apartheid while accommodating it; the USA somehow had to reverse world opinion that treated South Africa as a moral leper, this during the Vietnam period and the associated social unrest in "the empire." The USA was looking for a way in and a way out.

Sounds so familiar. In this case, the US had co-opted the emergence of independence in the Belgian Congo through the UN, destroying the elected leadership of Patrice Lumumba, and following his assassination, replacing him with army clerk Joseph Desiré Mobutu, to be protected and financed by the USA to take power through a military coup as a puppet of the West. Mobutu was then to be regional interpreter for the West, and allowed to become the major military force for Western economic and political interests. The USA would continue to pull the strings without their influence being reported in the media.

Once the MPLA became a serious force, Mobutu would carry out the US plan to set up a pro-Western liberation movement such as the FNLA, headed by Mobutu's brother-in-law, Holden Roberto, an Angolan who had never lived in Angola and who was as corrupt as Mobutu. The US could stay in the background and let corrupt Africans kill and eliminate any opposition to Western economic control. Exposing this plan was one of our tasks, best done by supporting the UN decree that the MPLA was the legitimate representative of Angolan aspirations.

And then there was the role of the Catholic Church, which supported without reservation the political ideology of Salazar's fascist regime. Portugal was on a *Mission de Civilization*—Mission to Civilize. Local Catholic priests said mass on top of tanks and armoured personnel carriers while ignoring the brutal labour laws, terrible medical conditions, and lack of educational facilities.

Aquino and I agreed. The vital international support component of this war was lacking. Support for the MPLA with information and materiel was urgently required. He was very pleased with the help that I was lending in the communications network, and we, Barnett and Harvey, were planning further significant support. We became good friends and travelled together for the entire mission.

Every day, new MPLA cadres arrived at the P.C. (*Poste de Contrôle*). Barnett and Harvey showed up in one of the armed detachments. They were a welcome sight. Our focus, due to our different experiences in getting this far, was clear. Before bringing any other persons into the MPLA fold, serious planning and training had to take place. Finally,

Dr. Neto, Anibal de Mello, and many of the MPLA leadership came. It was also my first meeting with Kabuloo and Tutu, the two Angolans responsible for radio communications.

The following day, the historic conference was underway. The Third Region was a new military and political front. The Portuguese government would not like this. Angolans would delight to hear, via *Angola Combatent*, that the leadership of the MPLA had been inside thisnew front. The ever-expanding war front, the continued backing off of colonial troops, and the exodus of more and more settlers to larger centres increased the insecurity of the occupiers.

Following the daily discussion, Dr. Neto briefed us on what had transpired. Kabuloo and Tutu arranged a discussion to develop a plan for the new radio communications network. They brought out very detailed maps. We addressed the antenna location problem. The most troubling need was for a power source. With no electricity in the war zones, an alternative source was required using a new approach. They dreamed of the impact this new radio link would have on the war. Angolans were training in Morse code. A security division introduced these new recruits to secret coding methods and languages. We spent much time getting to know each other. Kabuloo spoke French, English, Portuguese, and German fluently. Tutu spoke the same, plus one or two Angolan languages. Both had trained as electrical engineers. Kabuloo was an intense man, while Tutu was more poetic and relaxed.

Meanwhile, Barnett, Harvey, and I got down to serious talks on how to help the MPLA; in particular, how to integrate North Americans, based on our experiences. Barnett and Harvey had endured the long wait at a high cost to their friendship. In these new surroundings, we all accepted that this was a lot more difficult to do than we expected. Dr. Neto met with us on several occasions. The enormous pressures of his presidency made us reflect upon our little knocks and bruises and shift our attitude to something more realistic and less self-pitying. Angola needed weapons, food, clothing, seeds, schoolbooks, and medical personnel and supplies. The list was very, very long. And we were facing the international disinformation propaganda campaign by the South Africans, Colonial Portugal and the United States of America. Countering this force would be quite a job.

August 24, evening: Dr. Neto told Barnett he would go farther into Angola to do his newspaper stories and research material for the next book. Boavida would also continue. Harvey would (from Diary) ". . . go to Zone A and reach the Benguela Railroad. This was to show that the MPLA will not destroy the railway so long as Zambia allows passages of goods from Tanzania to Angola." Kabuloo, Tudu, and I would go to Lusaka to assemble and test the new radio system.

August 25, 19:45. End of the regional conference. Usual daytime activity. This day is far from over.

Diary: After the 2000 broadcast, we are at the centre of the camp, unusual but with no military activity in the area a less tense situation Silence shattered by the explosion of a grenade, guerrillas in motion to go to noise, armed and swift, commotion yell for help Boavida come quick. A young soldier in his quest to light cigarette bent over fire and dropped grenade from his shirt pocket, guerrilla sees this and jumps on the flames and takes hit to save five others, carried to medical sector, crying and moaning.

Very dangerous situation, after dark noises had carried far . . . night conditions . . .

Lumbala is less than 4 hrs by foot . . .

[G]uerrillas tell that injuries are too serious to bring out to Zambia, no medicine. Boavida steps in. Moans and crying stops. Time is 2300 hours. Quidado is dead, has laid down his life. My very good friend is gone, sadnesseverywhere . . . *a lutta continua.*

Off to our usual sleeping quarters, no sleep, sadness abounds.

August 26, 0300 hours:

Since our location is marked by the explosion, we must vacate P.C. now.

Goodbyes to Barnett, Boavida and leadership, time is precious. The outgoing trip seemed much shorter. 4 hours on, 30 min rest, same routine, sand and more sand. Land mines in identified fields, burned-out fields by the newly introduced napalm against MPLA food production.

Two hard days of forced march, a final rest stop before leaving Angola. One- half of our group went for a bath and swim. This lasted half hour. We had begun to have some food when the guardshouted *"aviaó."* We scrambled, ran following guerrillas who knew where to go. Other parts of group are in the water, fortunately all Angolans, a black bottom of water and reeds gave them shelter, no time to come out, 3 minutes later DC-4 heard by all and seen direction Zambia. Can't move till it returns . . . 25 min later aviaó signal and visual confirmation.

We continued out of Angola, tired, hungry and dirty. We have made it back to our launch point. It is dark and cold. In the large hut a small fire to help us warm. Hot tea served and off to bed.

The next day was only for resting. My legs were paining and the right knee swollen. All of my movements catered to my limp . . . listened to the MPLA radio broadcast, shortly after Dr. Neto, de Mello, and other leadership arrive by jeep. It had been driven to the inside of the border. The mood is very somber as the thought of losing Quidado still hangs in the air. So far this year, MPLA has lost another great leader, Commander Henda, killed in the attack of Karipande. The evening is short-lived.

Now, the return trip to Lusaka. After breakfast, Dr. Neto announces that we have a fuel problem; it will be up to three days before we can get enough fuel to make the trip. MPLA leadership meets to continue planning of the war effort, logistics, food, and medicine. After the evening meal, Dr. Neto asks if I had any thoughts for activity. Dr. Neto was like a big brother. He had allowed me to grow politically and spiritually. I answered: "Let's go fishing." He liked that idea. So the next morning, Neto, bodyguards, a few guerrillas, and I set out and walked twenty minutes and found the riverbank. It was two metres from the top of the bank to the water surface, allowing for some military protection if required. Our fishing poles were baited and strung in the slow flow. The next four hours or so are embedded in my thoughts.

We discussed the politics of how to build a country, exploring the question of how to ensure an equitable distribution of the large economic wealth that is in Angola, its people and land.

Neto had been branded a communist and terrorist in his student days. This 1940s label gave carte blanche to Portugal and apartheid South Africa to tell their Western economic backers that they were doing the dirty work on the protection of the Cape Route, stopping the dominoes from feeling the weight of gravity.

The racists with the poorest state in Europe were upholding the dominoes. America really liked this formula. The African also knew how shaky this theory was.

Neto was very sad at the Russian-led invasion of Czechoslovakia. He said, "How can Russia impose military might under the banner of freedom?" The MPLA had been receiving military and technical training from members of the Eastern bloc and did so because the West did not want to see independence in Southern Africa.

"The West is supporting the colonial situation in Portugal's 'Overseas Provinces' and minority rule in Rhodesia and South Africa. So the MPLA, pushed by sheer need and African philosophy, sought help where they would be heard and respected. Hundreds of Angolans are trained in medicine, engineering, and economics. This type of training will give us professionals so that when we do get our independence, we will have the infrastructure for an independent country. We have seen the ill-prepared countries of Zambia, the tribal effects in Kenya, and the corruption and continuing neo-colonial regime in Zaire.

Can you imagine—we Africans who have seen and lived in the mess of a corrupt dictator, Mobutu, are all too aware that we must not repeat this. We must develop Africa. We *must develop Africa for all*. Even we, the MPLA leadership, won't bring a better life to our people if we squander the wealth that this country has; I expect the Angolans to rise and overthrow us.

As you saw, our people are very poor. Many live today as they did 800 years ago. Bad water, poor diet, no medicine. The statistics say it all. *Notre peuple souffre,* [Our people suffer].

Due to the pigheaded fascist government in Portugal, we have no choice but to conduct our war of liberation. In the areas that are free, we have our schools with textbooks that reflect what is Angola, its culture, music, and poetry. We have Angolans who will soon graduate as pilots, engineers, and administrators. These Angolans will be able to hold responsible positions. The Angolan struggle is against colonialism and those who help to perpetuate this terrible exploitation of our people, which imposes slave labour conditions for the profit of companies who pay a war tax on the goods from Angola.

Angola in many respects is like the family having the most beautiful daughter in the village. Everyone wants her."

Neto wanted to know my thoughts on Angola. My response: "*Président Neto, c'est incroyable, pas possible*"—unbelievable, not possible.

About my mother and father, I said, "They are very proud of my actions because your aspirations are fundamental to a decent life. It is not possible to negotiate freedom, it must be taken. Nothing I have done in my life has been so demanding, or intellectually fulfilling. I am very happy with the objectives you have identified to attain independence."

I thanked the president for his wisdom and foresight.

It was a short time, and as I review my diary notes and photographs, the magnitude of what we were discussing is a little overwhelming.

We walked back to the hut for a late lunch and a siesta. I was out of emotional energy.

The political thoughts of this great man and famous poet gave me a unique insight.

I summarized it as follows: Neto was a leader with an African Nationalist political platform stating its intention to create a climate to allow Angolans to direct their own destiny based on the UN Charter for Human Rights. He did not want a repeat of the Zambia and Kenya independence experience that was based on tribalism, nepotism, and absolute corruption, independence that was "granted" with an entrenched colonial system and a pitiful, small, educated African elite. MPLA has sent thousands of its youth to countries that supported self-determination. These were Cuba, Romania, East Germany, Russia, Bulgaria, Romania, and Algeria. Some church bursaries were given in

Canada and the US for Angolan studies. The West was not interested in promoting self-reliance or programs that would build the African infrastructure, so naturally the West would accuse the MPLA of being communist and manipulating its population in "showing the spread of communism" and demonstrating the need to intervene when aspiring nationalist movements would not bend to the West's will.

At the 1975 independence of Angola, the USA through Kissinger vowed to not give the MPLA any room to develop. The USA would promote a civil war resulting in a million Angolan deaths, four million refugees, setting some fourteen million land mines, while supporting apartheid as their local military saviour. When the anti- apartheid forces mobilized and presented a comprehensive overview of Southern African oppression, the West, in particular the USA, was shown to be the terrorists and perpetrators of a massive genocide. When Canada was asked to take specific actions, the results only amplified the conspiracy of economic interests. The coffee boycott showed Montreal-based General Foods supporting the colonial war through a war tax on the export of coffee beans. The missing link was the consumer's role, which was mobilized in a successful national boycott, which was then applied to South African products, oranges, wine, etc. Zola Budd, the white barefoot Olympic runner, was not permitted to run for Great Britain. As the information campaigns expanded in content, urgency, and relevance, public opinion shifted and the true intentions of the West were exposed. The label of communist sympathizer was thrown about, but accusing the churches of being communist was not sticking.

The calm delivery and clear understanding of these fundamental issues made me see Neto as a great Angolan and African leader. I could certainly see that a Kissinger would be incapable of understanding the African aspirations. Kissinger, an opportunist and member of the ruling class, a racist who could not process the humanity of Vietnam's NLF, facing an African who could articulate African needs, would rebuff and treat him as subhuman. *In Search of Enemies,* by John Stockwell, gives an insight into the apparently constant American need for war, for enemies. Find an excuse, any excuse—such as the Gulf of Tonkin Resolution—to justify military intervention to discourage the local people from aspiring to the development of their country for their own benefit. Kissinger was given the mystic role of negotiator *par excellence* in the Southeast Asian conflict until the American media caught on to the criminal acts their country was engaged in. Walter Cronkite's words, "America has lost the war," finally admitted the reality that Dr. K had lied and the outcome was defeat.

When Neto spoke, he spoke in terms of all of colonized Africa. Mandela was in jail, a distraction for Pretoria's racist regime. But it was the liberation movements that were creating the military and political clout that was getting the attention of public opinion. My presence was a testament to the need for the international community to support the United Nations Resolution on support to the liberation movement.

In 1961, the mutiny amongst the Portuguese sailors and soldiers on the *Santa Maria* had been reported on the television news and in *Time* magazine. Led by conscripts bound for a five-year obligatory service, the boat carrying these soldiers was anchored just outside the Luanda harbour. The world was learning of the terrible slave-like conditions in Angola. The news was so brutal that it was nearly impossible to comprehend the character of Portuguese colonialism. Branding anti-colonial progressive forces such as Neto, Machel, Mbeki, Tambo, Mandela, and Njoma as terrorists and communist subversives would soon be understood by world opinion as a smokescreen and a lie. The demonization process of Vietnam was yet to be applied to the African leaders.

The daily activities of the camp continued. In my conversations with Kabuloo and Tutu, the subject of what to do tonight, our last night, came up. Here we had an international gathering of anti-colonial fighters, so we decided we should organize a cultural evening. Harvey adapted *Yellow Rose of Texas*. I came up with two French Canadian songs, *Un Canadien Errant*—a wandering Canadian story on the expulsion of Acadians to the USA—and the second song was *Sur la route de Berthier*, on the road to Berthier (a town east of Montreal), telling of a historical period of hardship.

The Angolans produced chorus after chorus of songs from Angola. The variety in music and words in different languages added the final rich dimension to the evening. Angola has an international reputation for literature and poetry. Having Neto read one of his famous poems was pure magic.

The Angolan words and music, melancholic for the most part and influenced by church music, reflected their pain and hardship. Harvey and I used places, leaders' names, and historical dates and events from Angola to fit the easily learned melodies.

Diary: The evening was a total success. Afterwards President Neto and many of the MPLA cadre congratulated Harvey and me for suggesting and preparing the evening . . . we had impressed the need for cultural development within the struggle.

. . . my own feelings . . . a very positive vision on future tasks and possibilities.

How about the production of an Angolan Revolutionary music album?

How about a calendar celebrating the history of the armed struggle?

Art work by Angolan artists for the calendar!

This would further the education campaigns required to show the building of a new nation as well as exposing the supporters of this poverty and exploitation.

The battle for the hearts and minds of North Americans was on.

Back to Lusaka

Diary: Prepared to leave. Said goodbye to Harvey, Neto, de Mello, Monimambu, and Lingatti. On board, driver, Kabuloo, Tutu, myself, and an Angolan mother and sick child going to hospital in Lusaka. The trip to Lusaka is direct and stops for fuel in Mongu. We carried a drum of fuel in the Land Rover.

The MPLA houses in the Lusaka outskirts were full of people, therefore, I returned to the Annex. Room 19. The radio equipment had arrived so we planned the workload.

After daily breakfast, I walked over to taxi stand and got in a station wagon heading for the township, near the MPLA houses.

Diary: Election campaigning held in Zambia . . . all non-Zambians to be considered suspicious . . . radio and newspaper write-ups, all good Zambians had the right to stop any person who they thought was suspicious. MPLA workshops and people lived 6 miles from city so I had to take a taxi and everyday different taxi driver would ask me what I was doing here and where I was going. After getting out of taxi, a 15 min walk brought me to the workshop.

The month of Sept was full of hard work and surprises. Harvey returned by Sept 15 to Lusaka without filming railway. The military activity in Zone A was too heavy. Film project abandoned.

He moved into Room 19 with me. In Lusaka, the CID followed us closely. Shortly after Harvey's arrival, on the street near the library in daylight, we were stopped by an undercover cop on a motorcycle and detained by the CID. "Why are you here without passports? What are you doing?" They questioned us separately. We had agreed to tell the truth about our MPLA connection. It was then we learned that the CID had been following us since our (my) arrival in Lusaka. The questioning lasted three hours and then this complete ass finished his questioning with, "Well, if you are a Portuguese agent, may you have a miserable life, but if you are helping to tell the struggle of the MPLA— he could barely pronounce this—then may God bless you."

As soon as Harvey left on September 20 for the US, a CID

agent was put in Room 19. No certainty exists that he really was CID: he did not take money, 100 shillings, four US dollars, given by Barnett. He did not go out to work and would not talk. He remained in the room when I left every morning for the day. A few days later, he was gone. On the following Saturday, a new person moved into Room 19.

Diary: A second theft took place . . . a European stole tapes of Angolan music, interviews, to be translated into English I discovered this on returning from an evening walk. Goods were gone and he was asleep. I waited till he got up to go to the bathroom situated down the hallway. I found the tapes in his pillowcase. I returned and faked sleep till he returned and dozed off. I went down stairs and called the Police. All of the goods were put in a bag and we all went back to the police station. He sat in the back while I was up front with the 2 officers. Following the written statement indicated no charges to be laid, the police returned the tapes, sugar and tea. There could not be public record of this incident.

The guy volunteered to give me back my shirt and pants that he had put on under his clothing—we had missed these items. Once this was accomplished, and while I was wrapping returned goods in my shirt, the drunken thief dropped a stool on the floor behind the main police desk. It was very funny and I was glad to get the hell out of the CID office once again.

Regular interaction with the liberation movement of the African National Congress—ANC—took place because the Zambian government had given housing in a certain area to the liberation movements, so due to this proximity I met Mbeki, Nzo, and Tambo. Dennis September arranged more serious meetings with Mbeki. Due to lack of a friendly border with South Africa, the ANC were hard-pressed to create a military front. However, an underground intelligence unit needed to be formed. Getting accurate and up-to-date information was absolutely essential. My participation was to think about it and come up with a plan.

Dennis was the CUSO Director for Zambia and would make things happen. The name "September" indicates that his family was "bought" or sold as slaves in the month of September.

September 25: MPLA decided that I should be at the work site and with the working group. The security and daily transport by taxi from Room 19 to the outlying area where the liberation movements lived were woefully inadequate. A small room with a typewriter and a spring bed were assigned at the residence of Comrade de Mello. This was so much easier and much more secure.

The routine continued, radios into final assembly. We still needed dummy antennas for system testing. Before lunch, a shortwave radio crackled from deep inside Angola . . . fierce military battle this morning killed four Angolans including Dr. Boavida. Tugas have his body and his diary. The shockwave is catastrophic. Another big loss. No other news on Barnett.

Obtaining Boavida's diary was a valuable tool of propaganda because Boavida wrote on the horrors of war and of his anti-war deep feelings . . . a pacifist. He understood the purpose of pushing back the Tugas with guns.

Meanwhile, the work of establishing a reliable power supply for the communication equipment was still unsolved. After serious thought, the radio gang of three came up with a solution for power needs in the field inside Angola. By using a series of three-kilowatt generators and motorcycle-type wet cell batteries, we were able to design a system to supply the required voltage for the radios and hand- held units. The cycle was as follows: Charge battery, remove acid for transportation, refill battery with acid at usable spot. Generators to be installed in underground locations with fuel to charge batteries as required.

October 5: Barnett arrived in Lusaka, weak, tired, stressed, shocked. Tells of the Tugas attack by helicopters, the wild scramble as circling copters shoot into the camp. No ground troops. An Angolan guerrilla, on a pass to visit his family, is captured and becomes traitor. He was spotter for the 10:00 a.m. attack. Commander Janguinda had broken the mobility rule, which states, if a person does not return at the scheduled time, vacate the area immediately. The MPLA had waited and paid the price.

October 14: The MPLA failed to get Zambian government permission to extend for my stay. I must leave by the 18th at the latest. On the 15th, I look into air schedules and fares. "The most difficult problem was where do we get the money to pay for the difference of the expired ticket and the new fare of plus $45.00. I had nothing, the MPLA nothing."

Thursday, October 17, 15:30: The solution was to go to CUSO and tell them I wanted to go home. I went to the CUSO office sporting a beard; the secretary had seen only a picture of my shaven face and short hair. Chris Brown was out, so I told the secretary that I would be back at 1700 hours. I returned to the MPLA house; an Angolan cut my hair and I scraped off my beard with an old razor blade. I ate with my friends and said goodbye to Kabuloo, Tutu, and others. M'Binda and a driver took me to the area near the CUSO office.

We said goodbye at the Annex and I walked over to the CUSO office. Chris Brown was very surprised to see me and was puzzled about the missing beard. That was easy. I presented him with my quandary— the air ticket.

The expiry date had come and passed, so in reality the ticket was null and void. Big Problem.

I was polite but aloof in response to the inevitable "Where have you been?" We looked at the options, including CUSO's buying a new ticket. By 2200 hours it was rest time. I slept on the floor of his apartment.

Diary: On Friday morning the sole flight to Dar leaves at 0800. CUSO director drove me to airport. Arriving at the check-in desk, the Zambian clerk asked for the ticket and checked in my luggage. He could accept the ticket if permission from East Africa Airway to travel Air Zambia because of expiring visa. A phone call gave me permission to board the Dar plane with a short changed ticket. The original 45-day ticket now into five months plus made it a non-negotiable ticket. The airport people had overlooked this fact as they were looking at the visa expiry date. A bit of good luck. I thanked Brown and said goodbye. He must have been happy to see me go. I sweated all the way. The loading of the plane went smoothly. Only possible screw up was the stop at Ndola for customs clearing. I became very diplomatic. If I made it here, I was on my way. More luck, no questions, just a warm wide smile with a "*Zikomo kwambili*, sir," thank you, sir.

In a few hours, we reached Dar. Clearing customs was very easy. My volunteer card did the talking. I took the regular bus into Dar and headed for the Luther House to find Berhan. He was there and we were very happy to see each other. Berhan had given up the house and moved into a small apartment in the outskirts of Dar. I accepted his invitation and stayed there for the first two days, thinking about the next move. How to get from Dar to Ottawa, 3,000 miles, with no money?

We shared great Indian food at the local restaurant. Berhan wanted to hear every detail. As a former guerrilla in Asmara, he knew the daily drills and hardships. He had mailed the letters for my parents as requested, which made me very happy. We took a bus to his apartment in the outskirts of Dar.

While he was at work, my thoughts turned to planning my trip back to Canada.

I went to Dar by bus and found the CUSO office and was greeted by a new secretary. I said my name was Jacques Roy. Her reply was, "We have a lot of mail for you," as she handed me a five-inch stack of mail. She continued, "We have been looking for you for a long while." In my smart-ass way I said, "Look no more! I am here and I want to go home."

She continued, "Mrs. Baker will be back tomorrow." We agreed I would return the next day at one-thirty. The secretary marked the hour in the appointment book. This was a start. But now my buddies Sinclair and Fleming were gone. It was a whole new game. Who was this Mrs. Baker, anyway? How much did she know and how did she feel about what she knew?

So the next day, I came to the 13:30 rendezvous. Mrs. Baker, a middle-aged woman, had lived in Tanzania for many years. Her husband was in mining exploration for the Para-State Diamond and Precious Stones Corporation. I probed her intellectual skill and tenacity. I wanted to find out how hard I would need to push and how to lean on her. She related that CUSO Ottawa had no idea what had happened to me. They had called my parents, but they would only say that they received regular mail from Dar.

Now the pitch: "Listen, Mrs. Baker, CUSO brought me to Africa and I expect that CUSO will bring me back home. The lousy working conditions at the college were well short of what I would consider acceptable. Even Sinclair agreed with me (this was a little exaggeration). I'm sure he told you about me."

She kept nodding.

"So I took a little holiday; now it's time to go back to Canada."

In my most empathic voice, I offered the following scenario, a way out for CUSO: "Send a telex to Ottawa about my situation and ask them for a return to Canada ticket. I will return in three days. Thanks for your time."

I left, not holding my breath. My first salvo was launched.

In the meantime, I rested and kept in contact with the MPLA office. My political maturity was very evident to the MPLA office staff. Mrs. Boavida was present. She continued to grieve, but she continued. I was received like a brother; the Angolans were very curious about my opinion of the war of liberation. Among them were Petroff, Loy, Pascal Luval, and Elsa, to name a few.

The amount of work to be done in Canada to support the MPLA was going to be enormous, but it I was determined that it would be done.

On my return to the CUSO office, Mrs. Baker had tightened up her vocal delivery. She said "Ottawa says no to paying your return ticket."

I answered, "I see. Well, Mrs. Baker, here is the game plan for CUSO. If Ottawa does not pay for my return ticket, I will go to the Canadian High Commission and throw stones at the windows. I will then tell the arresting officer that CUSO recruits subversives like myself. I will return in two days and I expect a positive response."

This seemed to get her attention. Shades of red and white descended over her sixty-year-old face as she stared at me.

In two days, I returned and she announced that Ottawa had approved the air ticket, with a proviso that it was to be a loan. My collateral was to be my passport. Failure to pay back meant the lifting of my passport.

I thought it over and agreed, knowing fully well that the conditions could not stick. CUSO had no power to seize anyone's passport.

She handed me the CUSO credit card and advised me on the next flight out.

I thanked her for her co-operation and left. My shoes did not touch the two flights of stairs as I headed for the travel agency.

The ploy had worked; the deed was done. I had put into practice the best lesson in life: Don't quit, Don't lose. I took a bus to the airport, and Berhan insisted on coming. Our friendship had become deeper and stronger; someday we would meet again.

Next stops were London, Montreal, and then Ottawa.

I would stay with my brother, a Carleton University student. Getting healthy was a priority. I was physically and psychologically depleted. I needed a real medical tune-up.

I knew I needed time to decompress, to adjust to the affluence and security so taken for granted here, to reflect upon and assimilate what I had experienced. I knew that it would be very difficult to convey what I had lived and how the experience had transformed me, made me a more serious person. My dream was clearer than ever: to be part of a successful liberation movement leading to independence.

Setting up an organization that would respond to the needs that we had just witnessed required a long-term plan. There would need to be an education component and a strategy for applying political pressure on Ottawa.

CHAPTER SIX

Values are like rabbits . . . they multiply.

On the 23:00 flight from Dar, it seemed as if I were in a dream. Going to Ottawa with a clear mandate from the MPLA and all this responsibility just fourteen months after my arrival with CUSO gave me a sense of accomplishment. As the aircraft taxied for takeoff from the beautiful city, I felt a little sad; my stay in Tanzania had allowed me to grow and view the world from a different rung. I loved Dar, its wonderful people, white sandy beaches, palm trees, the warm, green Indian Ocean. Just sheer beauty.

With a brief stop in London and Montreal, the final leg of the trip was a train ride to Ottawa. My brother was away on emergency matters and he sent an uncle to pick me up. His presence was discomfiting and difficult, as our opinions and outlook on life were not compatible. The next three days were restful, long walks alone and the obligatory meetings with family. The best questions were the ones dealing with the game parks and animals.

My brother returned and lobbied successfully on my behalf with his roommates so that I could have a short stay at their 42 Glen Street residence. It was a very old and spacious residence close to Carleton University. After settling in, I visited the International Department at Carleton University and met Professor Doug Anglin. His knowledge of Southern Africa was confined to the scholarly side; he was a sympathetic person. Clyde Sanger and Penny were introduced at a Southern Africa public meeting. Clyde, a former journalist with the *Guardian*, continued to freelance for the *Guardian* and the *Globe* in Toronto. Ottawa provided an intellectual milieu for the launch of a support group. The Sangers and other literary sympathizers could provide the research and fact sheet material. Public education was an important ingredient in our material aid project.

By mid-November, I began making calls at St. Patrick's College and met the dean, Father McDougall. He was in his early forties and was very sympathetic to my concerns. He introduced me to Professor John O'Manique. As a sign of his good faith and support, John invited me to speak to his class. My presentation was based on my experiences, but was intended to seek out students who wanted to help the project. The emphasis was on the moral and ethical drive to better, to unmask, the colonial realities of Southern Africa. George Best, a mature student and a serious man, came forward. Within a few weeks, he found time to research the economic links between Canada and Angola.

This consisted of coffee and oil imports, and exports to Angola of military parts and unidentified spare parts. These lectures were my first speaking engagements for a fee. Though it was only fifty dollars, it covered my food needs. My share of the rent was waived, as the other residents gave full approval of my efforts. I was grateful for this contribution. I re-established contact with Barnett, who had been hired to teach at Simon Fraser University in the Political Science, Sociology, and Anthropology Department in Burnaby B.C.

Barnett had contacts with UBC professor Kathleen Aberly, an expert on Southern India. Professor Adams, a progressive white South African, and Professor Gerry Sperling were at SFU. We agreed that I would come to Vancouver, but first I needed to visit my parents in Kirkland Lake. So in early December I took the overnight train, arriving at six a.m. in Swastika, a small village ten miles from Kirkland Lake on the main train line linking Moosonee and all the small communities along the way with Toronto. My dad was waiting for me, and we were both very happy to be reunited. I hugged him and thanked him for coming to get me.

His favourite expression when I was growing up, in lieu of driving me somewhere, was, "Here is some money, take the bus." The ride home this morning was without radio, to give time for my dad's questions. "Are you okay? Did you see anything important in your travels?"

"Well, Dad, the Americans are planning another intervention after Vietnam, and I had the honour to work for the Angolans who are leading the war of independence. I met the president and his shadow cabinet. They are serious and I want to help them." My dad answered, "That's okay. Just be a little careful with your mother. She has been sick. She'll like your project," added my wise dad.

The reunion was relaxed, homey, and full of news. My mom was very happy. She only had one inquiry. "The CUSO people from Ottawa kept calling to find out where you were. I just told them you were in Dar and that you were sending letters on a regular basis." I laughed and then had to tell her the truth and extent of the letter-write-home campaign.

She shook her head and said, *Mon chez-ti*—"You little rascal." I explained that I did not want them to worry, and it seemed to be only way; she agreed. I stayed close to home and occasionally saw the neighbours, who asked about Africa. My response was, "The people are wonderful and many of their problems could be solved if they were able to be in charge of their destiny." Most would say, "Are the Americans involved?" When I replied in the affirmative, they would comment, "They can't mind their own business." The animal stories were a tension breaker, and I heard "Better you than me" quite frequently.

After five days I returned to Ottawa and flew to Vancouver, where Barnett and his family opened their Coquitlam home to me. Within a few weeks, members of the U.S. support committees and friends of Barnett came to Canada. We legally established the African Relief Services Committee with Barnett in the chair, Carol as secretary, Harvey on audio- visual needs, and myself on the technical portfolio. The ARSC was launched, and the first forays into the community were planned with United Church.

I needed a vehicle and an income to keep me going. So I scouted up a used 1955 Pontiac for $200, and started a job search. Through the newspaper, I found an evening job polishing new cars as they were unloaded from a Japanese ship. My next stop in search for dollars, as the focus of the technical projects for the MPLA took priority, was the Burnaby School Board. The schools always had a need for skills to cover the shop options at the secondary level. I also applied to the adult education sector dealing with French teaching.

Christmas with the Barnetts was the next-best thing to being at home in Kirkland Lake. Little Jomo was my favourite of the three kids. However, the tensions began to grow as Barnett's expectations were not met. He still seemed to need to control my life. This also tainted his teaching at Simon Fraser. The students respected Barnett for his knowledge of anthropology and for the support project that we were getting off the ground. Students had many other preoccupations and they were young and had not become politically sophisticated.

Credit goes to the students: the likes of Larry Field, Liz Brooks, Steve and Linda Kelleher, Dwight, Jim, Paul Knox, and the many others who came and left the project. This was all volunteer work, and we all needed to learn how to do new things. For the SFU students, it was the confrontation with the faculty on student representation on council, faculty dining room privileges, and others, indicative of a changing time. There was also Vietnam. Vancouver was the last stopoff point for the GIs before heading to Southeast Asia, so the women's group organized the last-minute marriages to give these young men a legal right to stay in Canada. I met one lady who had been married twenty times. No sex, just the paperwork, and the GI could start a new life. The large anti-war demonstrations required participation as well.

That need was immediate and focused. Speaking of the anti-colonial struggle in Angola or the anti-apartheid efforts of the ANC was part of the same struggle, but it would be integrated in time. Hanoi was in, Mandela was in jail.

In early January, I got a job in the manufacturing of trailer homes. The boring Meccano set approach was very revealing, as I had had no previous experience of a production line. It was hard, alienating, and gut-wrenching work. I appreciated the role of booze and other escape mechanisms. Around the twentieth of January, the Burnaby School Board called me in for an interview.

The electronics teacher at the Burnaby Central High School had broken his legs in a skiing accident. The immediate need was much greater than the availability of qualified staff. Soft questions at the interview indicated the school believed that I could teach and had full knowledge of the technical jargon and the required enthusiasm. Provincial certification could be arranged. So after the one hour face to face, the board interviewer offered me the teaching post

Start time was the next day.

This job really lifted my spirits. The technical demands were under control. I needed to learn to connect with the students.

The morning was devoted to the Grade 9 and 10 students who had the shop option as part of their study load. The after-lunch classes were devoted to the Grade 11 and 12 students who were majoring in electricity and electronics. The principal checked up on my work regularly, and the students responded positively to the new guy in the classroom. As early February rolled in, the Adult Education program started up, and I began to teach French two nights a week. As a promoter of self-reliance and independence, I applied the learning concept to my afternoon group.

We had a discussion and agreed that with my help, they would each present course topics. It was a super learning experience for the students. They found it challenging and enjoyed the practical applications.

Bob F. was the Grade 12 class joker. He invited me to join the school hockey team for pick-up hockey. It was something that I knew how to do and this gave me a chance to get in shape and have fun. I needed to smile and be happy, since other elements were often conflicting with my inner peace.

In March, I moved from Barnett's house to a Vancouver apartment. We continued to work and plan the support committee activities. I guest-lectured in different classes at SFU and met with some of Barnett's students to help with the information and recruiting for the material support to the MPLA.

While walking through the SFU cafeteria, I noticed a very attractive lady sitting alone. I introduced myself. She was Linda H., a teaching assistant in the English Department. We spoke and agreed to see each other the next day after my class. Over the next few weeks, we solidified our friendship and soon we were lovers. Linda's outlook was a new set of eyes and brainpower that met a neglected need in my personal life. She was not vocal with her politics and let her actions speak for her. She was a very fine person who could laugh and put a smile on my face.

In March, the school board did a teacher evaluation and survey with my students. The results were very positive. With this behind me, it was time to do something for the Angolans. One afternoon, Bob F. requested on behalf of the class that I speak about my African experience. I limited it to the technical side and how it affected me, but left out the timeline. The story impressed my senior students. The best student, Gordy R., suggested that he could design and build different power supplies that would run off wet batteries. The stockroom was well equipped, and a project was created.

Our first technical project in support of the MPLA was the fabrication of tents. They could be rolled up to fit in a backpack and would be the ideal housing during the rainy season. As well, the most forward guerrilla front could sleep in these instead of under the stars. It had been an MPLA idea.

I was able to source a company that produced large, plastic, flexible tubing. These heavy-gauge, green plastic tubes came on an eight- foot roll and were perforated for easy separation every six feet. We required a location to mount the grommets on the tubes so that a triangle could be created, supported by ropes. We then folded and prepared them for shipment to Dar es Salaam. A core of the committee agreed to get a house with a basement. Within two days of beginning our search, a cottage across the railway tracks on Alderside Drive in Port Moody was found. It overlooked the Pacific Ocean with a harbour view. We were treated to the changing tides, the smell of salty air and the fumes from the local oil refinery, weather permitting. We negotiated the rent at a reduced rate and, with materials supplied by the owner, we converted the garage into a bedroom for Jim. I upgraded the electrical system. The front porch solarium overlooking the water became my room while Steve and Linda occupied the third bedroom.

The living room became the ARSC meeting place. The round kitchen table had a large wagon wheel above it decorated with small lights controlled by a rheostat and the food was cooked on an old wood stove.

The *pièce de résistance* was the workshop located in the basement. We purchased the required materials and tools and launched the tent factory. It was now late March.

Research organized by Barnett and some of his students advanced very well. The amount of information on Portugal, military and non-military goods, and its relationship within NATO became a valuable learning tool for our members. With this information, we created numerous fact sheets. The vast store of information at the SFU library allowed our project members to focus their term papers on Angola or other countries in Southern Africa.

The accumulated information was sent to the MPLA Lusaka and Dar offices. They responded positively, as the MPLA had few resources and personnel to do such information gathering.

By mid-April, my health was showing signs of my African experience. My liver was paining, and I was easily tired.

During the afternoon classes, I occasionally had to lie down on the floor in the storage area to get some sleep. The students required little supervision and understood my situation.

Time marched on; by the end of the school year my health had deteriorated. I sought help from a Vancouver doctor who had lived in South West Africa. He gave me some medication, but it was not helping. On my return visit he suggested a spinal tap, which I underwent. Nothing useful was found by this painful and dangerous procedure.

Meanwhile Barnett's behaviour had gone awry. The faculty members at the university went from tolerating him to excluding him, while his acceptance within the project dropped. On many occasions I told Barnett that he needed to change his pattern of ticking people off, but to no avail. An expulsion order was introduced at an ARSC general meeting and carried out. It was an easy decision on my part, because the Liberation Movement needed not only goods but people who were empathic towards human beings.

The African Relief Services Committee would continue without the Barnetts.

The tents, clothing, and electronic supplies, all paid for, were sent by ship to the MPLA in Dar es Salaam.

In early August, Linda convinced me to go to Toronto and seek proper medical care at the Faculty of Tropical Medicine.

I said goodbye to my friends at the Committee and a sad farewell to Linda at the train station. For the next five days, it was to be long ride. The cross-Canada trip did not provide the expected appreciation of my country. The sick liver pained continually.

On my arrival in Toronto, I looked up my old friend from Dar, Griff Cunningham, who had returned to Toronto. After a short telephone conversation, he invited me to his home. He was teaching at York University and approved of my work. Griff's central location on Spadina allowed me to be an outpatient. With my medical card in hand, I walked into the clinic and was interviewed by a medical nurse. Feeling quite conscious of my politics, I offered western Zambia as the location of my CUSO service and the pain was in the liver. A short time later, a tall, worn-looking man in his fifties, with deep ridges in his face and thin gray hair, came in.

"My name is Dr. Lenzler. Good morning, Mr. Roy." He pronounced my name correctly, and I said, "Good morning, Doctor."

"Your chart says you have travelled a little." "Yes, sir," I responded. "I've been working in the western part of Zambia with a group of

Africans." I measured his response before giving a more accurate and detailed statement. "These Africans are seeking their independence from fascist Portugal."

The Doc's eyes lit up and he nodded his head, indicating some form of silent agreement or understanding. With his large, bony, right hand, he unbuttoned his left shirt cuff and rolled his shirtsleeve up slowly. After three folds, a tattoo and numbers on his arm appeared. "Mr. Roy, I know about fascism and the Holocaust"

"Thank you, Doc, I needed to know that . . . I need to get better, so I can continue." We shook hands again, but this time it was a bonding. I may have reminded him of his youth. One way or another, he approved of me politically and now would get me back to good health. He pressed his large thumbs under my eyelids to force my eyes to an exaggerated open position. He calmly added, "You have jaundice. With a little medication and a controlled diet, your liver should clear up." This was great news.

Over the next few days, I did some planning and visited with the United Church and its African director concerning the Angola situation. Situated on St. Clair West, the United Church House had seen many supporters of Angola come through its doors, with the most famous being Dr. Sid Gilchrist. I went to the designated floor, and the secretary asked if she could help. "Yes, ma'am. Is it possible to meet Dr. Legge? I got his name from the board near the elevator."

"And your name, sir?"

When I said, "Jacques Roy," her expression indicated a slight hesitation. However, she asked me to sit down. She returned to ask the purpose of the visit, and I obliged with, "I work with the MPLA in Angola and I've just returned from the war zones."

She replied, "Just a moment, sir."

This time she invited me into Dr. Legge's office, and we introduced ourselves.

"It is a pleasure to meet you, Dr. Legge," I said.

"Well, Mr. Roy—is that how you pronounce it?" he asked.

"Yes sir, I mean, Doctor. That's the correct French way; a pleasure to meet you." Our conversation flowed from the political to the personal. It turned out he knew my hometown very well, as his first church was the small one situated near the railway track in Swastika.

Somehow, Legge felt that this was a good omen. We covered many topics, but the essential one was, "How do we help the Angolans? How do we publicize the plight of the Angolans?"

We ended the hour-long discussion in agreement that we should and would work together. We said *au revoir*.

I took the Colonial [sic] bus to Ottawa and visited an old acquaintance, Bob Caddo. He was the assistant at CARE Canada and offered me a room at his apartment, which I gladly accepted. With school still not in session, I could not lecture at the Ottawa universities. I took on a temporary job as a furniture mover. It was hard work, but my medical condition did not stop me from carrying out a day's work. The crudeness of some of the drivers made the job even more difficult. I kept trying to find an organization that would be interested in getting involved with Angolan civilian needs. The NGOs fled when I approached. Some individuals, such as Gabrielle Dicaire, a defrocked Jesuit priest, who had spent years in South America, were responsive and positive. The real difference between his experience and mine was that the Africans had decided to use the armed struggle to liberate themselves: no discussion, just liberation. Dicaire gave me a room, and this proved very appropriate. It was a refuge, since Dicaire was often away. I saw my friends from St. Pat's and continued the research project, this time with a link back to Port Moody. The information campaign needed to be carried out. I spoke to any group that would have me.

Here is the outline of information I shared in sessions during the fall of 1969:

Portugal occupied 35,000 sq miles in Europe with some nine million people and attempted to rule fourteen million in nearly 800,000 square miles in Africa and Asia.

Portugal's colour classifications are different from apartheid: it had colonial Europeans, *assimilados*, African or *mestiços* officially *equal* to the Europeans and *indigenas*, the native population. After the five hundred years of theoretically civilizing rule, only one percent of the African population had reached *assimilado* status. The structure and theory of Portuguese colonial power was economic, social, and political; not specifically racist, but the effect was the same.

The Police State Apparatus

Portugal's police state extended into the colonies. Premier Salazar built firm control of Portugal through an elitist coalition of business, military, and Church power. At home the opposition is silenced through imprisonment or exile; in the colonies by imprisonment or execution.

The most feared arm of the government was the Gestapo-like PIDE, the International Police for the Defense of the State, renewable detention of six months without arraignment, the constant "unavailability" of legal counsel, the use of torture to extract confession, with threats of "fixed residence" in concentration camps. When ninety percent of the overseas people do not understand the language of the ruler, the police can be more ruthless, and the State is *personified* in any Portuguese citizen, particularly an employer.

The *indigenas*—Africans—are subjected to a passbook system, containing tax and labour records of the bearer and names of members of the family, with photographs and fingerprints, to be shown on demand and stamped before the bearer can travel. If lost or not in order, the bearer may be sentenced to correctional labour, a convenient labour-supply system.

The *assimilados*—intellectuals—including journalists,

authors, and artists, regularly detained and accused as national subversives. One example detained in December of 1964 till February 1965, not placed on trial till the following year because of unsubstantial evidence. Yet in April of 1967, brought to trial again and now in prison.

Colonial Administration

A three-layer bureaucracy of civil, military, and PIDE Africans are excluded as most officials, including governor for each overseas province, are chosen in Lisbon.

Land Use Policy

Ninety percent of Angolans and Mozambicans live off the land.

Poverty in Portugal is a strong inducement to go to the province. Land policy favours the settler; the land acreage occupied by Europeans is sixty times that of Africans.

Five hundred fifty European plantations produced seventy-five percent of Angolan coffee, the major export crop.

Approximately twelve thousand settlers enter Angola annually, lesser numbers in Mozambique.

Agricultural Settlements by Local Administration

A *colonato*—white settler—is granted 125 acres with technical and financial aid. Annual revenue average $16,200.

An *ordenamento*—African person—is allotted twenty-five acres. Annual revenue $600, one-thirteenth of the *colonato*.

Labour

Recent reforms have modified the traditional system of forced labour in the colonies, which *differed little from slavery*. For the system to function, the local administrator must have the power to indict the Africans as malingerers without having to prove it in a court of law. Under existing laws, accused are faced with the alternative of being conscripted for public works or signing a voluntary [sic] contract with private employers.

The extent of exerted pressure is revealed indirectly by statistics showing that less than ten percent of the male population live and remain at home throughout the year.

Wages

A skilled worker in Luanda may earn up to $116 per month; the minimum monthly subsistence for a family of five, $200.

The average daily earning for an agricultural worker is 18c, while the cotton worker in Mozambique is less than $30/annum.

The European profit from low African incomes can be seen in price differential.

Annual per capita income for independent coffee farmers in Angola is $42, and their coffee sells in rural markets for $175/ton. The export price paid to the European exporter, $630 a ton.

Europeans receive up to three times the wages of Africans in the other sectors.

Migrant Labour

On average, 100,000 Mozambicans are recruited annually for an eighteen-month contract, which is between the employer and the Portuguese government rather than the men. Portuguese recruiters collect a service charge of $5.25 per labourer.

In South Africa, the primary recruiter is the Witwatersrand Native Labour Association. American Financier Charles W. Engelhard sits on its board.

Another 300,000 leave annually to find work in South Africa.

Social Services

Little is recorded; however, life expectancy is only 28 years, infant mortality up to 60 percent.

Education

Rural schools are almost completely African, while urban schools vary from African to integrated to wholly white. At the advanced levels of secondary schools there are progressively fewer Africans.

Estimates are that more than 90 percent of the people are illiterate.

United Nations

In 1960, the General Assembly declared that Portugal's colonies were under the jurisdiction of the UN Charter and requested that Portugal report to the Secretary General about her non-self-governing territories. Portugal refused, stating that the territories were a domestic concern.

In 1961 the General Assembly established a subcommittee to examine conditions after the war began.

The report of the year-long study called upon Portugal to cease its war of repression and to transfer power to the Angolan people.

In 1963 and 1965, the Security Council called on all nations to refrain from offering any assistance, including arms and supplies.

In 1965, the UN asked all nations to break off trade and diplomatic relations with Portugal.

On all of these resolutions, the United States abstained. In 1966, the UN Special Committee of 24 on Decolonisation called for the sanctions of the 1965 resolution to be made obligatory for all members. Due in part to United States' opposition, the action did not take place. The Assembly has continued to call for an end to military, financial, and other aid to Portugal . . . and has recently added a call for the moral and material assistance to the African people. Congo, Senegal, Zambia, Tanzania, and Guinea had submitted complaints to the UN about Portuguese military actions against their countries.

Portugal's Response to the War of Liberation

In 1967, military expenditure accounted for 45 percent of the national budget.

Compulsory military service extended from 2 years to 5 years and the troop numbers from 130,000 to nearly 400,000.

The presence of South African troops has been reported in Mozambique, and S.A. equipment in Angola.

It is also obvious from the South African press that South Africa considered defense of white minority rule throughout southern Africa—including Rhodesia and the colonies—as an integral part of her own self-defense.

May 8, 1963, Commander of the Allied Forces in Europe: "Portuguese soldiers while fighting for the defense of principles, are defending land, raw materials and bases, which are indispensable not only for the defense of Europe but for the whole Western world."

Portuguese officials have pressed NATO to extend its official sphere to include the southern Atlantic and Indian Ocean.

The Liberation Movements

MPLA: headquartered in Congo Brazzaville, a left-wing party led by Dr. Neto.

GRAE-FNLA: based in Kinshasa, led by Holden Roberto, brother-in-law to Zaire dictator Mobutu; CIA funded.

UNITA: based near the northern border of Angola and Zaire, led by Savimbi, financed by Portugal and settlers to combat MPLA.

Later, they would become the favourite conduit for pro-apartheid activities to combat the MPLA and the political, military front for the CIA.

The United States

The US maintained a permanent military mission in Portugal. US military and naval officials have accompanied Portuguese officials on tours of the African territories.

In 1965, a group of international salesmen and pilots were indicted in the US for exporting without a license seven B- 26 Bombers to Portugal. The aircraft, part of an order of 20, were flown from the US through Canada to Portugal. The defendants claimed to be working for the CIA (denied by CIA) and were never convicted.

Napalm and defoliants similar to those used in Vietnam showed up in Angola.

The strategic hamlets and the free-fire zones concepts were introduced along with military propaganda campaigns on the radio; and the pamphlet drops in the countryside used demonization terms such as terrorists, baby eaters, communists, and subversive to the ideological directives of colonial rule.

Trade

The United States is Portugal's third-largest partner, taking 9–10 percent of Portugal's exports worth $68 million; a comparable figure for imports.

On the tourism front the US is third on the income- producing tourism.

The US took 26 percent of Angola's exports valued at $57 million in 1965–66, with a 9 percent flow of goods to Angola worth $21million in wheat, automobile parts, machinery.

Fifty to sixty-six percent of Angola's coffee and more than half of the fishmeal went to the United States.

In 1965, the US imported from Mozambique tea and cashews worth $7.7 million while exports to Mozambique were $9 million.

Loans

InterAmerican Capital Corporation of New York made

large loans to Angola and Mozambique for the construction of a textile factory, paper mill, hydroelectric installations, roads, and airports.

The Export-Import bank loaned $2.5 million for the purchase of 30 locomotives for the transport of Angolan iron ore. Another $5.5 million loaned to the Portuguese government since 1961 for other items.

Bank of America was financing the Cabora Bassa hydroelectric dam project in Mozambique.

Other American-backed loans were arranged through the Dillon Read and Company Brokers.

Investments

Allis Chalmers had nine branches in Angola and had a contract for the processing of iron concentrates.

Firestone plans a $5 million factory in Mozambique.

General Tire holds stock in an Angolan manufacturing firm.

Standard Electric produces telecommunication parts in Luanda.

Pfizer Laboratories and Singer Sewing Machines have branches in the territories.

Anglo American Corporation holds growing interests in Angolan fisheries, a cashew business in Mozambique, and mineral prospecting in Angola copper.

Angola Diamond Company—net profits *four times the amount of the wages paid to the more than 25,000 workers.*

Oil Companies Gulf subsidiary, Cabinda Gulf since 1957, and after spending $125 million, struck it rich in 1966. Angola received

50 percent of the profits providing revenues of $10–20 million a year, the other 50 percent went to the oil company. The Cabinda civilian population was displaced and new military arrangements implemented.

Projections are for self-sufficiency by 1970 and world's fourth-largest producer of Arabica coffee.

Therefore strategic importance to the entire economic system—the system of southern Africa.

This encouraged South Africa to commence oil exploration off its coast.

Diversa of Dallas received a twenty-thousand-square- mile oil and diamonds concession in Angola. Mobil Oil and Texaco act as distributors of fuel and lubricants in Angola.

Life in Ottawa

My friend Dicaire was getting married and giving up his Bank Street apartment. I moved back to the Glen residence. Medical advice and medication slowly returned my body to normal. By Christmas, I could smell and consume a beer without feeling a pain in my liver.

This 1969 Christmas holiday was spent in Kirkland Lake at a lumberjack camp. My dad in his last working years had been hired as the resident electrician. However, during the holiday season the camp was shut down, so he was asked to supervise the vacated facilities. He was on duty 24/7. Located some ten miles from Kirkland Lake in the middle of nowhere, off the Goodfish Road, the setting was ideal for Christmas. Everyone had a task and that was to have a good time. Plenty of Mom's home cooking, a winter postcard setting with a beaver pond and snow-covered trees, and a lot full of modern tree-cutting machines.

In early January, my brother and I returned to Ottawa.

Father MacDougall introduced me to Mrs. Weston, president of the Miles for Millions NGO, the brainchild of former Prime Minister Pearson. It consisted of raising funds by having sponsors pay you a fixed amount for each mile walked or run. The circuit of twenty miles meandered through the Ottawa region, and at certain intervals proof of completion of a certain distance was registered. Water and medical facilities were also available.

The M for M needed an operations manager. Following a meeting with Mrs. Weston, I was hired.

This gave me a salary and visibility. The offices were located in the YM-YWCA situated near the Queensway. My old political friends were happy to get together and felt more comfortable now that I could say I worked for the M for M. It allowed them to be seen with me and to socialize without drawing much attention. I met old, and made new, CUSO friends. They all knew my story and seemed sympathetic to the cause. They would talk a good game but the involvement was peripheral except for the B. man and a few others. A letter arrived from CUSO Ottawa, addressed to me. I opened it and read it slowly. I burst out, "Screw you, you jerk!" It was from the East African director, Lawrence Cumming, demanding payment for the air ticket from Dar in October of 1968.

I picked up the phone and called him. I was so furious. "Lawrence, you are a jerk. You know what I do for the MPLA and if I had $800 it would go to the liberation movement. You could have told me face to face about the need for administrative purposes when I saw you this afternoon, but to send me a cold call letter—you're a louse." I slammed the phone into its cradle.

A few days later he called and gave me the good news that he had found monies to cover the air ticket.

Life without these little self-created messes would be dull. I kept reminding myself: Don't quit, don't lose.

Following a lecture at Carleton University, the roommates at Glen Street turned over three telephone messages marked urgent, which I ignored. A huge snowstorm had covered the Ottawa area and city life was on hold.

At four the following morning, my brother was awakened by a constant and hard knocking at the front door. He was able to see him through the small window and made out that this man was looking for me. His business card showed that he was from a prominent business family in Ottawa. My brother woke me up and I went to see what he wanted. I let this "new friend" into the house and heard him out. He wanted to talk about Angola and some business opportunities. I asked him to step outside so I could speak to my brother. I needed to see what he wanted, so I instructed my brother: "I'll go with him; you register the plate number as we leave, and if I am not home by lunchtime, call the police." I got dressed and went outside to the waiting car. The sidewalks and large snowbanks made getting to the blue Benz difficult.

We drove to his residence. I felt okay; however, I was to be educated. We went into the upscale house via the side door and went to the basement. Facing the couch was a wall-to-wall communications network, shortwave radio sets with direct links to different parts of the world. This was a serious set-up. We sat down on a luxurious black leather couch and he opened a file folder. It was my portfolio. He had been following my public speaking engagements. Following the usual polite introductions I said, "What is so urgent that you had to come and awaken me at four a.m.?"

He said, "I am going away soon and needed to talk to you."

It became clear that he could and would supply military hardware to the MPLA for a price. He understood the military situation very well and that the MPLA looked as if they would win. The supply of diamonds, industrial and social, from Angola, would fit well in his line of business. The CIA plans. Angola, a very rich country in diamonds and oil, had to be forced into the Western camp, without regard to the aspirations of the Angolans. In the early sixties the CIA had engineered the assassination of the elected leader of the Congo, Patrice Lumumba, then through a series of coups designated a military clerk as the American puppet and dictator. Mobutu was to be the figurehead and agent of American influence in Southern Africa. The FNLA was receiving military help from the CIA. This new friend offered more of the same to ensure American influence in case the CIA-backed group didn't work out. This new friend was not so certain as to the viability of the FNLA–CIA plan.

He, my new friend, might just get another foot in the door of Angola.

The offer: delivery of what was needed, at the MPLA location of choice, a "do it all" operation, with discretion assured. The hook: diamonds, preferred diamond exploration rights after independence. Mr. X provided photographs of the military equipment, tanks, SAM missiles, planes.

The large diamond vultures were now in the open. Other offers of cash were laid out.

"Can you set up a meeting with Dr. Neto?" he asked. "We just want to talk to him and offer our services."

I registered the request, turned down the cash, and said I would get the message to Dr. Neto. He drove me back to the Glen Street residence.

My brother was still home and was relieved that I had returned safely. I gave him a brief outline. He laughed and shrugged his shoulders, "Just more American imperialism." Now the question was how to get this info, which for the MPLA was critical, to Dr. Neto. Knowing that the industrial interests were coming out so openly meant that the MPLA and its military strategy were making certain people uneasy.

I wrote out the details of the conversation. With the help of a friend, the letter was carried to the MPLA. The mystery man was the son of a well-known Ottawa businessman.

As the M for M project continued, the African National Congress connection was rekindled through Dennis September, the CUSO Zambia director. There was a lot of contact between liberation movements, in Zambia, where the UN-recognized movements were given homes some ten miles outside Lusaka, and at international conferences. Having established my credibility with MPLA to the extent that I had meant that I had contact with some ANC cadres like Uncle Hector and Oliver Tambo. The ANC was always on the lookout for outside comrades to help their cause. After dark we mingled with cadres and exchanged views on the strategies for advancing independence. The word went back to

ANC leadership that there was a Canadian comrade who had helped set up the MPLA communications network, had integrated as a full member making no demands for special treatment or perks, had lived the experience on the ground as a friend and fellow guerrilla. I could be trusted. One area of weakness that kept being identified was intelligence about security measures in South Africa and data for evaluating the attitudes amongst white South Africans toward apartheid.

The catalyst to my involvement with the ANC was the arrival of Dennis September, an ANC comrade from Cape Town who had fled to Canada, obtained citizenship, and was hired by CUSO to be the country director for Zambia. His main job was to identify, evaluate, and recruit young Canadians to help Zambia train teachers, engineers, and people in other skilled roles that the Brits had ignored. He was hired by Frank Bogdasavich, executive director of CUSO since 1965. Frank, "the Bogeyman," was a progressive thinker, saw the potential for influencing developments in South Africa from a solid base in Zambia, and chose Dennis September, a mulatto with credibility in the ANC, to head up the Lusaka office.

Following the MPLA information campaigns throughout Canada, I had acquired experience in public speaking and community-based organizing, and I came to a number of important conclusions. One, the lack of images and testimonials made the message difficult to put across; two, my credibility in Southern Africa was limited because I had no track record with the ANC, which had the highest profile and were tackling the most challenging opposition in a well-established, sophisticated military and security culture in South Africa; three, my public persona was MPLA- focused and perceived as not very serious, creating a false impression of a naïvely optimistic Jacques Roy spinning his wheels, not seeing the big picture. Number one would be taken care of with a documentary film about the liberation struggle. I was putting some wheels in motion about that. When I heard about September and understood his role, I was inspired to approach the ANC with an intelligence-gathering proposal. Things were militarily too hot in Angola to take a film crew in, and the MPLA agreed to second me to the ANC.

My Miles for Millions job gave me enough respectability that I could approach the Bogeyman. Without it, I was a little too radioactive.

He agreed to have lunch. Since I trusted Frank with my life, talking with him was always a pleasure and a learning experience. He was directing CUSO to give support to developing nations, and was very interested in my plans. Seldom in life does one meet another human being who connects the dots so quickly.

Our cover would be a newly married couple, willing to travel, to accomplish tasks for the ANC.

Here was the story:

On their honeymoon, a couple of unassuming white Canadians explore a move to South Africa.

The scenario was my creation. Given my trust in the Bogeyman, I asked him to find a good woman who was sympathetic, capable, and willing to fill the role as a partner in a serious ANC operation. The consequences for failure were to be mentioned only when brought up. In time the person would get it.

Failure meant arrest, detention, and possible execution for crimes against the state. Espionage was a dangerous game, and if we were caught, our Canadian passports could be our ticket out. Apartheid leaders saw themselves as defenders of Western civilization, at war with the enemy, the African National Congress.

I read the newspaper want ads looking for employment as a teacher in Zambia. I looked for two months, and then one day there it was, in black and white.

"Canadian recruiter for the Zambia Institute of Technology ZIT" interviewing for technical teaching staff. Mr. Ford was the man. The ad was pure joy. The capacity to wait proved invaluable again. Following the advertised instructions, I prepared my resumé, filled in the blanks, and mailed the document. My work for the walkathon now required much attention and detail. The May walk was on schedule, but my presence at the office was required.

The man from ZIT called and asked to see me ASAP, so we agreed to meet at the Y. I did some relaxing exercises before the one p.m.

meeting and meditated. In his fifties, Mr. Ford was pleasant and wanted to do a good job. He was cordial, and we sat down in the large leather chairs in the YMCA foyer. He showed genuine interest in the M an M fundraiser.

First impression, a good connection. We both needed something, both willing to deal.

Mr. Ford was impressed with my African teaching experience and the successful completion of the Burnaby fill-in job. He expressed frustration at the difficulty in recruiting for Zambia. I listened attentively for the "desperation level" and possible weaknesses in his overall scheme. I heard them loud and clear, and there were plenty. Working in Zambia was a tough assignment. The ZIT was situated in the Copper Belt, 400 kilometres north of Lusaka, near the Zaire border, and had campuses in Ndola, Lunanshya, and Kitwe. The meeting was easy: salary, conditions, holidays, advancement, and professional development in a good working environment.

We agreed to get together again in seven days. I could discuss this matter with my fiancée, still an unknown quantity, and if she was in agreement, we could sign a contract with a memorandum of understanding that would bind both parties. My sleepless nights began. In order to be in control of my life, my political life required a tight scenario with an escape clause. I hated Zambia, but the inefficiencies of the bureaucracy gave me some leeway.

This was an enormous opportunity for me. I could not believe Ford's disorganized work habits. I was able to write my own ticket, knowing that he would simply glance through it at our next meeting and sign it. He would not see the wiggle room I was creating for myself. I was very excited.

I sat for many long, hard hours and designed the Memorandum of Understanding—tight, with potential to create loopholes:

- Teach in Luanshya, but to begin with would live in Kitwe some fifty miles away

- Transportation to school to be arranged

- Housing before November in Luanshya

- Teaching load at a senior level, subject: electricity, electronics, physics

- My fiancee to arrive before Christmas

- Rate of pay on par with other expatriates on staff

Failure to meet these conditions would render the contract null and void. That held for both parties.

Seven days later, the smiling face behind the spectacles arrived at the Y. The conditions in the Memorandum presented no problems for the ZIT and Mr. Ford.

It was time to sign on the dotted line.

We shook hands and planned for an August departure with details to be forwarded.

I was so happy . . . another step, another project.

With the end of the walkathon in late May, I gathered my thoughts and revisited the B. man. My message to him: "The first phase is complete and the fix is in. What about your inquiry, any results?" "Soon," was his response.

The Glen Street home was no longer available. After June, I got together with George Best from St. Pat's and rented a house near the Civic Centre in South Ottawa. It was functional and I could tolerate it for a few months. June went by and still no partner. Early July, a phone call from the B. man. "Come to my office tomorrow and we'll have lunch. You will meet someone who has what it takes." Yet another sleepless night.

I met the B. man at his Slater office and made my way to his office. The door was closed. A phone call later, he opened the door, invited me in to meet Colleen. Her long, blonde hair covered part of her face, but parted as she rose to shake hands. Hers were cold but firm. She was a beautiful woman, five feet six inches, thin with a small face with blue eyes. Her face was slightly elongated and the skin was smooth and tight.

The tight miniskirt made it clear that she was very presentable. We went for a long lunch. The B. man had explained the project and excused himself after the meal. We carried on our conversation. I was quite bowled over. I needed to know her inner strength, what mattered to her, what kind of adversities she had known. These details would come later.

The intentions of our first meeting were met. There was compatibility, seriousness, and laughter. We set up another date. The next day was Friday, so after her work, we met and headed for a restaurant off Bank Street. She warmed up to the idea of working and doing something positive with her life. A great meal and good wine; Colleen could hold her own with the booze. She also had great wit.

Personal trauma as a young girl had made her a little timid, but I could tell that she had a good heart. Her brains were also excellent. As for courage and tenacity, they were still to be measured. I asked for her observations and feelings on the project. She expressed a clear understanding of the implications. At age twenty-one, to understand such a proposal and to be prepared to carry it out with a twenty-seven-year-old stranger required guts—lots of guts.

So over the next weeks we spent a lot of time together. I met her father, a wonderful, warm man. As young men, he and his brothers had constructed a plane. When one of the brothers was test flying the plane, the Ontario Provincial Police in their infinite wisdom arrived at the landing area and gave the pioneer pilot a ticket for flying without a licence. It went to court, and the boys paid the five-dollar fine. Colleen's mother was a former schoolteacher and was now a computer programmer.

Our relationship had solidified, but the reason for it necessitated "discretion on all fronts." No one was to know how or why we got together.

Colleen continued to work, and I prepared the school materials and raised the discussion level of the project. August came and went. So did September. The predicted inefficiencies at ZIT were working. More time to spend with Colleen and to work on personal issues. I had come to care deeply for her and realized the direction of our flourishing and emotional involvement as well as the security for her life were in my hands. She trusted me. We could grow together and make a political contribution. We spent time at her parents' cottage west of Ottawa.

Colleen read a lot and had an artistic flair. She painted and wrote poetry. A very sensitive person with an introverted personality, she offered a view of life that allowed me to see something new. She was not much of a cook or a housecleaning freak, but that was a secondary issue. Her most important qualities: she was highly intelligent, had a dependable photographic memory, was articulate, gorgeous with natural, long blonde hair, and a smile to mask her poker face.

She brought to the forced joint venture more than I had expected or imagined was possible.

During this waiting period, I went to Montreal to meet with Oxfam Quebec, a progressive-thinking and action-orientated NGO.

Under the leadership of Pierre Rivard, Oxfam had established itself as the most daring in its support of international projects. Rivard was for the underprivileged. During the war in Biafra, he had been dropped behind the lines and worked as a photographer and knew the hardships of war. He took in the needs for information and material help in Angola with ease. He said, "This could be done." The board of directors—the *Conseil d'Administration, C.A.*— included comedian Yvon Deschamps, lawyer and physician Dr. Pierre Marc Johnston, hockey star Guy Lafleur, and well-known business people and personalities from the world of the arts.

These two days were filled with meetings with the staff. Hean Foisy-Marquis and Jean Pozatski were the experts in communication, written and visual. They worked very well with other NGOs throughout Quebec. Province-wide support for the MPLA could be managed. It required an action plan. I told Rivard that I was going back to Africa. He suggested that the visual material now in short supply was fundamental to the education campaigns. I promised that upon my return I would have a visual picture of the MPLA structure. In the meantime, I gave him a copy of the existing material. He liked the Boavida interview, because the content was descriptive and his death was a powerful reminder of the war in Southern Africa ignored by the Western media.

This new friend and I formed a very strong bond.

Early October brought the reality of "the next step." The air ticket and documentation for the ZIT contract for five years arrived by registered mail. Colleen and I spent the last few days alone, intimate, in thought and seriousness. I rented a furnished suite in the Ottawa downtown area. The large wooden staircase covered with a heavy piled runner led to the indirect lighting of the hallways of the upper landing. Large dark wooden doors opened to a sitting area, and behind a wallpapered wall was the bedroom and still farther on was the bathroom—a picture-perfect setting for a luxurious holiday. It was tastefully decorated with antique furniture, landscape paintings, and floor- length curtains. She would come to Zambia for Christmas. The tears of separation flowed. Somehow this was bigger than the project.

CHAPTER SEVEN

Make the impossible possible.

—Charles Garfield

On November 10, 1969, the Air Canada flight took me to London, England. The day's stay at an airport hotel allowed me some sleep and a small body clock adjustment. Later that night, the Zambian Airways flight, after a two-hour delay, left for the capital of Zambia, Lusaka. The late-morning arrival proved uneventful. Nothing to declare. The ZIT people had booked a room at the Lusaka Hotel and they were expecting me to stay at least three days. Within two minutes of reaching my room, I had connected with my good friend Dennis September. His response over the phone: "I don't believe you are here!"

"Come to the Lusaka Hotel."

"Stay in your room. I'll ring you up." Dennis spoke with a Cape accent, clearly South African.

He came up to the room, and as he entered we embraced. "I still can't believe that you are here."

"Well, Dennis, I am here to do a job," I said as he interjected, "Let's go to the house."

Off we drove, past the CUSO office, around the traffic circle, past the Riverside Hotel, and headed for an area of Lusaka that I did not know. The semi-circular driveway covered the front of the property. To the left there was a long drive leading to a garage. Numerous trees, small and large, gave the house a canopy and a secluded look. We entered through the right front door to be warmly greeted by Mrs. September—Hazel.

These two persons had suffered a lot under apartheid and now had a chance to help defeat the racist regime in South Africa. They had been active members of the ANC in Cape Town and, like many activists, were forced to leave or face prison sentences or the dreaded house arrest. This meant no more than three persons in the same room, no leaving the house, no income. The Septembers, classified as coloured, came to Canada and settled in Winnipeg with their children. Obtaining Canadian citizenship and qualifying as a teacher, Dennis was ready for a new part in the anti-apartheid struggle.

CUSO was recruiting a field officer for Zambia and given the quality of their political awareness, the CUSO leadership hired Dennis to run the very politically sensitive office in Lusaka. The Bogeyman and the CUSO leadership stepped up to the plate and hit the big one. Competent, articulate, and very sociable, the Septembers—Dennis, Hazel, and youngest son Steve—moved back to Africa to help in any way they could. Responsible for the Zambia desk, Dennis soon expanded his activities beyond the geographical boundaries of Zambia.

In my view, Dennis was furthering Canada's stated foreign policy by helping the liberation movements. CIDA would not do so, instead imposing projects that paid dividends in Canada, like a bakery that used Canadian-grown grain, displacing local farmers and bakeries. The liberation movements had a real friend in Dennis, a comrade in arms, creating more links and friendships in order to advance the independence of five nations still under minority rule.

It was another historical meeting. Dennis made a phone call, and within the hour Thabo Mbeki and Chris Hani arrived. We embraced and exchanged warm greetings. Revolutionary greetings, because our lives were driven by the struggle against oppression and racial division: our personal lives suffered tremendously as a result of the hours we devoted to this noble cause.

"Comrade Jacques," Mbeki said. "Welcome back." Hani doubled the salutation. We all wore huge smiles; we had survived to meet again and to perhaps accomplish another project. The focus was on working with our capabilities, giving more time to making things happen, and less concern about structure. In our view, effective teamwork called for knowledge of the business, and commitment to performance, accountability, and accelerated learning. Interpersonal and intercultural sensitivity were prerequisites. Deception and thinking on our feet certainly were developed skills, but the fundamental values of our personal lives guided our push towards results.

Our involvement contained an inherent danger. The enemy would dearly love to get rid of us. Assassination and disappearance were the preferred methods. However, their attitude of superiority and racist views created an illusion of invincibility. Smugness and self-deception would be their downfall.

Mbeki was responsible for the political side, while Hani looked after the military wing called "Spear of the Nation." These two men were the co-directors of the ANC. The old guard, including Mbeki's father, Mandela, Tambo, Slovo, and other leaders were either in jail or too old. A Hani-Mbeki duo represented the future and today were the brains and co- coordinating centre. There was no competition between them, just co- operation and determination to succeed. To become part of the movement and to take action with these men and women of the ANC was a privilege and an honour.

The youngest of the September children, Steve, was still in school. For this twelve-year-old boy, living in a household that was a rotating political Who's Who of Southern Africa could have been overwhelming; he just smiled and observed.

Our conversation centred on the personal and the status of the latest political problems in South Africa. The Zambian reality had not changed very much since October of 1968. The South African Air Force had penetrated all the way to Lusaka's southern suburbs and bombed the Liberation Center once again. In response, the Zambian government denounced the action but would not find the political and moral courage to purchase anti-aircraft equipment. The government failed to educate the population and its armed forces as to the plight of the people living in South Africa.

Zambia was free and had not lived in a racially divided society; the understanding that all of Southern Africa was implicated in the struggle was missing, and the Zambians suffered. They did not understand the need for armed struggle and had little sense that independence in the bordering countries would make their own lives better. The Portuguese had struck Zambia and killed civilians in western Zambia near Kalabo as well as villages near the Mozambique border. If their government was not willing to explain the reasons for the attacks and the need for continued support for the liberation, then the liberation movements had to operate with continuous vigilance. The ANC's efforts were getting the racists to ramp up their military bravado. Zambia had to be tolerated for their weak effort, and no public criticism was permitted. It was a base, not a home. The focus soon shifted to the "project." In carefully chosen words I said that it was a go, and within a few weeks my friend Colleen would arrive. Perhaps by April or May we could be free to carry out the plan. I would keep Dennis informed.

All other details were superfluous: the teaching job and the hoops that we needed to jump through, the legitimate and the plausible. Hani and Mbeki had a team available for a project.

Teams that are led effectively are the most powerful and productive means for accomplishing work. With my MPLA experience, the ANC could count on the accurate completion of the project. Their part was defining the project, assuring financing, and providing proper training while minimizing our exposure to Zambian authorities. But for this get-together, there was a social dimension to enjoy.

We consumed a few cold Zambian beers and savoured a home-cooked meal.

The reunion had lasted three hours and covered a lot of issues, but now it was time to take the next steps towards freedom. Chris and Thabo exited, and a half hour later Dennis drove me back to the hotel. The luxury of the rooms and the efficient service made the stay very enjoyable. My first walk after dinner on day one was in the direction of the Annex. From a distance, I saw the ugliness and nondescript façade; it had remained etched in my memory. I looked at it from the steps of the library, my former place of refuge, for meditation and calm. Time to rest. The "reality" of ZIT would soon be upon me.

The ZIT officials introduced me to the scope and depth of the education syllabus designed to train Zambians for integration into the main industry, copper production. I knew the mining industry and associated mining procedures and skills required. The orientation was a breeze. The overall focus of the Education Plan shifted my mindset to survival with a focus on the required ploy for extracting myself from the contract. I learned that a number of Canadians from the Canadian International Development Agency—CIDA—were on site in the Copper Belt. Was this the first clue that it was a well-financed project? Had I been short-changed on salary? Was this therefore a possible loophole in my contract?

A few Americans and a leftover group of former colonial Brits filled out the teaching staff.

On day three in the early morning, there was a knock at my door. "Who is it?" I asked.

"It's Chris, Jacques, open up."

It had to be Hani. He had a very distinct voice. I opened the door and extended my hand on positive recognition. "Just dropped by to see how you were doing, Comrade Jacques."

I responded, "So nice to see you, Chris."

Hani had bypassed the front desk as usual. He enjoyed our get-together, as it gave him some genuine human contact. He could talk freely while appreciating the efforts of outsiders in exposing apartheid. Progressive Europeans turned into comrades, playing the maximum role according to their abilities. We were brothers because of our shared views and the tasks that we carried out. He had only praise for Canada and its voting record at the UN; that is, continued support for the ANC in political and material aid.

It was not a good idea for us to be seen together. There could be no reason for public togetherness. No public hellos. We spoke for a half hour. Hani was a big man, 220 pounds and six feet tall. His smile revealed a broken front tooth and his speech contained a small lisp. He was a muscular person with enormous presence and charisma. I was in awe, because he represented the South African youth and had been a popular youth leader in South Africa till he joined the military wing, and was part of the first wave of guerrillas to enter Rhodesia. On South Africa's Most Wanted list, Hani was charged with subversion of the state, along with a litany of fabricated accusations. His capture meant the firing squad. When cornered by Rhodesian troops, the ANC guerrillas slipped into Botswana and were captured by an independent African government, which charged them for entering Botswana without proper documentation. They served a sentence of two years less a day and then returned to the ANC base in Zambia.

Apartheid leaders feared Hani because he knew how to confront, poke at, and undermine the racist regime. No bravado, just push and pull back, hit on the left, jab, duck, and disappear. An evaporating target, the ultimate guerrilla.

Hani had seen the repression, the political assassinations, the 1960 Sharpeville massacre with sixty-seven dead, one hundred eighty injured, the constant humiliation of Africans because of the Pass Law.

The Boers had such hatred of the Africans and demonized them with the "K" word—Kaffir. I have tried to imagine what were the long-range effects of this continuous assault upon the dignity and self-worth of Africans. Fanon in his book *The Wretched of the Earth* looked into this lingering abusive behaviour by the French colonials on the Algerians and on the haters, the French settlers themselves.

Mandela was on Robben Island, and the ANC was the only organization with a political and military structure capable of defeating apartheid. ANC president Oliver Tambo, after so many years of struggle, though just middle-aged, was a tired and worn-out cadre. In the white-only parliament, one woman had the guts and wisdom to question the actions of the racist. This was Helen Suzman. She was the only voice to question and to show the absurdity and futility of apartheid. In early 1967, Suzman visited Robben Island and its infamous RIVONIA Group headed by Mandela, Sisulu, Govan Mbeki, and many others.

A tireless opponent of minority rule, Suzman was under constant attack by the white press and parliament and was constantly under the eye of the Bureau of State Security—BOSS. This fascist and secret organization had Gestapo-trained personnel. Feared, loathed, and powerful, this apparatus operated outside the law with no accountability or consequences. The names of Terre Blanche, Milan, Voster, Botha provided the manpower to sustain the enrollment in the secret society.

The international organizations and service clubs remained silent in spite of having codes of conduct. The vast majority benefited economically from the racial divide. I recall being invited to join Rotary and refused since the four-way test (Is it true? Is it fair to all concerned? Will it build good will and better friendships? Will it be beneficial to all concerned?) did not apply in South Africa.

Hani got out of the chair, extended his hand, and drew me into a hug. It was time to carry on. I met another time with September before heading north to the Copper Belt. As CUSO Director, the flexibility of his time lent itself to doing many tasks, official and non-official. We would only communicate when absolute necessity dictated. Day four meant time to go to the Copper Belt. Another flight, a new experience with a defined task of teaching while following an undefined time line. A window of opportunity had to be opened within five to six months so the "project" could be started.

On arrival at the Ndola airport, a driver from ZIT picked me up.

Dust, the red dust that I knew so well, was everywhere. The drive to Kitwe made me very sad. Faced with this red land, my courage drained away. Arrangements had been made by the ZIT administration for a temporary stay at the Kitwe Hotel. I settled in, and late that first afternoon, a Canadian, a former teacher at the Ottawa Technical High School, came to the hotel and welcomed me to the new teaching post. He filled me in on the structure and personnel at the Luanshya campus. Some teachers drove the fifty miles every day and therefore transportation to and fro was not an issue. It was, however, an issue for me. We had a few beers in the well-kept garden terrace at the hotel. This CIDA man was very enthused with his power from shop teacher in Ottawa to department head in Zambia within three years. He was a rising star in ZIT and CIDA. He knew of my African teaching experience but he knew "how these Zambians think." His remarks had paternalism written all over them, in a different accent, one that I recognized.

Next morning at seven a.m., I headed out on my first drive to the Luanshya campus. The Kitwe-Luanshya road surface was paved, but the edges of the pavement had been eaten away by the rains. The usual road maintenance required to make it a safe surface had been duly neglected. It was designed for two cars, but the large trucks hogged the majority of the tarmac. You either moved to the jagged edge of the paved surface or challenged the big lorries for right of way. Driving on the left-hand side enabled the passenger to clearly look into the crater along the road, ditch, and burial ground all rolled in one. The meeting of two large lorries carrying mining ore and a double lorry carrying fuel gave the blistered edges a further shake and narrowed the good driving surface.

Ninety minutes later, we entered the parking lot of the school. ZIT was a two-storey building made of brick, painted white with a courtyard of neatly trimmed grass and flower trees. I also knew this picture.

Looking at this predictable layout I could only conclude that during the colonization period, only one architect and landscaper had been available, since the same model appeared again and again. We entered and headed to the faculty room and met a dozen staff, who had convened for coffee. With introductions out of the way, we all headed to a meeting on ZIT business.

Mr. Goodine, the principal, and CIDA senior staff gave the welcoming words. This whole exercise of bureaucratic banter drew out for an hour. I met the head of the electrical/electronic department, an American engineer, a recent arrival to the continent.

Teaching courses were handed out and the routine started. My courses, due to the lack of seniors, focused on the entrance-level students. A possible first loophole in the original contract?

Classroom time represented some fifteen hours per week. Having prepared the basic courses in Ottawa, my free time gave me room to think. I met other Canadians and Brits in Kitwe. Social outings were intentionally limited and the move from the hotel to a hostel in Kitwe made for much better surroundings, meals and laundry included. I bought a used 150cc motorcycle for use in Kitwe, and this time had it properly licensed and insured. The nearly daily run to the campus was the responsibility of the school, and in a short period of time I learned that it was also a very dangerous stretch of road. Frequent accidents between cars, trucks, and pedestrians made the front pages of the local paper.

Another loophole? Just maybe.

With my new mobility, I explored the Kitwe area, found the library and booze store. The housing for most expatriates was small and functional. No colourful landscaping or trees like Dar. Just a lot of bare, dry, red dusty surfaces made worse by the annual dry period. The sterility of the surroundings gave the impression of a large minimum-security prison.

Living in a hostel limited my contact with the expatriate community, which was compatible with security needs. We could not trust Canadians, Americans or Brits; anyone could pick up a suspicion that I was not all I seemed and a careless or deliberate word in the right ear could make life very difficult. Likewise, I confined my contact with the Zambians to teaching. I was simply not available for social events. With the end of December approaching, I felt obliged to attend the simulated good cheer gatherings, drink a little booze, and listen to the gripes of the "imports." It amazed me to realize that so little cultural and history training had been offered to the expatriates before their assignment.

Whatever lessons of living in Africa were followed, the results were neo-colonial in day-to-day events. A grasp of the consequences of colonialism in terms of economic and psychological effects would give a newcomer a start in understanding the underdevelopment and a clear direction away from the "treat-them-like-children-they-can't-do-anything- right" mentality, which was very prevalent.

The English department had Canadians, Brits, and Eastern Europeans. I made it a point to have lunch with Murphy, a Canadian and CUSO volunteer, who lived in Luanshya with his wife. Over lunch, Murphy opened up on his views of neo-colonialism and the sorry state of Zambia. I prodded to measure his political development. At best, he was left of centre, somewhat alienated from the political arena, and basically putting in time. He could be a useful person if properly massaged.

Murphy provided an in-depth analysis of the housing difficulties that plagued ZIT. Having been part of the college for a few years, he had heard the promises and witnessed the non-results. Kitwe, barring a miracle, was the only place I could live.

I responded, "You've got to be kidding." Are you telling me that Mr. Ford cannot deliver on his promise for Luanshya housing?

He answered, "Look at the number of expats who are travelling from Kitwe."

I confined myself to a shrug of the shoulders. Murphy gave me a lift back to school, where my ride to Kitwe was waiting. The expat community knew that my fiancée was scheduled to arrive by Christmas. Any personal interaction was limited by this event, no politics, no visits or promises of future engagements. No Christmas parties. Just school.

Once back in my hostel room, situated on the second floor and away from the court, I talked to myself. If what Murphy said was correct, Ford had exaggerated, perhaps lied. The promised housing did not exist, and this, this was indeed super news.

I wrote to Colleen regularly. I missed her a lot and did not write about my feelings regarding Kitwe. Only the progress with the "project" in unwritten words made it to paper. Her responses were slow and out of sync with the developing events on this side of the ocean. My follow-up answers to her queries gave her more uncertainty and disconnect. Some days I wrote three letters, intended to reassure her that she would be coming soon, she just had to be patient.

Christmas 1970, more trials and tribulations. More reflection time.

ZIT persons living in Kitwe had family and did their Christmas

thing. Being away from Canada meant putting up a tree with a little green, a few lights, and the familiar strings of incoming cards on doorframes. Hostel food had been upgraded, so I enjoyed the nearly deserted dining room with a book on Ethiopia, the history of Selassie and the queen of Sheba. This 500-page book was banned in Ethiopia and anyone found with it placed under death sentence. Welcome to Africa and America's friends.

I still had the copy of Boavida's book, *500 Years of Portuguese Exploitation*. It provided an ongoing economic lesson, and as a tribute to my disappeared friend, I decided to write a review and sent it to *Afrique Asie* in Paris using the pen name B.J. Quidado—B for Boavida, J for Jacques, Quidado for the military commander killed in 1968.

I got through the Christmas holiday without contact with the Canadian expatriate community. Food and drink were plentiful, and this "downtime" was a reminder of past experiences, filled with variable emotions and forcing me to come up with scenarios that would be needed to fulfill the next step with the ANC. Still learning how to wait.

In mid-January, the MPLA sent a cadre to Kitwe to meet with me. His name was Kamalata, and the meeting was away from the hostel. The talk centred on a message from Dr. Neto, who ". . . was glad to see that I was close by and that given the severe military engagements in Angola it would be better to stay in Kitwe." I had a film-making project in mind. All of the questions and lack of information in Canada could be resolved with a documentary film. MPLA needed to be put up on a screen. If the Vietnam War was on TV in North America, why not the Angola war? The secret war in Laos and Cambodia, the secret wars in Southern Africa, the definite decision not to have these conflicts in the news made it difficult to rally support. It was up to the progressive forces to speak of these conflicts and to show which countries continued to support the minority governments while ignoring human rights and the founding principles of a democracy.

Kamalata agreed to come back at another time. For now the film was on hold. I also began to pressure the ZIT officials regarding my housing. This exercise was designed to test the contract, and within three days a small one-bedroom apartment became available. Freshly painted, clean, this arrangement got me and my housing complaints out of their hearing range. ZIT had bought time. Luanshya housing confirmed, a nonstarter. With this move, Colleen needed to make travel arrangements. Though it was part of our contract, we could not allow the ZIT people to fulfill this part. So we arranged and paid for the flight. This would be another argument for breaking the contract. Next move.

Arrangements in Ottawa by Colleen included final inoculations and closing out of her job.

My mood at school changed. This ZIT teaching assignment had nearly run its course.

I needed to find out what was happening with the project. With the help of a colleague who would cover three of my classes, I took the early morning train to Lusaka. On arrival, I called September, who took me off to his home, as this meeting needed to be under wraps. Following the details of the ongoing saga, September agreed that the ZIT relationship was heading for the correct results. Mbeki came to the house later on that night. He had set out an objective and the tools to attain it. The time line seemed to okay.

Hazel produced great food and companionship, as Dennis needed to go on with his "show." The evenings were shared in the warm environment of a loving household. The discussions certainly made time fly. She and Colleen would get along very well. The companionship of these few days re-energized my spirits and refocused me for the next step. The return trip to the Copper Belt was Sunday night by Zambia Airways. While waiting at the airport to enter the craft, I noticed a beautiful, healthy-looking blonde woman standing by herself. I knew this woman, but from where? I racked my brain and really pushed my memory. Finally, the connection—this could be trouble.

She was the English teacher at ZIT. What now? I believed she was Russian, which meant that she knew the politics of Africa and the liberation movements but she would be unaware of my connections. If I could get her to talk, then I could explain what I was doing in Lusaka during teaching days. The best scenario was that I was visiting the Canadian Embassy regarding my fiancée's documents relating to her arrival.

Offence is the best defense. I walked over to her and extended my right hand as I said, "Good evening, Madame la Professeur."

She extended hers, but with a slight hesitation. She was trying to remember where we had met. It gradually came to her that we had crossed paths in the hallways at ZIT, Kitwe Campus. Once this link clicked in, I asked if we could sit together for the return flight. "Yes," she answered. Situation under control now, "Excuse me for a minute."

I was off to the washroom. Time to regroup.

The return flight proved to be more than interesting. They were in fact Russian, and her husband was a surgeon at the Kitwe hospital. She was an intelligent and well-informed person. She wondered why the Canadians were measured in their friendliness towards them. I explained with the intention of demarking myself away from these Canucks, that they were not very politically aware. The anti-communist bias was very alive. It was probably the first time Canadians had met and spoken to a Russian person, but their anti-communist view blurred the relationship. Somehow, I felt that she already knew this.

She invited me to meet her husband and family. This was getting better. Her husband was at the airport to pick her up. No other persons from ZIT were about, so they agreed to drop me off at my apartment, and I accepted their invitation for dinner on the following Friday.

Life at the apartment seemed a little unreal. The evenings, following the schoolwork, were spent listening to the shortwave radio.

I still liked the French overseas radio service. This combination radio allowed me to listen to the MPLA daily reports as well as the ANC news from Lusaka.

The Friday night dinner at the Russians' house was very relaxed. I knew that the Russians were helping the MPLA, and therefore more than likely he had some connection as a surgeon, perhaps on standby to help if required. I continued to press on the liberation movement issue. They seemed very comfortable with the subject, so I opened up as to my past work with the MPLA. They accepted this and were pleased that other nations were helping liberate Africa.

I gave them my method of how to deal with the Canadians at the ZIT. We would remain friends, but with limited contact. I would attend a party at their house as long as other Canadians were present. The good doctor offered his services if required.

The results of the Lusaka agreement with the ANC required a telegram for Colleen stating that at her convenience she should arrange to come to Zambia. Her reply cheered me up.

On February 15, I was at the Lusaka airport to welcome Colleen. She was exhausted, and the customs people implemented their return ticket policy. Despite my speaking with the officials we needed to purchase, as condition for entry, a return ticket to Ottawa.

This was okay. Colleen required a lot of attention at this time. We still had the flight to Ndola. Humour, lots of humour, seemed to help.

Colleen co-operated, and we made it back to the apartment. Frazzled and sporting a Canadian winter tan, she had made it. Seven days went by before she could talk normally. She was suffering serious jetlag. Seeing Colleen gave me real pleasure, as I had missed her wit and personality. Her delicate body looked so good. She desperately required recuperation time and adjustment to the hellhole we were in. She shook her head at the building, made of cold concrete blocks, cold concrete floors with one small window in each of the three rooms. Furnishings consisted of a wooden table, three chairs, a small fridge, a stove, and a few dishes. The bedroom had one chair and a three-quarter-size bed. There was one small bathroom with bath and toilet.

From February 22 to the end of the month, we celebrated her arrival. Good wine and good food, plentiful.

The intimate evenings were followed by long nights of warmth and passion. We both expected so much and were willing to do our best. Because this apartment had so little natural light, we left the front door open, and of course a mouse got in and was soon discovered by Colleen in the bathroom. The monster mouse from Kitwe was tracked down and removed, and the excitement was over.

Colleen was very curious to know how the project had developed. In measured quantities, she grew to understand the scope of the events leading to the project. It seemed like a good movie in a bad town.

The last event in the overall scheme was the M.O. for our project. We needed to establish our reasons for travelling around the country.

As agreed in Ottawa, we would get married. On my next trip to Luanshya, I reached Murphy and told him the good news that my fiancée had arrived and that we were going to get married. He congratulated me, and I asked him if he would be the witness. He agreed, and with this assurance I went to the Kitwe Municipal Offices and purchased a marriage license for 10k and set time and date: 10:00, Saturday the 24th of March, 1971.

The only people we wanted at the wedding were the Murphys. The intention was to establish and control legitimacy for travel with as little knowledge of this wedding as possible. What we feared most was the CUSO gang in Lusaka, known for their indiscretion. This short time span gave us the desired edge to get to Lusaka to break the contract and enter the next project.

Colleen was back up to speed and had accepted the temporary nature of our living arrangements.

My school presence continued with no mention of nuptials there, either. I drew as little attention as possible, just carrying on as a good teacher.

So, on Saturday the 24th of March, we got dressed in jeans, helmets, and a change of clothing, and drove to the Town Hall. We arrived at the Municipal Offices, and were met by the clerk. It was 9:45 and no sign of the Murphys.

Colleen went and changed into her special-day attire as I stood scanning the empty street. It was now 10:00. The town clerk had arrived, ready to perform his legal duties. Colleen was ready. I was ready. Still no Murphys.

Time to intervene. "Mr. Clerk, sir, it seems our witness is delayed. Could you grant us another ten minutes?" I asked in my best grovelling voice. He said, "I will return in ten minutes," and left the office. As the minutes ticked off, it became clear I had to create a new plan in order to get this thing done. The wheels were spinning.

Bingo. Here was the plan. First person who walks in front of this building, I would tell the story and beg for help.

A young Zambian woman, Vaste Kunda Phunny Malokotela, approached my position in the doorway to the Municipal Offices. "Madame, I was wondering if you could help me.

"My fiancée and I . . ." she was still listening ". . . our witness has failed to show, so would you be our witness? We'll pay you for your time." She agreed to be the substitute. At 10:20, the clerk came in and asked the relevant questions. The ten-minute ceremony, key to the project, was now over. The rubber washer from a plumber's toolbox sealed the deed. Another example of Colleen's attention to details. She had brought the ring. The legal documents were signed. We thanked the justice of the peace and the clerk for being so obliging.

We gave our witness a 10k note and thanked her profusely. Colleen and I set out for a walk intending to find a bar restaurant.

This day needed a little celebration. As we explored the dining options, the Murphys showed up for an 11:00 wedding. The four of us went out for a meal.

After lunch, Colleen changed back into her jeans and we headed back to the apartment. Colleen was always so witty and funny regarding our new arrangement and sent her aunt the following telegram, "Married for bureaucracy, not pregnancy."

During the next week, we thoroughly discussed all the steps leading up to the project. We needed to dismantle the ZIT engagement:

1. Complain about elementary teaching level.
2. Press for promised housing.
3. Reinforce the dangers of the daily road trips.
4. Stress ZIT incompetence regarding Colleen's arrival.
5. Note lack of working permit for Colleen.
6. Note salary discrepancy.

These factors would have a cumulative effect. If presented to Mr. Ford without notice, in his Lusaka office, he would be taken aback by the seriousness of having to deal with all these issues, especially without our co-operation in the negotiations. The trip into Lusaka would be a test, perhaps confirming that the leadership in Kitwe was not taking care of business.

He would have to ask, "How is it possible to have someone so upset that he is prepared to quit? How could we lose a good, experienced teacher?"

What could he offer as reasonable answers to the six queries?

What issues could he not resolve when pushed with the original contract?

The trip to Ford's office would make or break the deal. Colleen and I agreed: we were confident he would blink. The next question was timing: When could we spring this?

Due to work schedule, a five-day period starting on Wednesday and over the April 15th weekend was available. We prepared and left Kitwe for Lusaka by motorcycle. It was a cool, sunny day. What I had forgotten to consider was the sun's intensity, leaving the top of my hands unprotected to the sun and wind. The first stop in Kabwe revealed severe sunburn. We purchased skin cream from the local store to ease the pain.

This was just the halfway point of the journey.

The rest of the trip turned out better, as the sun set on our right side. We arrived at the September residence and were greeted so very warmly. Immediately Hazel and Colleen were sisters. Following a shower and a little rest, we sat down and had a great meal. Friends like these are so rare. We celebrated Colleen's twenty-second birthday.

Dennis gave us an update of the Mbeki plan. It had a definite date and purpose. We now had to be available, and we discussed the "contract-busting strategy." They agreed that the surprise visit to Mr. Ford's office with no compromises was the best strategy.

On Friday morning, Colleen and I rode our motorcycle to the ZIT offices. Following the usual questions by the guards, we were led to the offices of the director of the Zambia Institute of Technology, Mr. Ford.

He was surprised to see us. He stumbled in his speech as he invited us to come in and sit down. What could be so important that we had made the trip for this meeting?

"Mr. Ford, we have some real concerns on our ability to function at ZIT."

I gave him a copy of the written document and watched his eyes read the lines.

As predicted, he tried to eliminate certain issues. We listened, and I added, "It's not acceptable."

We went over the same material three times. Finally, he ran out of sticking power or valid arguments.

I said, "Dr. Ford, here is a copy of the document that we agreed upon back in Ottawa. The memorandum of understanding is clear that housing would be in Luanshya.

"My fiancée would arrive in Zambia before Christmas, that my teaching level would be at a superior level . . . and the pay scale would be compatible to the other expats from Canada.

"How about the travel on this highway from Hell?"

I must have sounded like a crazed man just pausing to catch my breath to keep up the barrage.

"My good faith has run out of good faith. The contract has been breached, and—" a long pause, "—has to be terminated."

He remained speechless. We left it to him to break the silence. "Mr. Roy, I feel very bad about this situation, housing is really a problem." His voice went back to silence and another deep breath. Over the next fifteen minutes, Ford massaged the argument and recycled his weak arguments. His eyes kept dropping to his desktop. He was on the ropes . . . when will he blink?

"What do you want to do now, Mr. Roy?" he asked.

"Well, Mr. Ford, I just want my final paycheque and our return air fares to Ottawa."

"That can be arranged, Mr. Roy," said Ford. Bingo, he caved. We held our joy in reserve.

He picked up the phone and dialed, and a long thirty seconds later someone answered and Ford gave his instructions. He put the phone down and got out of his chair to shake my hand. He started to walk us to the door, adding, "I'll take you to the department that will handle this." So Ford had walked the walk, we were now on our way. We shook hands and agreed that it was a mutual disappointment. I lied.

We spoke to a person taking care of the travel arrangements. He needed to see our passports. Colleen's passport was under her maiden name, and Mr. Ford had given the go-ahead for tickets for Mr. and Mrs. Roy. We needed to defuse this little problem.

So back to thinking on my feet.

I told this man that we had just gotten married and had not received the passport reflecting this new marital status. He seemed confused, adding, "In Zambia a married woman always has her husband's name."

I responded, "In Canada that is not always the case." He finally accepted that this was a different situation.

Now the question of the expiry date for the ticket. I asked, "Can you give us a twelve-month open ticket? We were going to visit Zambia, so an open ticket is best." The tickets were issued. This one-hour task had given the finance department enough time to complete and issue my last cheque.

In my best Chinanja, I said, "*Zikomo kwambli.*" Thank you very much.

We left holding hands and shaking our heads, our faces wreathed in huge smiles.

Six weeks after her arrival, Colleen was on the move again.

We drove back to the September residence to give them the news: no hitches, money and ticket in hand. Let's celebrate.

Dennis said that the "project" would start within four weeks—the end of May.

I called the MPLA office, and Paulo Jorge, my old friend, wanted to see us. He came over to the September residence and wanted to know the status of the film that we had talked about. Jorge was responsible for the Department of Information and Propaganda—DIP. The only thing we could do now was for Colleen to do an interview with the head of the Angola Women's Movement, OMA. So on the 24th of April, Maria Carlos arrived at the September residence and did the interview. I suggested to Jorge that we should plan for September or October. He agreed.

We feasted and drank to our success with the Septembers. To share the joy of creating an opportunity to help our comrades of the ANC in a significant way and to share this with three people who were so focused in this contribution was a very special moment.

Early Sunday morning, we left with gloves on hands and cream on faces and headed back to Kitwe. Later that night, we found our small bed in a cold cement block apartment. We required a warm nightcap.

Colleen had been a "real trooper." This nickname would stick.

Choose in Advance What Sort of Values We Want. (author unknown)

At issue now: organizing the exit from Kitwe. My teaching responsibilities were over. We required a period of reflection and rest. The next move was to Lusaka, and this was an unknown quantity. Over the next fifteen to twenty days, we purchased a few African dresses and two men's suits. The look for this voyage had to be authentic. We needed to be one of "them."

We also studied the maps of South Africa and Botswana. Our mental picture of the journey was jelling.

On May 11th, Colleen and I celebrated my twenty-eighth birthday.

Our Russian friends invited us for a farewell meal. It was a sombre event, as we all knew that it was a goodbye dinner. Nonetheless, the invitation to return to Kitwe remained. Zambia Railway serviced Lusaka on a daily basis. On day twenty, our return trip to Lusaka started. We carried only two suitcases and a travel cosmetic bag.

The ancient railcars were filthy and crowded. The first-class seats offered worn, cloth-covered padding flattened by years of wear and tear, seats as hard as dirty concrete.

The train was powered by an ancient coal-fed steam engine, the little engine that just barely could. Cold beer was available, and we used the mind-numbing substance sans reserve.

With many stops along the way and a major water and coal fill-up in Kabwe, the setting sun measured our late afternoon arrival in Lusaka.

We called Dennis, and he arrived from his downtown office within five minutes. The return welcome to the September residence was as warm as the last meeting, just a few weeks ago. Mbeki and Hani came over that evening to meet Colleen and lay out the details of the reconnaissance.

They connected very well. Hani had a sharp eye for beautiful women, and he really liked Colleen. Mbeki, Hani, Colleen, and I went to the dining room table. Mbeki started by saying how much the ANC appreciated our teamwork. Military considerations dictated that good reconnaissance was crucial to evaluating the next step.

Hani then took over. "In our strategy to overthrow this regime, a good supply of weapons must be brought into the country. Botswana has a long border in the Republic, but it is well supervised."

Without so much as a notepad, Hani began to spell out the requirements for a successful mission.

"We want to know the security status of the Gaberone airport. This means, first of all:

- Know the quantity and quality of the security, know who the persons responsible for the security are, know the persons in charge of the airport, know their habits, personal and professional. This means their drinking habits, sexual habits, and any other information we could use to bypass the authorities or squeeze them in another setting.

- For example, declare to the Botswana authorities via our inside man damaging information about the inability of upper management to do the job. This would result in the firing of existing staff and the hiring of a waiting associate, a friend of the movement. This new leader and associated team would rewrite the necessary schedules and on-site work personnel to facilitate the flow of goods.

- Measure and evaluate the presence of South African security at the airport and travel agencies.

- Look into off-road tourist attractions.

- Collect relevant info on the outside airports, how they are monitored.

- Check radar availability, military/civilian supervision.

- Meet and evaluate persons from the expat community in Gaberone and outskirts. Evaluate their words and attitudes to see how they might help with transportation and storage facilities for people and goods.

Secondly:

- Cross into the Republic and go to Mafeking. Measure train routines, visible and covert security on train.

- Look for security weaknesses on the train, at border check.

- Visit and know extensively Mafeking merchants or vacationing alienated Brits who dislike apartheid, express need for change, persons who could co-operate with logistics and housing needs.

- From Mafeking, take the train to Francistown. Spend a few days to assess security elements. Spend a few nights in Bulawayo; this will give the tourist story credibility.

- Proceed to Victoria Falls and look for the same information at train stations, sympathetic store merchants.

- Use the train to leave Rhodesia by the Victoria Bridge.

- Return to Lusaka by bus. The overall trip should be thirty days. On arrival, come directly to September's house. All of this information, you are to remember. Use notes as little as possible.

Mbeki asked, "Do you have any questions?

I looked at Colleen and waited for her approval. She now understood the scope of the project, and with my approval that everything seemed okay, Mbeki took over the meeting.

Here is the plan.

"In a few days, the flight for Zambia Airways to Botswana will be the last one. Service is being terminated. You have reservations and now with your passports we will have them picked up and delivered to you. The last nights in Lusaka you will stay at the Lusaka Hotel. The regular taxi run to the airport leaves from the hotel. No more communications with the Septembers. You are on your honeymoon, so go and enjoy it."

With this, Mbeki handed over an envelope. It contained the appropriate currencies, US dollars, Canadian dollars, Rhodesian dollars, and South African rand, and in an amount to dignify the trip. The meeting had lasted twenty minutes, but it seemed longer, and the weight of the responsibilities of the project seemed to go from pounds to kilos to stones. We hugged and received best wishes from Hani and Mbeki.

"Good luck, Jacques and Colleen," from Hani and Thabo.

We moved back to the sitting room, and the Septembers rejoined us. The ANC officials, comrades, excused themselves with a sincere thanks to Dennis and Hazel for their assistance.

A long calm set in. Colleen and I stared at each other. The moment was precious and engraved on our memories.

We sat down to another round of cold beer and Dennis just laughed as he spoke.

"How do you like the news?"

I shook my head, a little stunned by the recognition that we were now an integral part of the ANC.

Hazel joked about, and this seemed to reset the mood.

"First thing that we must do after the beer," I said, "is that we need to move to the Lusaka Hotel." He called a cab and within the hour we had arranged a luxurious room at the Lusaka Hotel.

We ate at the familiar dining room from 1968, but my co-conspirator was not there. We strolled the side streets and did a little shopping.

On the eve of our departure, Hani found his way to our room unannounced. He entered and quickly set out his business. "Here are your passports and air tickets. Good luck." He hugged us and left.

Following breakfast next morning, after making arrangements to get to the airport, we headed out to buy the last items for our trip. We were very well dressed and groomed and, as we turned the street corner to go back to the hotel, we came face to face with David Beer, CUSO's assistant in the Zambia program. He was the one guy that we had managed more by luck than planning, to avoid. Now I had to think quickly. With his usual and permanently attached smile he did his routine of, "I didn't know you were in the country," as he knew Colleen from Ottawa, and to me: "What are you doing in town?"

My brains somehow knew what program to go to.

"Well, Dave, we are just visiting for a day and going on holidays," I said, and he fired back, "Where are you going?"

I continued in the same hurried mode, "We are going to Dar. We are in a hurry, our ride leaves in thirty minutes. Nice seeing you Dave, gotta run." I wondered anxiously, *Did he buy the story?* To me it was obvious we were overdressed for a road trip to Dar. I was holding onto Colleen and gently nudged her in our desired direction.

"Can you believe our luck?" I said, "with all these many visits to meet him today."

We did our shopping and returned to the hotel. We still had a few hours before the taxi left for the airport.

At 11:00 we went to the lobby to the waiting taxi, still feeling very exposed.

The driver closed the back door of the station wagon and we headed to the airport to board the Zambia Airways flight to Gaberone.

Colleen returns from brushing teeth at the camp grounds outside Lusaka, August 1971

Trip Number One

This last flight from Lusaka to Botswana was significant, as the cancellation of the service marked an escalation of the South African apartheid government attack on the mobility of independent Africa to carry on the business of an independent state. In fact, this represented a great victory for the South Africans and another lesson for Zambia in its education as to the extent to which the war of survival of the apartheid state would be fought.

The two-hour flight from Lusaka to Gaberone (pronounced Haberoney) was uneventful, and following the airport formalities, we headed to a small hotel in the Botswana capital for our first night. Following dinner at the main hotel, we spent some time at the bar, not just to decompress but also to feel the reality of Botswana. We observed a small group of CUSO volunteers, so our controlled dialogue was curt and distant. We didn't want any new CUSO friends at this juncture. Other occupants of the bar varied between mining people, bureaucrats, and travel agents. We skipped out politely around eleven p.m. and returned to our hotel room. The cold night, along with a constant wind, reminded me of the Lusaka days of super-dry air making breathing difficult.

Colleen adjusted very well, and for the next few days, we observed the town layout and housing for sale, the general mood of street talk, and the presence of the war of liberation in the newspaper. South Africa dominated the news; the vigilance of apartheid justifying its existence had the Botswana government intimidated and neutralized. The ANC could do what it could get away with, but government and the administration of justice would not escape the heavy hand of apartheid. This meant that if Africans from the ANC fleeing apartheid were caught entering Botswana they would be charged with entering without proper documentation and imprisoned as common criminals. The political status of these captured freedom fighters meant that they would receive much harder sentences, as the international courts or the United Nations had not yet addressed the question. This lack of legal status for ANC members certainly pleased Botha and his thugs.

On day four, we met the director of the National Airport for Botswana at the bar. All flights at this time needed to go through South Africa—there were no international connections for the "independent" state of Botswana. This red-headed man was our *"pièce de résistance."* His knowledge of airport usage, South African army usage, and general and specific operating methods were key to our education. With bravado and a lot of whisky, the crewcut man sang the virtues of security with examples of the control of "terrorists" and the might of the South African military.

Secret airports throughout Botswana were controlled by the South African Ministry of Defense, and were dedicated to border control and the provision of advance airfields to intervene in South West

Africa from the Namibia border up to the Angola border. The Caprivi Strip was the entry point for the guerrillas of the SWAPO—South West Africa People's Organization.

The military presence this far north also permitted the apartheid regime to launch attacks into Angola and Zambia. This was to map out a South African military strategy with the Smith regime of Rhodesia and the Portuguese in Angola. Security was tight and frequent, so as we changed hotels, we were required to fill in documents and to prove with passports that our vacation was truly a vacation. Day seven meant time to move on, as our saturated lessons of Gaberone and the people who were running the show were complete. We made travel arrangements and seat reservations on the train to Mafeking.

We entered this phase with greater focus as the security presence on the train by the S.A. military increased.

The luxury of being white was indicated by the comfort and quality of the seating arrangements. The first-class cushioned couches upholstered in a spacious and richly decorated style made us uncomfortable but very aware of the unspoken mission. We were to behave like South African racists. We would not solicit answers or opinions. We were tourists looking for a possible business opportunity. This position was very effective because of the racist belief that white numbers needed bolstering, and that the international ideology claiming that only whites could run an independent country attracted the likes of Colleen and me.

As we reached the South African border, the Special Police Force came on board. Unsmiling and armed with machine guns, their presence evoked movie images of the SS while their accents in bad English with a Boer harshness set off alarms of fascism and dictatorship. Politeness and the miniskirt of the day distracted the "black shirts" from thorough questioning.

Along the grassy fields, Africans stood by, some getting on, some getting off, while the "K" word was thrown about, creating a tense and intimidating situation. Within one hour the train resumed its journey to Mafeking.

Relaxing was now a task. Creative chatter and dialogue at the bar car were required. As Colleen, with her angelic face, puffed on her cigarettes, I listened and practised controlled breathing to hold in my rage amid the racist, derogatory views expressed by most of the whites we encountered. At the Mafeking train station, South African blacks pushed and shoved in order to be our porters. The numerous languages, along with police surveillance, created a social tension designed to force arriving whites to enter the kingdom of apartheid. This kingdom of whites was under siege. Defending it was essential to survival of the white race. German shepherd dogs showed their teeth, and the handlers shouted orders in Afrikaans. It was noisy and chaotic. We gave up our luggage and followed the porter to a waiting cab. We set up shop in a modest hotel and decompressed with a shower and a beer, followed by a rest period. The charged atmosphere of minority rule enforced by constant police and military presence required some mental adjustment.

Mafeking was the first outpost of the apartheid system. It was

small and designed for military control of the city centre and the gated white communities, while the "stands," black neighbourhoods, were kept at a distance and easily controlled by the police and military. The other advantage of the stands was the ease of controlling of the flow of workers toward the white enclaves with the pass laws and the controlled transportation system, one bus line for non-whites and one for whites. Shopkeepers were white and the entrances were separate. This was difficult for us to take in. I was floored.

Same restaurant, but separate entrance and serving counter. I could only remember this scene from the Selma, Alabama, days on Canadian television in the early 1960s. We frequented the shops with the purpose of finding English arrivals and to evaluate their views of apartheid and their resolve for changing the system. The overall view of all parties, racists and non-racists, was that change was necessary. For the racists, it meant more whites were required in order to expand the frontiers of encroaching independence described as "communist threat"; and the majority rule position of convincing the Boers that planned majority rule with election of credible black leaders was the only way around a prolonged war similar to Vietnam. The players in this equation meant many Vietnams: Angola, Mozambique, Namibia, and Zimbabwe versus poor Portugal, isolated Rhodesia under UDI, and leper South Africa. Contact with these newly arrived Brits was easy enough, as we shared a fixed obsession with apartheid. They had come to South Africa to be close to their children and grandchildren, who had emigrated for financial and social reasons. Now the changes in their own adult children made them realize the extent of indoctrination and the likelihood of future confrontations. Their grandchildren would undergo obligatory military training and be part of the repressive regime, all for the social status of "Blank"—White—with all of the privileges, maids, good schools, holidays, and economic wealth.

Mafeking was very vulnerable. The large electrical distribution transformer was unguarded and protected only by wire mesh. We met a few whites in their stores and over dinner in public restaurants. They recognized the weakness of their situation and had little to say about accepting majority rule. They seemed spooked by reality.

This controlled society was vulnerable and showed fear and paranoia. It was an education for us, and over the seven-day period we had learned what we needed to for the project. We retraced our train trip via Gaberone and stopped in Francistown. This railway town, though very small and militarily weak, had a relaxed atmosphere. Eating, drinking, and asking about available investments were now our primary focus but not a routine. Our thought process had homed in on the quick, unrehearsed answers to the regular questions, while our "Canadian puppy dog look" seemed to smooth over the tough ones. The round hut accommodations were cold and drafty. The town had a few eating places, and the largest hotel gave us night outings to fulfill our mission. In two days, back to the train station, and here I met a train conductor who felt comfortable enough with our innocuous presence to tell us of his anti-apartheid actions but now, after being threatened, in quiet desperation had become a train engineer. From the station we saw the prison where Hani had spent two years for having entered Botswana without proper documents.

We continued our travel towards Zambia via Bulawayo, Rhodesia. At the Rhodesian border, we now encountered new tactics and accents as the Rhodesian border patrol took over the security of the train. Same questions, same answers. Passport, medical documentation, and fill out the entry form. From our white-only rail car with few passengers in our compartment, we felt an uneasiness, a wearing down of our emotions. Colleen and I grew closer. I grew more confident our strengthened bond could withstand separation if imposed by detention. Bulawayo city, an old city with its minority citizens, offered the same racism, but with a different flavour.

Here the old ancestry of the Zimbabwe ruins forced the whites to acknowledge that at one time a great civilization lived here and that self-rule could not be granted, because ". . . you see the mess in Zambia, Kenya, and Tanzania; well, these blacks needed to be educated, and perhaps in forty to one hundred years some type of representation, but not an equal vote."

We met many Portuguese who had left Angola and Mozambique along with former British colonials from Kenya, Tanzania, and Zambia. Some were already planning to move to South Africa, as the world sanctions against Rhodesia meant hardship and ongoing guerrilla warfare. South Africa, the regional military giant, could resist and dictate the outcome. No one could defeat this military machine, the last stand against world communism. Our hotel was very British—morning toast, fried tomatoes, half-cooked bacon, scrambled eggs, and coffee; later, a two- hour lunch period followed by four p.m. tea and plenty of servants for cleaning rooms and clothing. After three days, we travelled to Victoria Falls by train. What a breathtakingly beautiful setting. From our hotel, we could see the deep gorges of the Zambezi River, splendid surroundings so perfect for international tourism.

But would they come if internal security was not assured?

This controlled society, so fragile, continued to putter along as world opinion slowly woke up to the repression and hardship of the black majority. Infiltrating this country meant crossing the Zambezi River, not an easy task. From the falls, our last leg was by bus, as train service through to Zambia was forbidden by the Rhodesians. The bus delivered us to the long bridge across a deep gorge where the powerful Zambezi flowed toward Mozambique and the Indian Ocean. We would have to walk 250 metres across this open bridge with our suitcases, now much heavier, and enter Zambia on foot with armed soldiers at each end of the bridge: at our backs, the Rhodesian Army, and in front the Zambian Army.

Where was Clint Eastwood? Where were the Hollywood moviemakers? I am certain this scene could have held a cheap thriller together.

As we walked away from Rhodesia, Colleen and I spoke softly and smiled a lot, as the trip was soon to be finished. The centre of the bridge had a large yellow line indicating Rhodesia on one side and Zambia on the other, and as we crossed, we drew deep breaths into our tired bodies. More steps, sweating as the equatorial sun baked the black road surface, which deflected a damp tropical breeze to the front of our bodies.

The end of the bridge appeared, so did the soldiers with pointed guns. As we got closer, it was time to diffuse the tension, and I said, "*Mulee bwanji*," and the familiar response, "*Teelee bweeno*," came back. We at least got a first hearing, and the guns were pointed to the ground. Home at last, and more paperwork, as the soldiers directed us to the small house that served as controlling point. The polite officials asked for and received the documentation while we kept our silence till requested to speak. No hardship, just a little time on a wooden chair while the sweat poured down our faces.

We were free to go, as our official documents stated that I was a teacher at the Zambia Institute of Technology and that Colleen was my wife. Good story, good cover. No hassles.

We walked over to a small hotel and booked a room, as the bus going on to Lusaka was leaving in the morning. It was time for decompression. Cold beer, with locally grown roasted peanuts, filled the tummy and calmed the mind. I was exhausted and so grateful for the results. Colleen had proven a capable friend, a real trooper.

Next morning, the bus left for Lusaka, and the many stops meant a crowded bus with powerful odours and livestock.

In Lusaka, our cab took us to the September residence, where we were warmly welcomed.

We washed, drank, socialized, and waited for the arrival of Thabo and Chris.

On their arrival, Thabo and Chris were grateful and anxious to get into the debriefing. We went into the far end of the house while Dennis and Hazel kept the food, drink, and hospitality. After four hours, we agreed to resume the debriefing in the morning. The evening meal was interrupted with friendly visitors and fellow guerrillas from the ANC.

Following a good night's sleep, the details of our objectives were elaborated and registered. The questions posed by Hani and Mbeki were very focused, obliging Colleen and me to dig deep for the observations and the clues that would allow the ANC to plan for the next step. It was a tough process, revisiting certain events was emotionally draining, and going over crucial details again and again was very challenging. The days just flew by. It took three days to streamline our complete answers and when it was over we'd earned a warm hug from Chris and Thabo for a successfully completed assignment. Thabo then requested that we reunite in a few days. In the meantime, stay low and out of sight.

On the Futility of Halfway Measures

No man can swim and take his luggage with him. (Seneca the Younger)

Thabo and Chris returned with a further mission. The first had been a success; this one involved a much greater risk and more specific details.

We would be driving from Lusaka to Rhodesia over the Beith Bridge into South Africa with many cities and specific objectives to attain. However, this mission required total secrecy. We would have to leave the September residence and would be housed with ANC members in Lusaka. There would be no contact with the host families, except they would provide food and lodging—but no social activity. We had no names or country of origin. For the next three weeks, travel documents, transportation, and assignment details were to be worked out. In the meantime, our small quarters were ideal to get us to return to our motivation and desire to help the anti-apartheid movement advance its tactics with good, precise information. I always had a shortwave radio, and it provided our outside link for information and as silence breaker. We had a daily link with the Radio Canada International broadcast and the familiar voices of Harry Brown and Bruce Rogers.

I listened for hours to Radio France International, always amazed at the accuracy and speed with which they got the news from Africa. Colleen, an avid reader, was somewhat limited in this, but the secure environment gave us a period of rest and bonding. The relationship had changed. We worked well together and our personal lives intertwined emotionally. How much stress could it withstand?

If the stress was a negative factor, where and when would it manifest itself?

We spoke of these concerns and agreed to dialogue them through, because failure to anticipate the unknown meant working around and accepting the consequences—hopefully only positive ones.

Trip Number Two

With documents in order, money in Zambian kwacha, Rhodesian dollars, South African rand, and U.S. currencies and road maps for Rhodesia and South Africa, we focused on Thabo and Chris as they outlined the final instructions for this fact-finding trip. Our transport was a Volkswagen Kombi, a German vehicle with complete camping facilities, a pop-up roof, and accessories for an attached sun shield, green and white canvas awning on a roller.

Final instructions:

Verify the telephone links from post office to London, England. This meant to link up with an ANC contact in England, using a code word to ask for money to be expedited to us via the post office. This was to test reliability as well as speed, as other foreigners working for the ANC would require funds under emergency conditions. We were to wait for twenty-four hours for the response, and failure to complete link-up and money delivery meant abandoning this item of the agenda.

Other items:

Check on storage facilities for weapons within and outside white areas. Check white areas of convergence for special holidays, say New Year's Eve and associated festivities, while measuring security considerations and geographical pluses and minuses as to accessibility by police or military.

Evaluate game park areas as military storage with locations, access, and supervision by whites and/or by hired black security. Extensive driving and continual evaluation of military presence, location of permanent and mobile bases; we also assessed co-operation of white community with law and order in rural areas.

Many other specific requests were part of a thirty-to-forty-five-day excursion and honeymoon.

The credibility of the overall planning and in-depth preparation using the friendly Canadian passport gave us an excellent chance of returning with the needed information.

Departure would be mid-morning in order to reduce our chances of meeting people. Thabo came to our hideout and brought us to our vehicle. Armed with our suitcases, the adrenalin flowed as our mission started on a back road of Lusaka. Thabo drove us to a waiting Chris Hani with the Kombi, and we made a quick transfer to our vehicle. On the back seat, Thabo, Colleen, and I did a systematic inventory of the documents, maps, vehicle ownership, international driving licence, and currencies. The turnaround was quick, and within five minutes Hani and Mbeki had left us.

I immediately thought of one problem: this vehicle had a manual shift. Colleen did not know how to drive a gearshift car, so I would have to do all of the driving. Shortly before 11:00 a.m., we were on our way, driving down past the Ridgeway Hotel around the circle and off to the south. Within minutes, we passed the drive-in theatre, my once-upon-a- time residence of a motel, past the trailer park, then 100 meters later, the road on the right leading to the liberation movement offices and out of the Lusaka region.

Within a few hours, we reached the Rhodesian border, but decided to sleep in our camper at a Zambian animal reserve. It was a secure area, so our first night out was peaceful. The events of the long day had taken their toll on our humour, and our weary bodies craved peace. From this day onward, Colleen was in charge of the map reading and choice of the roads, once we had determined the destination. As an early riser, I got the coffee ready and awoke the "trooper" to a beautiful African sunrise; the smell of the damp forest cover gave a special meaning to "good morning." Our home on wheels gave us a certain freedom— within a certain insecurity, as we were now vulnerable to theft and physical harm. Security was always on my mind but now with a new dimension: where we could safely park overnight. The daylight timeouts were made at supervised, designated rest stops, also the favourite spots for truckers who hauled food supplies into Zambia, the lifeline of the sanction-busting efforts of Ian Smith and UDI.

The border formalities at the Kafue River bridge got us into Rhodesia and within an hour we came across a Rhodesian military convoy of new recruits who were being slowly indoctrinated into the army: a period of forging of friendships and then to the front— Mozambique, Botswana, or the Caprivi Strip. They cheered as they passed our "designated" tourist bus and were gone forever. The Kafue River was fast flowing and part of Lake Kariba that ended at the Kariba Dam, a major source of electrical power for the Rhodesian farmers, the military, and small white cities and towns.

Northern Rhodesia also had pockets of tse-tse flies, and the medical authorities had erected a large building as part of the roadway to disinfect the vehicle and the vehicle contents. To do this, the vehicle was driven into this building, and an attendant sprayed the inside of the van, with us in it, and then closed the large doors for a period of total darkness. This thirty-minute stop refocused our purpose to possible distraction and potential response. We were mostly looking out for the military roadblocks and the security questions that would be asked. Tanks, large guns, and machine guns can be intimidating.

We spent our first night in Rhodesia, camping on the shores of Lake Kariba at a small place called Siavonga. Colleen was in a depressed mood and seemed to question the reason for this trip. I was really pissed off and over the half hour tried to reason with her about the significance of this work. Finally, I lost my cool and blasted her. She knew that I was no longer putting up with expressions of self-pity and doubt. My words were clear: "Shape up or else!" I regret having had to use these words. It seemed that the harsh reality of success or jail time could not be interchanged. We needed to win. With a little tenderness and patience, Colleen turned up the charm and got back into the game.

Back on A1 at Makuti and on to Chinhoyl, west to Kadomato Gweru, Bulawayo, and on to Messina in South Africa. Beautiful countryside, smooth roads, large trees, parched soil, always that red soil and dust.

Following the N1, we stopped in Pietersburg at a local campsite. Getting accustomed to the white mentality was very tiring, and for the next few days, we observed and absorbed the rhythm of racial prejudice. A real treat for us was the mud baths at Warmbad.

Not only did a bath in warm mud warm us up to the depth of our bones, relaxing our self-induced social tensions; it also cleaned the body pores, a definite benefit only appreciated following a long shower. We were white and clean.

Pretoria was our first focus, with banking activities to set and test the conduit. We stayed in a local camping ground and had our first experience with wild monkeys. They saw tourists as a promise of free lunch. Throwing food away from the vehicle would make them to jump off to fetch it. We then diverted towards Rustenburg. A short distance from Johannesburg, this city to the west was a step for the ANC military goods coming from Botswana into South Africa. Any movement to block the flow of goods and manpower meant that onsite reserves would enable some action and economic paralysis if required.

Rustenburg also had a large, unprotected, and easily accessible hydro dam. We set up camp at a local campground, and because this was not the usual tourist season, sites were cheap and available. Some of the top hotels allowed on-site camping with use of their facilities for a few rand. One hotel site in particular proved a real gold mine of social information, because with its location and level of luxury, it was frequented by the upper classes and the rich. The large annual Christmas party, followed by the New Year's bash, had a captive audience for the full holiday period. There were a swimming pool, tennis courts, horseback riding, and lawn bowling. The owners were proud to show off the list of their guests: CEOs, parliamentarians, military personnel, sportsmen from the rugby clubs. There were photos of previous parties and weddings that made the socialites and social butterflies throng to this place.

Most important of all, the open fields that surrounded the hotel were orange groves, flat and offering open access to the fenceless property. Throughout our stay, the owners expressed their conviction of the necessity of minority rule, but also had a back-up plan. Money was being put into British banks just in case ". . . communism flows across the Zambezi." They would say, "We treat these blacks well and probably better than most other whites, but still, the blacks are not grateful for the work and always try to steal from us." Interpretation: as a slave with a measly income, you should be grateful for foul water from the one faucet for twenty houses, open sewage in the culverts, and the rat-infested cardboard shacks that blow over in the rainy season and are flooded by the receding waters. Praise apartheid and the good labour force, they smile, and hope they don't rise up. From Rustenburg, we turned towards Jo'burg and camped out near an orange grove. That night, I left on foot to explore the orchard and get a sense of the land and possibilities of storage. Two hours later, I returned with plenty of oranges and found that Colleen had been very worried.

We travelled to Jo'burg and stayed for three days. This metropolis is all white after dark and very black during the daylight hours. The daytime revealed blacks on job sites and white supervisors, while the white children in school uniform had no apparent connection to the social conflict, the moral question of institutionalized racism. They were the privileged, the defenders of a future apartheid. But they had no clue to the thoughts of the majority. Their only contact was through the maid, sitter, and nanny. The presence of the servants seemed natural, they had no life of their own, they were there in the back of each white house, in a small hovel made of dirt or brick, with a tin roof, close enough to carry on their duties and to step in whenever necessary.

Colleen and I reflected often on the social tension and the overarching presence of different military and paramilitary structures and personnel. Our lives could be seriously compromised in a conflict of majority vs. minority. We needed to be on the lookout for potential conflict situations.

We determined to test the first link to the outside world: an encoded UK telegram to send funds for a car repair. "Thanks sis." was the code. Our home on wheels was parked in one of the numerous parks on the outskirts of most cities. Forty-eight hours later, we returned to the post office to see if there was a response. The negative response meant abandonment of this enquiry.

Next stop was the Kruger Park and the surveillance of a stocking area for the "chips" that would be entering. The ANC were master negotiators, and the poker approach was part of the strategy. The ANC would have to prove to the Boers that not only did they have the majority of people on their side, but ANC also possessed the military might to "soften" the non-negotiating hard-liners of Milan and Botha. These officials needed a wake-up call: "Show me what you can do and then I'll tell you if I'm impressed." The racists had a mindset so engrained with self-proclaimed superiority so eloquently articulated by UDI Prime Minister Ian Smith, when responding to the likelihood of majority rule: "Not in a thousand years."

How many times were we subjected to the racist litanies and dire predictions if majority rule were allowed to be achieved. "Not in a thousand years" seemed to be the final statement from these colourless beings.

We then moved our mission to the Kruger National Park. We travelled the N12 to Belfast to Lydenburg and turned east to Marite and Skukuza inside Kruger National Park. In this off season, tourists were scarce, and this meant little supervision by park authorities and little traffic. Our campsites were very comfortable, but as we explored, we decided to find one specific area. Deep in the Kruger, we found and evaluated rock outcrops, caverns, and accessibility, both easy and difficult for the storage of goods that would be coming into the country. With our self-contained travelling unit, we were able to get a good picture of the layout of the park. We toured Sabi Sands Game Reserve up to Satara, camping in designated areas and eating a lot of tomato sandwiches and drinking our refrigerated beer. Here we settled under the canopy of huge trees, lots of shelter, privacy, and a respite from the mission that had still to be accomplished. Life was uninterrupted in our silent milieu. We continued past Olifants and Letaba to exit at Mica and back to Lydenburg.

From Kruger Park, we travelled back to Jo'burg and towards Bloemfontein and the mining town of Kimberly. Soweto was always a big item in any discussion of apartheid, and to come upon it even when we were expecting it was quite a shock. Tin-covered sheds, one water faucet for dozens of mud houses—the picture that I was looking at represented the powder keg of South Africa. We stopped and visited Kroonstad, with a side trip to Welkom. Kimberly was of particular interest to me. It was now an abandoned mining town, not much left but a big hole, along with the remnants of how Africans had lived under the rein of racism, and the socially sanctioned humiliation of its true owners.

The large hole was proof that the wealth had evaporated just like my hometown of Kirkland Lake; it had similar large holes and the accompanying abandoned towns, schools, and churches.

As the days passed, our views and observations grew on a steady diet of anti-African contacts, along with our growing need to block the only topic Afrikaners wanted to explain to us: "You cannot understand this situation."

"Of having to deal with these K..." Boers could really emphasize the sound of their favourite word. The term "kaffir" has a long history, originally an Arabic term for non-Muslim Africans, particularly slaves. It became a universal ethnic slur in Southern Africa. Since 1976, use of the word has constituted the crime of *crimen injuria* in South Africa. We hadn'tgot there yet.

Colleen and I talked about the effect on our own sanity of this constant barrage of derogatory remarks with the knowledge that Hani and Mbeki intellectually and spiritually outgunned any of these shell-shocked "persons."

The Boers gasped for the alphabet of human compassion. They were sick and their continued put-down of the majority was born of their own lack of self-regard.

From Kimberly, we travelled through Bristown to Hanover, and rested in a campsite near Port Elizabeth for the next five days. We explored and visited the Addo Elephant National Park. This huge country offered so much, most of it denied to the majority, and everywhere we went, we felt the tension of constant humiliation and the silent depth of anger. We then moved on via King William's Town to East London. This large centre gave us some social cover, as we blended into the white community and away from the piercing eyes and grimaces of desperation close to the dividing line that was colour.

After parking the Kombi, we walked the sidewalks of these large streets and soaked up the atmosphere of wealth that was based on slavery. Now we were evaluating the weaknesses to give more bargaining power to the ANC.

On this warm day, as we wandered the streets, the aroma of fresh-baked goods filled the air, so we stopped at the source and entered the bakery. What we came for was not what we left with. The multitude of fresh-baked cookies, cakes, and bread were an easy sell to these two wandering Canadians. Colleen did the ordering as I looked around the countertop and the information sheets that were for the taking. I had to bite my lip reading one: "Warning to the Population" described the consequences to anybody helping the "Terrorists who cross the Zambezi" and continuing, "You will shot on sight." This was a chilling reminder of the context in which we were gathering information here. I picked up a series of pamphlets and joined Colleen at the exit to pay for the treats andgot out of this "sanctuary."

We still have that pamphlet.

As we returned to the Kombi, I showed Colleen a few of the activity announcements and saved the gem for the comfort of our camper. "Colleen, look at this invitation, do you think we qualify?" She read the words and the reaction slowly set in.

A pamphlet warning against helping the "terrorists"

"Pretty serious stuff," she commented.

We dropped the topic, but it remained as a reminder of our purpose and possible consequences. The stress of continued vigilance was starting to show. The extensive driving and continued physical punishment of the car motion made Colleen ill. Some days at the campsite were spent in nearly total silence as our emotional batteries recharged.

Part of this re-energizing process required that we leave the Kombi and take a room in a local hotel. So, near Queenstown, we rented a simple yet comfortable room. The always-accommodating whites were very curious to know what we were doing in South Africa, and at every opportunity, we would state the obvious, "We are on our honeymoon."

This elevated the level of welcome, a better room and at no extra cost, their contribution to the revolution. During our two-day stay, our conversations were light and friendly, which created a certain problem. The woman of the hotel took it upon herself to look out for our safety. She enquired what direction we were going and I indicated towards Durban. Without asking us, she telephoned her brother and made arrangement for our next stopover. He would take care of us as he knew "how to control the K's"; he was a police officer in Umtata. As Colleen and I looked at each other, we sighed a deep, ambiguous sigh. Obliged to respond this overture, we met the law and order man and agreed to stay for one night only as we needed to get more rest and had decided that the game park setting was best for us. We were polite and skipped out after the customary salutations, and still remember the standing invitation by the policemen, "Come back any time."

From Umtata, we followed the N2 to Port Shepstone and enjoyed the wonderful Indian Ocean and another rest stop in a designated area of Durban.

Our work and test scenarios had accomplished certain objectives. It was now time to back off the tension and indulge our senses to a level that permitted us to untie the knots in our stomachs. No travel.

After four days, we drove the N3 through Pietermaritzburg and then onto N11 at Frere to Mamelodi and to Pretoria, our slow exit from apartheid land.

Heading north on N1, we encountered the South African army on many occasions, but had no interactions.

Finally, we arrived at Beitbridge which crosses the fast-flowing Limpopo River, and entered into Rhodesia, one step closer to home and still fighting Colleen's fatigue and depression.

We turned right onto the A4 and headed for the Great Zimbabwe National Monument, also known as the Ruins of Zimbabwe.

Nearby Kyle Lake National Park gave us a new campground.

Our visit to this spectacular monument offered proof that a great society had left a structure and an imprint on the countryside. The cultural and sacred grounds were inhabited. I could feel the emptiness of a well- created monument that had been deserted and left to the wind and rain.

In nearby villages, local potters created from the red clay art as well as functional items based on a traditional method of allowing the unglazed clay to sweat and therefore, through evaporation, cool the liquid contents.

Here again, we could not escape the put-down of Africans as a local white Rhodesian who saw us as tourists took the occasion to state that this great work was carried out "by Egyptians, since no Africans could accomplish such a marvel."

Colleen was now getting very weak with pain and depression. It was time to head for Zambia, but Colleen's health required a stop at the emergency room of the hospital in Salisbury. We rolled into the emergency ward looking at all these white faces, the enemy. Colleen was put onto a bed and the questions started. I would not leave her side.

Would the questions overflow from the medical to other reasons for our travels?

Where have you been and why so much travel on your honeymoon?

I held her hand throughout the delicate medical questions.

Silence and another question as the tears flowed down Colleen's cheeks.

Time for the diagnosis: "Madame, you are suffering from extreme fatigue with a bladder infection, and what you need is a complete rest, medication, and no travel for three days."

I took Colleen back to the Kombi as my own fatigue seemed to disappear. Compassion for my friend took over. The trooper was hurting very badly and a regular hotel was needed.

As Colleen slept for hours, my mind worked overtime over the last push towards the Zambian Border. The delicate nature of the border crossing, the fragility of Colleen's health, my own mental fatigue, required that I back off from any stress and negative thoughts. Within three days, the trooper pronounced herself fit. Great news.

As we headed north out of Salisbury, we encountered no military and very few vehicles of any kind. At Chirundu, the tse-tse fly control was still operating, and after this brief stop, we approached the border point and stopped. The border police asked a few questions regarding the export of pelts from the five great animals, diamonds, or other contraband.

"Nothing to declare, officer." He replied, "Have a safe trip."

We were on our way. As we crossed the Zambezi River, we remained silent and grateful for the stamina to make this successful trip. The Zambian border authorities were welcoming and waved us thru. The Zambian plates gave us our last pass.

I said, "Tonight, we will celebrate. Colleen, you have done a marvellous job, we have accomplished way beyond our mandate."

We went to the local bar for a cold one, and it was evident that following a short rest period, the stress started to leave our bodies. It was very tiring, but Colleen wanted to get to Kafue City and the local campgrounds near a large lake.

Within five days, our strength and humour had returned, so the few hours up the road to the park south of Lusaka were easy.

We checked into the offices and obtained a spot near the washroom under a large tree. Our camping life would be limited and would be determined by the debriefing period. Under this large and precious shade, Zambia was now our decompression chamber.

After the shower and traditional beer, a long-awaited phone call was made to Dennis September. He was very happy at our return and would make the contacts for Chris and Thabo. That evening, Dennis invited us to a meal and our welcome was warm and full of the intensity that only comrades in a military situation can understand and share. Hazel and Colleen, two great friends, their friendship renewed, carried on their conversation holding their favourite cups of spirits.

Thabo and Chris arrived the next day and we began the debriefing.

These long sessions were supplemented with notes that we remembered as per our security outline.

Mental exhaustion set in following four days of intense questions and answers. All details were important, noted for use in planning future missions.

Now that we were back in safe hands, our thoughts turned to a young lady operating for the ANC and who was caught. Shortly after our second mission was completed, Swiss-born Barbara Hogen was detained and sentenced to ten years in prison for "advancing the aims of the banned ANC."

The ANC continued to develop intelligence officers based in England, Sweden, and other European capitals. Fighting Fascism required many approaches, and the ANC, long ago dismissed as communists and subversives, would grow an international network of friends and supporters.

We had carried out a very important mission. Here is how Chris and Thabo reacted to the end of the mission: "Comrades Jacques and Colleen, you have provided a very valuable service for the ANC in our struggle to end apartheid. We are very happy for all that you have done for us. Someday soon, we will have independence; we will be free in our lifetime. Thank you."

I was very choked up at this sincere recognition. I held Colleen's hand very firmly in mine.

So we all stood up and the final salutations were made. The ANC leadership, young and competent, would achieve independence. When and exactly how were still to be determined.

CHAPTER EIGHT

Develop a global capacity organization that is colour-blind.

Our mission with the ANC was over. The next project was a documentary film about the MPLA and the ongoing war in Angola. Colleen would return to Ottawa, but first we agreed to have a holiday in Dar. This would stabilize our relationship and separation, since Colleen would not be going to Angola.

We made our way to the airport by taxi without incident. Our carefully preserved ZIT tickets were our way out of this country. No regrets about leaving and many hopes for a good holiday.

The Lusaka to Dar flight had the usual Ndola stopover. Colleen and I laughed at the geographical implications in our lives, so many stories, but not for today. From February to September, we had lived a whirlwind tour full of love, decisions, and friendships that would impact us for life. So close to the decision-makers, we had contributed to the best of our ability, and now it was over. The prospects of a holiday in paradise, Dar es Salaam, Harbour of Peace, would allow Colleen and me to examine and share our lives in a very beautiful city by the sea. As we circled the Dar airport, the green Indian Ocean, its white sandy beaches full of coral, showed Colleen a picture of calm and restful surroundings, lush, green vegetation, and colourful clothing. What a stark contrast to Zambia. We really liked this place. We arrived at the Agip Hotel. A few more steps, we were at the Luther House Hostel by the sea. Our luck held: there was a room for the next few days. I could feel and see that Colleen was very happy in this new setting. We could walk around in complete safety and, with the Dar harbour behind the hostel, we sat for hours on the beach admiring Kivikoni College in the distance and watching the ferry slipping back and forth from the opposite shore of the harbour. We travelled to the beaches of Oyster Bay by taxi and spent many hours under the coconut trees. We were both fair-skinned, and the reflection of the sun off of the waves was sufficient in the shaded areas to redden the skin. I never liked the sun, I found it too hot and, having been burned in the tropics in a previous outing in 1967, I covered my feet and head. Tanzanian beach service workers provided coconut and papaya juice for a modest fee.

I met the new CUSO director, Jack Tittsworth. He was a very nice man and offered to share his flat, which was near the bridge leading to Oyster Beach. We thankfully accepted his gracious hospitality, and since this was the same residence as that of the former CUSO director, the same house help, Saaidi, was there. He remembered me, and though he was a small man, always wanted to lift me off the ground in joy when he saw me. When I was teaching in Dar, Saaidi had invited Rob Martin and me to attend his daughter's wedding, and we accepted. Getting there was quite a trip. We took a cab, and following Saaidi's instructions, we left the cab at a path leading to the wedding ceremony near Mbwamaji. We made our way on foot and found the party. Saadi was so happy to see his two white friends in his village. A locally brewed porridge-like substance, highly alcoholic, was continually served. This drink—*pombe*—gave a solid base while getting us a little tipsy. It was made from boiled cassava and fermented for many days; added spices ensured that the digestive tracts of these Mzungus were well maintained. A banana-based beer was also available. Meanwhile, the distribution of the gifts proved quite an event. One hut had been filled to capacity, and as the items came out and were given to the newlyweds, they had them placed in their new house. First, the linoleum, the tables, chairs, pots, pans, cloths and more housewares, then came the couch and other living room things, all deposited with care on the dirt floor now covered by the linoleum. Excitement was high as each gift was identified and transferred with cheering and laughter. The bride and groom rose in a regular rhythm to toast and thank their guests.

Saaidi was full of energy as he prepared our food and carried out other domestic chores. Colleen and I walked after sunset along the aroma- filled streets past the Indian shops offering Kitenge cloth, saris, and scarves for all occasions in colourful silk. We ate at various restaurants, and having a roof over our heads and being in comfortable surroundings slowed down the pace that had placed a lot of unwanted stress on our lives. Living as a young couple, sharing the simple comforts of life, the warm and tender moments of honeymooners, was a second start. Late mornings, afternoons at the beach in Dar, Kunduchi on the Kivikoni side of the warm Indian Ocean, we shared a lovely connection with laughter and harmony of idea and purpose. Our politics and reading material were the same, and Colleen's quick wit and my persistent need to discover made us a good team.

I maintained contact with the MPLA office, as I knew that in a very short time my life's focus would be fixed on going back to Angola. The separation from Colleen would be tough—and unhealthy, since she had given so much and this next phase would exclude her. Why could we not come up with a job at the liberation movement offices for her in Dar or Lusaka? This still troubles me. It seems that we the outsiders had needed to invest a lot of creativity to become part of this important struggle; and once we were trusted and aware of the dangers, we did exactly what was asked of us—and then were set aside. No one stepped up to advocate for my security. MPLA sympathizers were labelled evil communists in the prevailing cold war atmosphere. This created serious survival problems for me.

How does one massage a CV that contains ". . . guerrilla sympathizer and freedom fighter. . ."? The CUSO/SUCO description was bland: "*Agent de liaison* to the liberation movements." As an example, years later, in 1987, an opportunity arose that fitted perfectly with my experience: an energy conservation project in Costa Rica. Senior CESO project officer Don asked if he could submit my name to the CESO rep in Costa Rica. A few weeks later, the VP for CESO called me into his office. He showed me a letter he had received from the field office in Costa Rica. It was a hateful condemnation of me as a "communist" who deserved to die. He asked what I wanted to do with the nasty and prejudicial letter. To my lasting regret, I told him to destroy it. Eventually, the effects of this letter combined with the weak and nepotistic management structure of CESO assured that my time quickly ran out. CEO Don Haggerty called me to his office and told me I was no longer welcome in the organization. I had ten minutes to leave. Fired as a volunteer; match that!

I have found that, in any relationship, personal or working, trust is absolutely essential. Without trust, the freedom to release full creativity is inhibited. The soul cannot flourish. Essential to this trust is the ability to accept difference. We do not have to agree about everything; our differences, if we can accept them in a spirit of trust, stimulate the creative energy that will drive us toward our common aims.

As September slipped by, Colleen and I fixed a departure date for her return via Rome, including a stopover and hotel, then on to London and Montreal.

After the wonderful holiday with Colleen in Dar, MPLA business resumed. It was now time to travel back to Lusaka, some 1,500 kilometres, on the highway called the Tan-Zam Hell Run. Trucks carrying Zambian copper were renowned for their careless, death-defying drivers. Again I would taste the red sand. My butt would get beaten against the slippery leather seats and I for sure would get the middle seat. I moved to a downtown hotel, and this single room with mosquito net and washbasin was an excellent space to refocus my energies and political *raison d'être*. My room overlooked a traffic circle just up from the MPLA office; I could walk around and eat at local restaurants, still feeling very secure.

Finally, MPLA came, and from the Kurasini base, the loaded vehicles, one large five-ton truck and a Land Rover along with the passengers, started down the "Hell Run." With our own fuel, the stops would be calculated according to fuel consumption only. I sat in the middle back seat and the leather cushion made my butt very uncomfortable and hot. Leaving at night was a good strategy, cool and silent. As we passed Morogoro, I enjoyed memories of the water slide and cold dipping pools. Now, we faced dusty roads, jolting roads, and a lot of road. We went through the Mikumi National Park and reached Iringa and passed Ifunda Secondary School, some 500 kilometres upcountry. Boundary lights illuminated the school area, but we needed to refuel and move on to Mbeya and the border point of Tunduma for Tanzania. Nakonde was the Zambia entry point.

At the Tanzanian stop, the paperwork went smoothly. The *askari*—soldiers—were courteous and respectful of the MPLA. Within the hour, we left Tanzania, travelled the short distance to the Zambia side, and stopped for border clearance. MPLA made sure to keep me away from the office, as my white skin would create another issue. The Zambian had issues with MPLA, as Angolans come in many shades of white, given the assimilation over 500 years. Dr. Neto's sister, Ruth, was in our party, and it seemed that her name, being recognized, prompted a lengthy discussion as to her value as a hostage to be traded for money. A Zambian soldier wanted to see what was under the tarps, which created another point of discussion. In effect, the corrupt border soldiers, far from any supervision, could impose a flexible rate of entry tax. He who has the bigger gun is the most powerful. Just pay and you are on your way.

The Angolans were very unhappy, but their great negotiating skills and powers of persuasion over the next two hours cleared the tax problem, with "a little grease." It was a very unsettling situation, quasi-legal extortion, and though the MPLA could have wiped these two-bit soldiers off the map, the reality was they needed a functional border, so they just plugged along. It was known that Zambian soldiers near the Angola border had run when the Portuguese army crossed into Zambia, while the MPLA stood their ground and repelled the conscripts.

On to Mpika, down to Kapiri Mposhi, more than 1,000 kilometres, and more road to Kabwe and finally Lusaka, in all some three days, 1,500 kilometres, day and night. I was so exhausted and sore. On arrival in Lusaka, the driver took me to the September home with the notice that they would be back in a few days. After a shower and a cool one, I was just pooped and sore, but I was in great company. After a good night's rest, I would be just about okay. The next morning, I called Paulo Jorge; he would come around next day to the Septembers'.

Jorge was pleased to see me and showed me a magazine article from *Afrique Asie*. He said, "It's a great article, but I don't know who B.J. Quidado is." After a long pause I declared that I was the author of the review of Boavida's book.

MPLA wanted to do the film project. When I had organized the film making equipment, we would leave for Angola. The pressure was on to get CUSO to come up with the money.

The long and comfortable days with Colleen were but a memory. Dennis and Hazel continued to be my revolutionary friends and refuge till the film project started. I looked for a suitable super-8 mm movie camera; a package deal—$1,800.00 for film cartridges and audio cassettes, an amount beyond my personal wealth.

Who would be willing to give such a gift; who could also afford it?

The new CUSO assistant, Zambia program, had arrived. It was

Barry Fleming, from Dar es Salaam, and Barry, according to September, had learned since his arrival in Africa that the liberation movements were serious and trustworthy. He also knew that the United Nations policy stated that the UN-approved movements should be given help. From his point of view, he would look good by helping advance the struggle with no physical involvement and possible bragging rights.

I thought about how to approach Fleming. It would have to be soft sell with a moral hockey stick just in case he wanted to cross to the non-moral side. He knew better, but would he help? Best of all, he had not spoken with Tittsworth regarding our Dar holiday, so he would have no questions about Colleen and why she was no longer around.

I made an appointment to see him in the foyer of the Lusaka Hotel. Armed with product knowledge and sales material, I presented the film outline and the associated cost. His initial resistance needed to be attenuated. He was not in my face; however, he required some inducing. I knew how to do this.

We walked to the camera store for a demonstration of the camera's features and examples of film quality. Barry asked intelligent questions and requested a timeout for the two of us to discuss the plan. We went to the nearest coffee house. Friendliness and human warmth towards Barry kept the emotional temperature under control.

"Let me explain why this film needs to be done, Barry. Canadians are unaware of the needs of the Angolans living in the Semi-liberated Regions. The ARSC has as its mandate to inform Canadians about conditions on the ground, about how to help implement the United Nations resolutions to help the civilian population. After giving dozens of presentations to church groups and at universities, it is obvious that the message was stalled, not coming through loud and clear. Visual images are compelling.

"A visual presentation would be the missing piece of the information puzzle.

"Are there any valid reasons why this should not happen?" I asked.

"It's a lot of money," retorted Barry.

"Look, Barry, enough bullshit, this is a viable project and you have the power to sign onto this. CUSO will not have a problem with the rationale; all it takes is your positive response to make this film a reality."

I had said enough. He sipped his coffee slowly, looking for a way out.

"Jacques, this is such a risky project."

"I don't do risky projects, Barry, you know how I operate. This will work. This is your contribution."

"All right, the project is a go," said Barry. "When do you need this?"

"We leave soon for the zones."

We shook hands, and I showed measured gratitude. I returned to

Dennis's home and called Paulo Jorge with the news. MPLA had agreed to do the film; the story of the MPLA, its people, its base, its structure, would be told on celluloid. Paulo Jorge introduced me to Guinapo, member of the Department of Information and Propaganda—DIP. He was a short man with a beard, a protruding chin, great white teeth, and a large head of fuzzy hair. He spoke French fluently. We discussed the content and locations where we could film. This was the dry season, the Tugas period for military action. I required a constant companion, both for protection, as military action was now frequent, and as a guide to ensure the fullest possible coverage. We would start the film in Zone C south, deeper than the 1968 foray.

Next day, Barry had the financial arrangements ready. I purchased equipment, film, and cassettes. It was time to study the operational details and pack for our departure. Jorge came by and announced a seven-day delay and another piece of good news: Commander Monimambu would lead our group. This greatly allayed my concerns for personal safety. The Dar meeting and the subsequent interview with Moni gave me confidence and trust in a smart, dedicated guerrilla leader.

The *Times of Zambia* carried a series of articles on Angola praising the UNITA—it had the character of a planted story. Journalist Winter Lemba acclaimed the Zambian government's support for the UNITA group, without critical examination of the well-known political policy of tribalism. His regular printed articles praised tribalism and neo-colonialism. I kept up my diary, as this would be my only written source of information to accompany the film. I was constantly aware of the Septembers' connections with the liberation movements and the value of his cover as a CUSO representative. We all guarded this precious link. My presence was concealed from the CUSO staff, who seldom came to the house. The best visitors were from the movements. I met ANC President Oliver Tambo for the second time, Comrade Nzo, Uncle Hector, my former colleagues Thabo and Chris, and many other comrades who visited this safe house. One person who educated me about the effects of apartheid was Dennis's sister, visiting from South Africa. Though they were from the same mother and father, her skin colour was lighter than Dennis's, and this allowed her to be classified as a white person under apartheid. Dennis was classified as coloured. She was taken aback, scandalized, that the Zambian house help at the September residence ate with us. She was a coloured racist, a hater of her own kind. This was the evil of apartheid, the disconnect from nature and the rejection of one's heritage and culture. Another dehumanizing effect of apartheid was the skin creams used by men and women to lighten the skin. And the lengths to which Africans went to straighten their curly hair: they applied a hot iron and ironed out the curl.

I needed to hear these stories. Sociology 001: The Absurdity of Racism—Method of Determining Race Classification. When in doubt, the apartheid enforcers inserted a pencil in the hair and had the person give his head three shakes. If the pencil fell out, the classification was "coloured"; if it stayed in, it was the K classification, spelled K-A-F-F-I-R. In America, better known as the "N" word, while in French Canada, "F" stands for F-R-O-G.

This was apartheid; integrated and officially sanctioned humiliation, an absurdity imposed by a group of whites who derived their racially superior status by living off the self-appointed avails of racism.

The days ticked away, and I carefully prepared my packsacks, relying on my memories of the previous visit to the war zones in 1968. My backup food consisted of condensed milk; I had a towel and a bottle of J&B scotch for my friend Monimambu. Finally, on October 10, 1971, we were ready to go.

We loaded up the new Land Rover and headed for Mongu. The members of our group were Guinapo, Medical Director for Zone C, Dr. Toze, and four armed soldiers. Carrying our fuel, the good driver pushed on and stopped only to fuel up. The route was a new one. It was amazing how the Land Rover moved around water puddles and other obstacles. Within three days, we reached another MPLA border base. It was nighttime, and we needed to reach the small base where we would join up with Monimambu.

A ten-hour forced march got us to the well-hidden, fortified base camp. Some fifty Angolans, families and guerrillas, lived here. On arrival, Guinapo, Dr. Toze, and I were assigned to a straw and mud hut. The other four were integrated into an existing group. Moni's right-hand person was Diendengue, a well-known veteran of the early days in the Congo; this MPLA guerrilla became a valuable source of history and military stories. Trusted by President Neto, proven under fire, he was severely beaten by the Portuguese and Mobutu's thugs during the time MPLA was forced to set up in the Congo. A raconteur, the "Devil" spoke good French and many Angolan languages.

A military parade marked the formal acknowledgement of our arrival. Moni inspected the troops and introduced the members of the Angolan leadership at this camp. There was Mario de Andrade, Angolan writer, member of the Central Committee, from the 4th region; *Camarade* Lungwenia—"chameleon" in kikongo—leader of the National Union of Angolan Workers—UNTA; *Camarade* Emile, Assistant Secretary General for International Relations; and my old friend Lingatti, assigned as my bodyguard.

After the presentation of arms, Monimambu spoke about my presence. "Jacques is a friend of Angola. He has worked in the radio set- up and continues to mobilize Canadian opinion on our just cause. He is with the DIP and will make a documentary. He will put our story in pictures. Welcome to Angola, *Camarade* Jacques."

Some clapped their hands, and the villagers made their unique traditional greeting, that wailing sound.

We all sang the MPLA national anthem and Monimambu gave the MPLA battle cry,

> *Abaxe o colonialism* [Down with colonialism]
>
> *Abaxe o racism* [Down with racism]
>
> *Abaxe o tribalism* [Down with tribalism]
>
> *A lutta . . . continua* [The struggle continues]
>
> *A Vitoria . . . e . . . certa* [Victory is certain]

We exchanged our civilian clothing for military camouflage, and were issued weapons and instructions in camp procedures. The daily routine over the years had not changed radically. The defensive tactics and new military hardware of the MPLA had forced the Portuguese to withdraw. Tugas forays by helicopter were sporadic. Nonetheless, a war was being waged. There was just the matter of when the next military contact would take place. My instructions were to use the pistol I was given to defend myself, and, if necessary, to kill myself to avoid capture. I was fully committed now.

Monimambu invited us to his quarters. We exchanged greetings, and everyone expressed their pleasure to be serving in the national liberation of Angola. The evening meal, shared in the kitchen quarters, was the traditional *foo foo* with a spicy sauce. Our assembled teamwas ready to go in three days. For now, plenty of rest and mission focus. I learned a little of the history of this region. At the beginning of 1965, de Mello and Monimambu had recruited fifteen young Angolans, who were sent abroad for training, and fifteen seasoned guerrillas from Cabinda arrived as replacements. The formula for success: recruit new personnel before getting experienced soldiers.

With a further fifteen raw recruits, the first section, armed with a few grenades and rifles, attacked the closest Portuguese post. The overall strategy was to force the Tugas to abandon the borders and to fall back to Lumbala and Ninda. After some back and forth action, MPLA held on and established Zone A. Later on that year, a fifth region was opened some 200 miles from Zambia. Military supplies were obtained from dead soldiers and from captured military posts.

Packing for this long trip meant limited material: camera, film, tape recorder and cassettes, sleeping bag, small bag with towel and tooth brush. No change of clothing. This time I had running shoes. Though warm on the feet, they were flexible on the eternal sand. And given the high probability of military engagement, speed and agility to reach a safe tree or underground bunker was a must. This movie project was now part of the Angolan political-military structure under the *Forces Armade Popular Libertacao de Angola*—FAPLA: The Popular Armed Forces for the Liberation of Angola.

This base camp, inside Zone C, Third region, had a sizable population and was a miniature Angolan society. Education was obligatory and available through *Department Education e Cultura*—DEC, themedical services—SAM, the trade union—UNTA, women's organization—OMA, and the youth group—OPA. No forced labour. This area and its people were free.

I asked *Camarade* Diendengue, during this pre-walk rest period, how he got his name.

"As a youngster I was raised in a Catholic mission. The dreaded enemy of the Catholic Church was the devil. It was the same for Protestants. Their enemy was the devil. However, their common friend was Portuguese colonialism, and in my eyes, the enemy of all Angolans was Portuguese colonialism. In the overall scheme of things, all these friends are the same and I hate them all. Therefore I must be the devil."

So many other names with a message. Think of Max Schmelling. A big and tough guerrilla explained, "I adopted the name Schmelling because to be the best I have to be like him, strong and determined."

In the last days of the 1968 stay in Zambia, I had adopted the name Quidado, with the "B" initial for Boavida, "J" for Jacques. So the interviews were signed "B.J. Quidado."

We stored clothing and other items in an underground tunnel on the second-last day. Following our last meal and a short rest, we headed out at about midnight. A scrawny dog accompanied our column. Another lesson in guerrilla warfare. He was part of the security. Most water sources were tested by this dog; if he drank, then it was okay. The Tugas poisoned "all" water supplies in the free fire zone. This dog was our proverbial canary in the coal mine. The night sky was full of unknown stars and planets. The walking surface was harder, with less sand. My knee was holding up, no tightness. It was very dark, and I could just make out the boot prints in front of me. Lingatti was behind me and Monimambu led the way for this first section. At regular intervals, we stopped to rest and drink water. At sunrise, we put up in a wooded area, and soon we were joined by another MPLA brigade, travelling in a northerly direction. We were going due west. The warm exchange with these MPLA strangers, *camarades*, was a boost to morale.

MPLA successes and tactical information provided a military education. The long walk continued till two hours after sunrise. We would rest till 12:00. The MPLA had learned that the Portuguese considered their cultural habits more important than the war. The

Portuguese ate lunch from 12:00 to 13:00 with a one-hour siesta to follow. Their belief was that Africans were lazy and would not work in the hot sun.

"How could the Africans possibly defeat the 'superior civilization'?" seemed to be the Tugas' attitude to war.

Around 14:00, Portuguese military action resumed. The pattern was fairly predictable.

To take advantage of this, we walked in the hot noon sun while the enemy rested, and stopped at 14:00 till dusk for food and water. The population living in the immediate area fed us fairly well. We had bananas and squash to round out our *foo foo*. For the next days we walked, rested, and ate *foo foo*. Friendships developed, and my close friend Lingatti looked after me. He reminded me often that I had separated from my weapon. The effects of hunger and poor nutrition slowed my thought processes, and given that my existence depended on my bodyguard, further diminished my usual self-reliance.

At one long stop, I asked Emile what he thought about during these walks and stops. His response: "I make plans for meals. I imagine a well-set table with quantities of food on it, and have a feast." His imagination and knowledge of meat, wine, and cheeses told of a man who had tasted the good life. He shared the vision—cloth napkins to the left of the finest china plates with gold rims, three silver forks, two spoons, three knives, long-stemmed crystal wine and water glasses, on a white, starched tablecloth. Fresh, sweet smelling flowers from the garden, a big pitcher of ice cubes with a dash of fresh mint.

"Now," he added, "what kind of wine should we have?"

I shook my head at his creativity. My hunger pangs slept during this feast.

As we crossed certain barriers, such as open clearings, an established MPLA post provided the scout for the next leg of the journey. One night, Monimambu brought me over to meet our new guide. "This soldier, *Camarade* Jacques, is the best and finest tracker. He is an Angolan from the southern part, near the Namibia border, a Bushman." He spoke no Portuguese and I no Chokwe or Kwanyama. We shook hands and whispered *bon noit*—good evening. Night communication was by hand signal and whisper. Night air carried sound waves much farther than in the daytime. Monimambu listened to the interpreter's words re our direction. The Bushman stepped away from the group and fixed his eyes upon the sky. Reaching up with his hand, he studied his star-studded celestial map, learned over the centuries, and gave us the direction of our next leg. What a sight.

He knew the ground conditions as well as the hidden water holes.

I kept staring at this tiny man who had such intensity in his face. In the pitch-black African night, I could only see the white of his filed teeth.

The Angolan landscape: a vast savannah with sparse vegetation and an irregular distribution of trees. This allowed us to see long distances, but offered little cover. In these areas, underground shelters had been dug out and in an emergency would be our "home." We walked off trails, and every step was in the print of the preceding boot—land mine avoidance. The quantity and quality of knowledge required to survive in this jungle was staggering.

Every day we heard at a distance the sound of helicopters ferrying troops to another area. The Portuguese budget was taking a serious hit since nearly 50 percent was being expended for the war. This was accompanied by a growing reluctance on the part of the conscripts. Returning body bags changed the sparkling eyes of "getting the terrorists" to eyes filled with tears: the heart-wrenching pain of the mothers and fathers who had responded to the military call and sent their sons to die for the feudal state of ancient families and fascism.

More sorrow for the poorest fanatics of Catholicism, more hatred of blacks, resulting in more dehumanization. When military planes and helicopters were in the vicinity, we found shelter in an enclave of greenery. Monimambu in a mocking voice asked, "Do you know how to play 'musical trees'?"

"What is that?" I asked.

"Well, today we cannot move, so we will sit under this tree, and as the sun moves, we will follow the shadow of the tree."

It turned out to be a long day—a restful day, but always at the ready to move on Moni's command. The forced walk and rest had a few light moments. One night after the news, a woman guerrilla who had been in our patrol for five days approached me quietly. Lingatti, who slept next to me, noticed her advance and intervened.

The language barrier evaporated as she told me with hand signals, as Lingatti looked on, that *Action Social* was possible. I threw up my hands and shook my head, whispering, "No, nothing tonight, *camarada*."

It occurred to me then that, in these difficult circumstances, there was no privacy; the required ambience for intimacy was nonexistent.

Lingatti knew that all he had was the MPLA. His life was for the freedom of Angola. During the stops, words were few, but on a "musical tree" day, we talked. One day, I asked him the same question I had posed in 1968.

"Why did you join the MPLA?"

"After my *kazi*—work—in South Africa, I came back home to my mother and father. The *Tropas*—troops—came to our village and as I heard the trucks arrive I ran into the forest to hide. From the bush, I saw them beat my father. Soon the helicopter arrived and they put my father and mother in it and went *juu mingi juu*—high very high. They wanted my parents to say where I went. They would not tell, so to show the other villagers what happens with no co-operation, they threw them out the side door. *Ame kufa*—they're dead. It is then *nemekwenda Zambia*—I went to Zambia—to meet the MPLA."

Initially, FAPLA leaders were trained in Russia, China, and Cuba, but the incoming and aspiring guerrillas were trained in Tanzania near Morogoro, *Centre Instruction Revolutionar*—CIR—Center for Revolutionary Instruction. As the military front expanded, in-country training and upgrades were done in Angola's liberated areas. The structure of FAPLA was based on the guerrilla unit of ten.

Small, very mobile units that could strike quickly joined up with other units to hit harder or offer an elongated attack along a roadside. Success resided in the element of surprise.

Proven over and over, these ten-man and -woman tactical units could hold down 100 enemy soldiers.

For the Tugas, all areas of road surfaces, ditches, bridges, overhanging trees, streams, shorelines, and other numerous possibilities needed to be observed, evaluated, and investigated, as failure to do so meant trouble.

Just stopping to evaluate a bridge could take one hour, exposing the soldiers to a refined crosshair attack. For the Tugas it was a no-win situation. These conscripts, mainly from poor Portuguese families, were cannon fodder.

The psychological warfare of today was as important as the military warfare in the beginning. Now the retreat of the *Tuga Tropas* from bases that had been established for 200 years created food for thought in the actions of the soldiers. During this mission, I saw the application of this demoralizing tactic.

One day around 0900 hours our scouts shouted "*Helicop!*" and pointed. Immediately Monimambu sprang into action. "Hurry, over here, follow me!" I followed his hand signals and imitated his body motions as we walked parallel to an established trail in a semi-dense area. From the perimeter of this tree and bush area we watched the helicopters arrive. There were five of them, Alouettes from the French NATO connection. At about two kilometres from our hiding spot, they hovered high up. Onehelicopter lowered but did not touch the ground and discharged its *Tropas*. They ran to the immediate bush line in front of the helicopter. This scene was repeated till all five had completed their discharge duties. As the fifth helicopter rose to the level of the other four; they took off. Our scouts evaluated the *Tropas* walking direction so the leaders could plan our next move. Binoculars and knowledge of the nearly predictable behaviour of the Tugas gave the FAPLA the edge.

Plan of action of the MPLA: Move deep into the bush area and set up the offence in a "V" formation five metres back from the existing trail with four metres' space between us. Guns were set in a fixed direction at 1430 hours, pointing into the incoming traffic.

Two well-hidden scouts waited near the entry point of the monitored trail and the arrival of the Tugas. As they entered the trail and slowly advanced towards our position, the scouts observed. When the Tugas passed a critical, predetermined point, which put them in the trap, we needed to know when to go to our next step.

This moment was signalled to us when our FAPLA scouts exploded a grenade from their vantage point, which was behind the walking column of soldiers heading for the trap. We had the edge and allowed the Tugas to decide their move. The Tugas knew they were in a trap but did not know when and from which direction the shots would fly. Panic, the psychological pressure of the limited possible outcomes: alive, dead or injured.

Their move would determine the FAPLA response. Maybe the FAPLA would only hit the front man in their column; or maybe the middle, forcing the ends to scatter?

The Tugas could not win.

The cover made it so difficult to see; a movement of a branch might or might not indicate a human presence "out there." A war of nerves ensued as the lead soldier appeared with his weapon pointed to the ground, his right hand back and finger away from the trigger, always a good sign. He turned his head and spoke at a normal voice level to number two soldier; just another walk in the bush of Angola . . . Why are we here?

The column proceeded on the trail and into the preset trap of the "V." The jig was up. Within a few minutes, grenades and bullets would create more dead bodies, injured, and, for the married Tugas, widows and orphans. It could also be a silent trap to walk through and an indication that the will to occupy and fight for this hot and forsaken land would end. This slowly moving and talking group of conscripts had made a decision that for today, their guns would point to the ground, no finger on the trigger, and wondered, wondered, "where the guerrillas are."

As they passed my field of vision, my adrenalin pumped and heart beat shot up. I witnessed the power shift, acknowledged military weakness and the ultimate question: How do the Portuguese get out of this mess?

Not just the immediate situation, but the greater question: how do we put an end to colonialism?

I watched seventy-three men parade in front of my eyes. Their continual chatter was no doubt to reduce the nervous tension.

Then soldier number seventy-four followed, then soldier seventy-five, front profile, then side profile, nose, head covered by silly hat, then finally number seventy-five's back. A large target that slowly shrank as the distance between us increased. A FAPLA soldier shouted at them, "I'll get your ass next time. Go home." The Tugas shouted back obscenities about our sisters. We had witnessed the results of an evaluation by an unwilling military force. The morale was lacking, a beaten fighting force but not demilitarized—not yet.

We got up slowly and saw these young men back slapping each other as if they had scored the winning goal for the world soccer championship with no time left on the clock. What's for lunch?

We gathered back at the entry point and had some food and water. Every participant had a story and a vantage point, a humbling experience and a morale booster. I watched as the guerrillas, in different languages, spoke slowly and softly, relating their view of the slow-motion passage of dead men walking. Monimambu applied this "wear down the enemy" strategy often. It involved vision and value for life, underscoring behaviour that dignifies a civilized society. This must have given the Tugas plenty to talk about and jolted their colonial assumptions.

Both sides learned how to control their power. Good behaviour was rewarded. FAPLA still controlled the agenda. By sunset, our rested bodies pushed again against the effects of gravity, and later that night we reached the large open field. Lingatti explained that during the rainy season this land was under a metre of water. It was only passable on foot or dugout canoe. Foot travel in waist-high water represented a real danger from snakes. Here in Cuando Cubango Province, Zone C Third Region, the Ninda to Lumai Road indicated that we had penetrated nearly 100 kilometres from the Angola–Zambia border. Just south of us was the large Portuguese military installation of Lumbala. Its physical survival depended on air transportation. Fuel, food, and military goods were flown in. The ground belonged to the FAPLA. The air belonged to the Tropas, but less than formerly; the MPLA had shot down two helicopters during the past year. Far from quitting, the metropolitan-based military planners implemented the building of a pro-Portuguese movement called UNITA, financed by the war budget. The settlers saw this tribal group as the saving face of their dwindling power. UNITA's mission was created to fight the MPLA. The infrastructure of government, commerce, and agriculture would still be in the hands of the ruthless settlers. Enslaving other tribes while using the power of the Portuguese seemed a good deal for UNITA. In the view of serious political scholars, UNITA would turn Angola into another dictatorial state, another Zaire.

Portugal's friends, apartheid Africa and Rhodesia, with their 1962 Military Alliance Accord, would be capable of creating another racial category for the tribal Savimbi. If Chinese and Koreans could be classified as honorary whites, perhaps, just perhaps, the necessity of floating this new racial classification, similar to the Homelands, could be created. The United States in the meantime sought to keep racist South Africa in the World Community while trying to negate the "moral leper" label.

A few more days of walking, and we arrived at the village with the infrastructure to put on film.

The National Trade Union—UNTA—had the major responsibility of food production and fabrication of clothing and tools for food production.

Here is the edited version of UNTA's food production efforts in the 4th Zone. On December 12, 1970, all of the crops were burned, and this demoralized our sixty-three agricultural brigades. The air force bombers accompanied by helicopters flew very low and sprayed chemicals on our crops. The cassava crop, our staple, turned black the next day. Gone.

I saw these empty fields, scorched and unusable just like the crops in Vietnam. The role and influence of the USA was evident.

The United Nations Human Rights Commission on January 2nd, 1971, reported the events of May 20th, 1970, as told by Alfonso Hundandano.

[A] Portuguese plane dropped chemical substances over his village . . . which destroyed the harvest, the animals and fish, compelling the population because of illness caused by this act, to move away from the area . . . there was no longer anything to eat or drink . . . the Portuguese . . . destroyed everything that could serve as food . . . they dropped pamphlets saying they would return if resistance in the area continued. Investigation of the chemicals identified them as 2,4, D, 2,4,5,T along with cacodylic acid and picloram, a Dow Chemical product, Tordon, which sterilizes the soil for two years.

Other trades within UNTA were vehicle repair, bakers, blacksmiths, shoemakers, and tailors.

With a quota of 250 metres of cloth per month, Zone D with three tailors averaged twelve shirts and short pants per day. The poor quality of the cloth combined with the conditions of wear and tear gave their product a one-to-three-month lifespan. We arrived and settled into our new base for a five-to-seven-day stopover. SAM, DEC, CIR, OMA, and OPA units were in this village. During this prolonged stop, I started to record the activities and personalities of our home base. Guinapo arranged for the time and location. The emphasis was on structure and the personalities that made it happen. I witnessed the joy that comes of being outside colonial rule and its forced-labour practices, and building their independent nation.

Personal respect and respect for the war effort gave our visit an added educational tool, making the international component of the Angola war a two-pronged effort. The MPLA's success required international support, and exposing the "friends of Portugal" was the other prong.

I was learning; I was witnessing extreme poverty, disease, language barriers, and constant insecurity, and feeling the pulse of an emerging society.

I was living through the gestation period of the new nation of Angola. As time passed, my North American body was feeling less energetic. My brain functioned below full capacity.

Despite medication to ward off malaria, the fever came on with weakness, diarrhea, and an increased need for sleep. Dr. Toze, born of Portuguese parents in Angola, had stayed to build his native land. He looked after my medical needs, and within three days I returned to the interviews and camera work. The departure date was pushed back.

As I completed sections of the filming, the generosity of the Angolans made my heart glow. After I had filmed the fabrication of a shirt, the UNTA leader assembled the members, and through the young pioneers, OPA presented it to me. Emile, the UNTA representative, gave me a boa skin and a tanned Angolan otter skin. What generosity. The major workload for this Chiume location was now completed. Next step was a return march to the Kalabo region. The outgoing trip seemed shorter. We stopped at different villages and were treated to a feast. The UNTA hunters had shot a young deer with a bow and arrow a few days before our arrival. Our presence meant a celebration. The deer, covered in a sticky substance, was grilled and served with fresh squash grown under the overhangs next to a small creek, and the famous *foo foo*. The meal was delicious and recharged our batteries. The last leg of the walk had only guerrilla postings and little food. Dr. Toze told me that we could survive on squash alone, while meat alone would lead to extreme health problems and death. Early next morning, we set out for the last sixty miles. We came across burnt-out villages, abandoned military installations, and defoliated crops. The daily buzz of helicopters and the occasional reconnaissance plane kept us alert.

Monimambu informed us that within a few hours we would be in a safer area. By now our stomachs were growling. We also had discovered two large mango trees full of fruit—forbidden fruit, as Dr. Toze said. Unripe and hard, the moisture content quenched a little thirst. I bit into the flesh and consumed some of it. Within an hour, I and the others who had also eaten the fruit developed stomach pains with the dreaded "runs." We should have listened to Toze.

In the final hours, the scouts announced the sound of a motorized vehicle coming from the border area. We went and hid, waiting as the sound got closer and clearer. Moni whispered, "Jeep, a small jeep, stay down." The scout guerrilla gave the thumbs up as he ID'd the jeep. The MPLA Kalabo detachment had delivered guerrillas farther up the border; our meeting was a coincidence. The driver was frightened by our unexpected appearance. For us, a relaxed atmosphere, except for the stomach pains; we had finished the walk.

Within three hours, we were let out near a small creek to wash our faces and hands before going the last thirty minutes to our original base camp.

For the next few days, this would be home, so following a long time in the river, I went back to civilian clothes. It was time to celebrate.

After the first meal at the base, I told Monimambu that I had a surprise and hustled to my hut to get the bottle of Scotch. I reached into the army bag and immediately noticed the lack of weight accompanied by a broken seal. I turned around and walked back into the dining room. Monimambu registered my displeasure.

I asked Guinapo if he had consumed the liquor; he nodded.

I gave no response. I deferred to Monimambu to deal with the issue. The party was over, and Guinapo was just an opportunist. The next morning, Monimambu, Toze, Diendengue and Lingatti saw us off. We hugged and wished each other good luck. My parting with Lingatti was the most difficult; we had bonded as revolutionaries from different worlds, shared dreams for an independent and progressive Angola.

The second part of the film was shot in Zone A, to the north. We returned to Mongu and waited for the transportation to arrive. Luxury time. This portion of the trip was no longer by road. MPLA was using aircraft to move people and merchandise in Zambia airspace. This was another indication of how MPLA took the initiative and showed the Angolans the limited power of the colonial army to stop the expansion of the liberated regions. The DC-3 plane from Mongu to Zambezi flew at tree level below Portuguese radar. The MPLA plane signalled a new weapon, a new phase. Two hours later, we put down on a dirt road to a reception committee of one driver, one Land Rover; we left ASAP for Kalombo and Chavuma Falls bases. Dealing with Guinapo was an exercise in mental strength. No anger, just curt questions and . . . let's get on with the job.

The MPLA leader at this MPLA base was Daniel Chipenda. He and Guinapo were friends and they shared their bouts with the bottle. There were stashes of empty whisky bottles under the bed. President Neto probably knew of this behaviour and tolerated it because democracy must be the mechanism to root out bad behaviour. Leadership called for self-discipline and moderation, and micromanagement was not acceptable. The political structure with the peasants holding power would fix the problem or they would learn to live with it. The MPLA was always democratic and fair.

On December 8th, we made another entry into Angola. Guinapo and I were added to the reconnaissance team going towards Lumbala north. Our walking schedule varied slightly; the difference here was the geology of the soil. This was part of the Zambia Copper Belt, South Congo. Within three days, we had passed the ruins of Cazombo and Caripande. Military leader Toze joined us for this section of the walk and recounted the battle to destroy Caripande. The MPLA guerrillas fought hard and smart. The Tugas fired back as they ran away. The post was destroyed and burned down. As the MPLA regrouped, the commander for the battle, Hoja Henda, did not appear. Another tragedy of national proportions: MPLA's top soldier had been killed. In memory of Henda, April 14th was dedicated as a national holiday, and he was made a hero to the Angola Pioneer Organization—OPA.

Here is a brief description of the events surrounding the attack at Caripande. General Petroff had been assigned by the MPLA military planners to reach an area in southern Zaire and march back to eastern Angola with some 1,500 new recruits for the developing eastern front. The forced march proceeded with the emphasis on getting to the final base and giving military planners sufficient time to plan for the upcoming dry season. Unknown to General Petroff, Commander Quidado of zone B, home of the large military base of the Tugas, had convinced General Henda on the strategic and psychological importance of making the colonial troops who occupied these barracks to feel a little insecure in their base. Henda agreed that FAPLA had enough firepower to cause serious damage to the "cement monster" and its contents. Petroff continued to march his men towards Caripande unaware of the military action being planned.

FAPLA had carried out the plan on the run, costing the life of a great man, while other elements of FAPLA could have been decimated, as they did not know their surroundings and the details of military security, which they normally controlled.

There had been little military action during this dry season, and the Tugas were less aggressive in their outings. As the April 14th attack took place, Petroff kept marching and feeling quite secure, as much of the march was through the sparse vegetation and tree cover of the savannah. Following the successful attack on Caripande, the Tugas had to respond, and did so by helicopter, catching Petroff and his men by surprise.

Where do you hide 1,500 soldiers on short notice?

It was a near disaster, as Petroff recounted over dinner during a visit to Ottawa in November 2004, as head of the Land mines Institute of Angola, a signatory to the Ottawa Convention.

It took courage and constant improvisation to keep bringing the war effort to the enemy. The MPLA guerrillas quickly discovered that a helicopter could most easily be brought down if they aimed for the back rotor. The colonial army was constantly taken aback by the sophistication of the MPLA's military efforts. When Karipande was lost, the colonial army retreated to smaller bases. Local shop owners abandoned their stores and became refugees themselves.

Filming and walking filled our days and nights. The MPLA structure was evident every time there was a sizable population. Here in Zone A, food was more plentiful and the Angolan health conditions better. The many rivers gave excellent growing conditions on the shores; the surrounding forest grew large trees and dense green underbrush.

Information on the strategic hamlets, the role of the Special Forces, and the presence of American advisors was not fully exposed. On November 16, two Angolans had defected, in Zone A, from the Special GE, a counter-insurgency group trained by some 2,500 Portuguese officers, graduates from Fort Bragg. Green Berets were seen in the field, a confirmed sighting by a guerrilla that I interviewed.

In Luso, these soldiers at a strategic hamlet were identified by a red armband and matching neckerchief and spoke American English.

Further confirmation came when Toze took me to an out-of-the-way place, a military prison holding eight Portuguese soldiers captured over the last year. I interviewed them, and they confirmed the presence of American Special Forces, the use of the latest American hardware, and chemicals including napalm and defoliation agents.

Silence in the American press gave the US military carte blanche in defending colonialism and racism, while building a repressive alternative and destroying progressive nationalist efforts.

US law forbade the use of American soldiers on foreign soil, unless it had been sanctioned by Congress.

These prisoners needed a little uplifting; Commander Toze told them to prepare a letter for their families, delivery guaranteed. Grown men, peasants, barely literate, started to tear up. After the humiliation of being taken prisoner by Angolans, MPLA turning out to be human beings who did not mistreat them, and now the offer to tell their families that they were alive, stimulated profound emotions that overcame these abandoned soldiers, who sobbed *muito obrigad, paz e grace a Jesus*, thank you very much, peace in the name of Jesus.

This was a war with no name and no foreseeable end.

Psychological warfare was required in Portugal directly or via other European states. Non-government organizations—the Red Cross, Amnesty International—were aware of the war and needed to be integrated in the war's resolution. There was a considerable effort of disinformation and misdirection to oppose.

"With the advent of the Nixon administration in 1969, a major review of American policy towards southern Africa, the tar baby report NSSM 39, concluded that African insurgent movements were ineffectual, not realistic or supportable alternatives to continued colonial rule. The interdepartmental policy review, commissioned by then White House advisor, Henry Kissinger, questioned the depth and permanence of black resolve and ruled out a black victory at any stage."[2] The FAPLA training centre, CIR, was well equipped with modern shoulder-held rocket launchers and anti-aircraft guns, both mobile and stationary types. My short stay gave me an appreciation of the diversity of Angola. Here the spoken languages were Balovale, Swahili, and Chokwe. The proximity of Zambian villages created different challenges for the MPLA. Tribal connections with UNITA could be exploited easily, as the Zambian government did not address this issue. MPs in Zambia's parliament were working behind the scene in support of the tribal brothers, because the MPLA opposed this neo-colonial strategy of supporting factions instead of nationhood.

Tanzania President Nyerere always had time for the MPLA. In public statements, and in the offer of port facilities, he never shied away from supporting the armed struggle. Zambia's Kaunda, on the other hand, held back support for the MPLA whenever he could, and could not be trusted. His allegiance, largely because of tribalism, was to UNITA. During the turmoil in Luanda, President Kaunda, at a National Security Council meeting in Washington, on April 19, 1975, convinced

---

2   Henry Kissinger, Years of Renewal (New York: Simon & Shuster, 1999), p. 23.

President Ford and Secretary of State Kissinger that the Soviet Union was intervening in Angola with military advisors and weapons, so that the US would oppose the intrusion for the sake of Angola's neighbours.[3]

Kaunda urged the US to support UNITA's Jonas Savimbi. In an NSC meeting on June 27, Kissinger presented this generic cold war situation: deny increase of Soviet sphere of influence in Africa by countering efforts in Angola.

In ten days, we had completed filming in this northern region.

On December 23, 2000 hours, the large MPLA truck was loaded up with empty fuel barrels and MPLA personnel going to Ndola and Lusaka. We travelled all night and stopped at 1200 hours to purchase mealie meal and eighteen barrels of gas and to repair the truck.

By 1500 hours, we were back on the red road to Kitwe and arrived December 25th at 1800 hours and parked at the school grounds near our Russian friend's house. We had travelled more than 700 kilometres in the red dust of Zambia. With no mirror, we could only observe the face in front of us to appreciate our true colour.

We walked slowly towards the Russian's house and used the side entrance, and knocked gently on the locked door. Sergei peered through the glass and recognized my face. He let us in and met my three Angolan friends. Our state of filth was secondary to our hunger and happiness to find refuge. Little Mischa, age seven, asked about the girl with long blonde hair—Colleen. I explained that she had gone back to Canada but was sure that he would like my black friends. He seemed terribly confused, as two of the three black Angolans spoke perfect Russian. A quick hand and face wash-up, then a splendid meal of Soviet canned fish, cooked bananas, and fresh fruit. However, during our meal, taken in the back room of the house, Canadian Principal I.

3   Ford Presidential Library, Collection on NSA Meeting file 1974–1977 Folder 16/27/1975. Talking points for Secretary Kissinger NSC meeting on Angola. We did not know at the time what Kaunda was doing, but we could measure the effects of his hostility and gross interference in MPLA activities. I have asked many Angolans what they think of Kaunda. Many defend him, and cannot believe he was party to what I describe here.

Goodine from the ZIT College dropped in without notice, no doubt to share the traditional Christmas good wishes, thus creating a security risk for Sergei and his family.

A nervous Sergei and I agreed that we needed to leave ASAP, as no doubt more aspiring "communists" from CIDA would continue to drop in unannounced. My presence would have negative consequences on the work of our Soviet friends. I escorted my three Angolan *camarades* back to the truck, and they were off to Lusaka and I back to the house.

Sergei gave me money and dropped me off at the familiar hostel in downtown Kitwe. I bathed three times in an effort to get free of the "red plague."

Christmas day plus one began with a big breakfast in the nearly vacant dining room, consisting of eggs, ham, dry toast, and plenty of fresh fruit. Next meal would be dinner, so, to get me there, I filled the large pockets of my pants with cheese, oranges, and nuts. I spent the next week reenergizing body and soul while transcribing the audio interviews to paper, followed by translation into English, to a background of recently taped Angolan music.

This experience had tested my will and revolutionary spirit, and sharpened my focus. I liked this life and my friends Monimambu, de Mello, Diendengue, Neto, and Lingatti and I cherished my memories of my past friends Boavida and Quidado. They had all trusted my wish to be part of their revolution. The creativity that went into survival was beyond anything I ever imagined. Strong values had been tested—shaken but not broken: skills known and learned; spiritual challenges; political illiteracy developing into political savvy; believing in democracy; and understanding the enormous cost to the Africans of the privileges of the ruling class. A society will believe its leaders and the lies they tell. Vietnam can be lied about till the lie is exposed; it seemed clear to me that Angola was America's next Vietnam. The lie must be exposed, or this US presence will push Southern Africa into another fiasco of corrupt foreign policy, and the brunt of the civil war will be born by the Angolans.

Our task as progressives and supporters of the anti-colonial and anti-apartheid movement is to create an opposition and point public awareness towards the consequences of consumption beyond our ability to pay a fair price and therefore put the finger on the ruling class, who cajole, ridicule, and silence those who expose the lie.

On January 6, 1972, at 0700, I headed back to Lusaka on the train arriving, at 1700, after a five-hour delay. The train crew was drunk—another sign of a crumbling society in a rudderless environment.

On arrival, I called Kamalata from the train station and headed for the slums of Lusaka to complete the filming of the movie. A small room with the same old typewriter was my new home. Food was scarce, but the companionship of De Mello, Paulo Jorge and other MPLA made it a pleasant stay. Our neighbours were the ANC, SWAPO, and FRELIMO. Exile is the greatest challenge to hope. The role of this place for those who lived here was to organize, accelerate, defuse events, starve, and continue to push for the day when the hellhole would be a memory.

Dr. Neto was so correct in saying that forcing the MPLA to exile was an unbelievable hardship, complicated further by other decision-makers and government corruption.

Will independence come in five or ten years?

Radio South Africa announced that The Pierce Commission is in Rhodesia to "test the acceptability of proposed white rule and independence in twenty-five years." How does one react to the absurdity of this timetable?

Political discussions, in particular with Jorge, are intense, a methodical analysis of world politics pushed by greed and ideology and with little regard to the effects of the West's decisions on the Third World. Angola is a rich country, with diamonds, oil, agriculture, and forestry adding up, inevitably, to a powerful reason for war.

Jorge was very satisfied—delighted—with the results of the trip. We discussed the American involvement and the information that I had gathered. He had heard it all before, but coming from a non-Angolan made it a matter for a press conference. The liberation movement centre was the chosen location, on the condition that there be no photographs and that the true identity of the Canadian journalist not be revealed. The Zambian journalists hungrily peppered us with questions. The implications, especially the Zambian government's complicity, were not lost on them. The news would require a response from Kaunda's cabinet Ministers of Foreign Affairs, the Interior, and Defence.

Jorge and Kamalata agreed that if they published this news, remembering Zambia backed UNITA, it would be a wake-up call to the world. We expected that the US embassy would deny any US involvement.

The Times of Zambia headline read, "US Troops in Angola." The shocking news and the ensuing denial kept the story alive. Winter Lemba, the Zambian journalist, could not be found. We wanted him to explain his past writings in this same *Times of Zambia*. MPLA was very happy. We agreed that world opinion needed to be shaped to know the Angola story accurately. From Lusaka, I contacted support committees in Rome, Paris, Denmark, Switzerland, Holland, and both Germanys to offer my services on my return to Canada. The response was fabulous. The established network of MPLA supporters drew up a schedule, and by the end of February, the information campaign was launched; the Angola coffee boycott in Europe had started. It was encouraging to see the emergence of this double-edged campaign.

More information on the coffee plantations meant more reason to boycott Angola coffee imports and less income for the Portuguese war effort. More information on the colonial war meant more awareness on the friends of the Portuguese alliances and intentions.

Security risks in Lusaka were a given, a constant reminder of the danger associated with all wars. The bombing of the liberation centre south of Lusaka was a reminder that the anti-liberation forces were only a few flying hours away.

Leaving Zambia could be complicated now that I had spoken publicly. Another European, a beautiful woman and a friend of the MPLA, agreed to carry the raw film footage to London.

February 4th, the anniversary of the beginning of the armed struggle, had come and gone, and five days later, the *"a lutta continua"* to my *camarades* completed, the MPLA drove me to the September residence.

For a few more days, I relaxed with Dennis and Hazel, true to their actions, fellow revolutionaries.

The MPLA Department of Information developed the still photos, as they would be the visual basis of the upcoming presentations. The power of pictures supported by witness accounts by Angolans and outside eyes gave the liberation movement moral support and greater credibility in the ongoing world campaigns. With my return ticket to Canada from the prearranged agreement with the ZIT in May of 1971, a Zambian taxi took me to the airport and a hands-on experience of police corruption. About four miles from the airport, in the middle of nowhere, a Zambia Police roadblock "discovered" that my driver was "wanted for violations," so an immediate arrest occurred. Of course, if I paid the police a holding tax, they would let him drive me to the airport and get him on his way back. Otherwise they would seize the taxi and the driver, leaving me to walk to the airport. It was now 22:00 hours, there were many reasons not to walk; I handed over ten k in service of the noble objective of getting out of Zambia.

That night, I vowed never to go back to Zambia. All future transit stops would be confined to the airport lounge.

First stop was Rome. Italian support committees received me warmly, having arranged public presentations to MPLA support committees, anti-apartheid groupings that featured a twenty-minute presentation of personal observations on the war, followed by a Q and A session. These public meetings focused on the political pressures on National Parliamentarians, and concluded with the material assistance dossier. Helping with material assistance was very important.

The Rome, Milan, and Torino support committees were joined by the progressive unions to keep up the flow of aid to the Liberation Movements, and to keep up political pressure on their respective governments. The Milano stop was very exciting, as I saw my old friend from Dar, Giovani Arrighi, now a professor at the university, who had helped organize the speaking engagement in his hometown.

From here, I repeated the same appeal in Düsseldorf, München, Stuttgart, and Berlin. Support for the MPLA was very strong, as Europe understood the Western position of its own liberation movement. However, they could not find political footing in Europe. The *Angola Comite* was by far the best organized and politically powerful group due to the committed personnel of former university math professor Bosgra and his friends. Sophisticated, relentless, and great researchers, this focus group was a creative clearing house for all support committees. The letters that I carried from the prisoners were turned over to the *Comite* and delivered by Portuguese citizens working in Holland. These volunteers provided valuable input, photographs to the enemies of colonial wars and news of the humane treatment of prisoners. In return, the families provided photographs showing conditions of the Tugas and their equipment.

I went by train to the designated stations, and a large placard read "*Angola Comite,*" held by a waiting committee member. There were two full days at each stop. The organized schedule led to Switzerland, where a group dedicated to the support of students from South Africa had organized under the International University Exchange Fund—IUEF— banner. The director, Lars Ericsson, provided full scholarships to selected South African students, most from the ANC Youth Movement, a target for BOSS, South Africa's secret police. Dedicated members such as Canadian Tim Broadhead and Anna Paludan from Denmark, with excellent African experience, recognized real needs and delivered. Too many NGOs wanted their organization to be the face of every project. Instead of delivering what was needed, such as materials and training for Angolans to produce what they needed themselves, they seemed to want to make themselves the hero of every story.

Unfortunately, lack of security at their offices and in the vetting of staff made them very vulnerable to infiltration. South African Security,

BOSS, Bureau of State Security, trained by the SS, operated freely in Western Europe and had not overlooked this small IUEF NGO. Gregg Williams had been assigned to infiltrate, and carefully planned the theft of student files and turned them over to the Pretoria BOSS office. BOSS now had a list of ANC youth and started to arrest and detain. The weakest link had been security at an ANC support group in Europe.

Williams was the expert at sending book bombs to ANC leadership and their friends. Ruth First died from such a book bomb, and the Minister of Education, a Catholic priest, in a new Mozambique had his arms blown off by such a device. His attack was recorded by a film journalist. The horror of a man bleeding and trying to get up off the ground while the skin dangled from the stumps of his blown-off arms made good evening news footage. This is how a fascist state behaves. Williams appeared before the Truth and Reconciliation Commission, and before Bishop Tutu, and admitted calmly to the many terrorist acts that he had carried out for BOSS.

Denmark and France brought the continental portion of the tour to an end. However, my Paris hosts, filmmakers, and serious political *camarades*, showed a deep interest in the photos and the accompanying story. I had kept two reels of raw footage, and they were delighted to have them developed. Six minutes of raw footage, visual testimony to the building of a nation, energized my hosts, who could hardly contain their emotions. As we celebrated long into the night, they told me that serious film producers needed to see this. So we drove to a studio and witnessed again the shaking heads approving the content. There were immediate offers to make it happen with a call to Montreal. Over the phone, the description by my French friends to Rock Demers sorted out the production and editing costs. This was a dream come true, because, although I was determined to make it happen, I had no idea how to put a film together.

Individual strangers who wanted to help the MPLA opened their hearts and doors. A weekly blood drive was organized with an overnight delivery to the MPLA hospital in Brazzaville. Future collaborations to get a mobile hospital in the field were planned.

The London Committee operated out of a huge house, and dedicated members put on a full complement of events to support their programs and projects. I got through the requested appearances over two days, then it was time to go home. And so with my African stories, gifts, and raw movie footage, I headed to Montreal to meet Rock Demers, renowned film producer and promoter of progressive causes.

CHAPTER NINE

A rock pile ceases to be a rock pile the moment a single man contemplates it, bearingwithin him the image of a cathedral.

—Antoine de Saint Exupéry

After going through the re-entry procedures at Mirabel, I booked into room 23 at the Hotel Iroquois in Old Montreal. This was my favourite room in a third-class hotel that Oxfam used for out-of-town guests. Demers's office was also on St. Paul Street East. I called Colleen, and she was very happy at my safe return, but somehow her tone of voice betrayed other emotions. I promised that after the Demers meeting scheduled for the next day, we would reunite in Ottawa.

At 10:00, I walked to Demers's office, situated above a small movie studio. Up the stairs into a reception area where a Québécoise welcomed me in soft and clear French and ushered me into Rock's posh and luxurious surroundings. Ten minutes later, the bearded man, heavy-set and slightly balding, came in apologizing for the delay, which was a non-issue for me, for this get-together represented another important step. Rock heard me out while looking at the still photographs and, wanting to see the sample six minutes of film material, led me down to his studio.

We saw images of life in the semi-liberated regions: schools and textbooks, small medical facilities, agricultural projects, fishing the Zambezi, defense capabilities, all showing the building of a new society and the desperate need for goods and services.

"This looks like a very good project, so let me call Jean Pierre Lefèvre, a friend and filmmaker; he will have something to add," said Rock. One phone call from his office, and within two hours, Jean Pierre arrived at Hotel Iroquois to discuss the project. Rock Demers had opened the doors; as a highly respected producer and a good human being, he had given the MPLA a well-deserved break.

Jean Pierre arrived and we went to the café on the main floor to explore how this movie could be made. This was an important part of the revolutionary strategy, and there were no funds for the production.

He asked many, many questions about MPLA history, leadership, and details as to the objectives of this war.

Though very well read on current events, JP did not know about forced labour, illiteracy, and other statistics, so he accepted my description and analysis of the Angolan war. In his words: "*Je vais faire de mon possible pour assurer la réalization de ce documentaire.*"—"I will do my best to see that this documentary is made."

He asked for a second meeting in two weeks, which allowed me time to develop the other film cassettes and to see Colleen while JP planned our next step.

By late afternoon, still standing, I went back to St. Paul East and dropped into Oxfam Quebec, situated in a stone building dating back to the 1600s on the old Montreal harbour, to see Pierre Rivard.

I climbed the wide wooden staircase to the open-concept office, still showing the original wooden architecture, trusses, and fire-scorched beams. There in the right far corner, smoking away, was my friend Rivard.

In a loud voice that got everyone's attention, Rivard said, "*Ah ben ça parle au diable,*"—"speak of the devil"—as he came out through an opening in the glass wall, offering a warm handshake and embrace. "You made it back. Come and meet '*l'équipe*'—'the team,'" as he continued with introductions to Jean Foisy Marquis, media person, and Jean Pozatsky, public education. I gave them coffee boycott documentation picked up from the *Angola Comite* in Amsterdam. The education kit contained all the elements, statistics, war tax kickbacks, and large photographs showing numerous gross atrocities by the Tugas. The most effective one in the Dutch coffee boycott showed a severed head on a pile of coffee beans with the subtitle, "Coffee for you, blood for Angola." *"Pas possible,"* was the Rivard response, with Marquis saying, *"Écoeurant , dégoutant"*—"Heart- wrenching, disgusting."

They wanted to hear about the latest developments and get a reaction from two of his top members about the context and the feasibility of Angola as a project for Oxfam and its NGO partners. This lasted till 1800 hours, and the general attitude was excellent. An overall plan of action was needed to realize support for humanitarian assistance. Another offer was that from now on my room at the Iroquois Hotel would be paid by Oxfam. Rivard drove me to the bus station. Destination, Ottawa.

By 2130, I reached the Ottawa South home where Colleen's parents lived, and found my friend in a very depressed state.

Since her return from Zambia, Colleen had lived in the basement apartment of her parents' home in south Ottawa, unemployed and discouraged. Her parents welcomed me and were very happy to see me back. I asked her father to fill me in on the details of Colleen's mood. According to her father, Colleen's African experience had made her very happy. She discovered unprecedented self-esteem because the ANC work had opened her spirits to living a fulfilling life. He did not remember this happiness from his little girl's past. The shock of returning to her parents' house with no project had pushed my friend into lethargy; no smiles, lots of smoking. She had not contacted any of her old friends. Our discussions were morose and the delicate balance required that my enthusiasm for the upcoming film and other yet-to-be-defined projects be relegated to the background.

I needed to get Colleen back on her emotional feet, so this no-sex

reunion added more stress to a difficult time. Within two weeks, she perked up a bit, and we found an apartment in the Sandy Hill area; 510 Besserer was the top floor in a town house owned by an elderly couple. A quiet, centrally located apartment, close to a large park, it had a back porch with a huge willow tree overhanging the sitting area. Our April moving date coincided with Colleen's birthday. A new job reset the emotional clock of our fragile relationship. Colleen had bonded, but was deeply dependant on our relationship, an unexpected factor I needed to deal with while pushing the African projects as the two-track approach gained traction. My return to Montreal tested my work ethic and emotional balance.

I met with JP to review the full raw footage. He liked the context and focus of the film, adding that he knew just the person, probably the best 8mm producer in Quebec, Michel Audi from Trois Rivières. Michel had promised to work on the project, so it was time to meet my collaborator. I had the script in my brain, so the frames needed to have a story line, complemented with a bilingual track. I spoke to Michel and arranged to come to his home in seven days with a written outline of a story. He estimated a production time of three weeks.

I went to the Cote-des-Neiges offices of SUCO to speak with an old acquaintance, Jacques Jobin, who was not only sympathetic but gave me an opportunity through the magazine to write a French article about my experience with the MPLA. It was an economic analysis, a political assessment of the players with a forecast about the military situation. It also contained military photographs given by the Tugas prisoners in Zone

A. It was a clear indictment of NATO armament, trucks and planes and helicopters. Most of all, this April 1971 feature story, distributed throughout the NGO community in Quebec, set out the historical background of Angola as well as Canada's role, another project that told me a creative journey starts with a lot of soul searching and sleepless nights.

On the return bus trip to Ottawa and Colleen, I pondered the ongoing saga of our relationship.

The delicate nature of our relationship demanded extra tact and emotional savvy so that the project could fly; Colleen had to become an accomplice in the project. Her revolutionary spirit needed to be rekindled with the rebuilding of her self-esteem. Our new apartment allowed us to discuss and love our way to stability, to laughter. Her old friends started coming around. In particular, there was Janine, who knew how to speak with Colleen, a very good friend. Colleen was getting better.

Time for the production of *Angola Liberation and Development*, and the long, three-hour car ride to meet a generous stranger. Michel, age twenty-four, lived in a small house with his mother on the third plateau in Trois Rivières. They accepted my presence as a family member; it was a warm household. After the initial viewing and the rough outline, Michel wanted to talk about the reasons for the film, the target audience, and desired impact. Our first day had been a shock for him—the reality of Angola coming through in the pictures and footage without any background context or knowledge of African colonial history. Michel began to understand the type of documentary we needed: an educational tool for project support with a shocking revelation of the way the Portuguese, their racist friends, and the USA were prosecuting the war.

We worked very well together; his skills guided the visual message that emerged as I worked on the script. From 0800 to 2200 hours, a meal break at 1800 hours, Michel showed up to work, devoting his energies to the support of the unknown MPLA. On the eighth day, we had a connected visual message, without soundtrack, retracing the trip on foot to the description of leaders and the infrastructure of the MPLA. We agreed to take a five-day break, so I returned to Ottawa and to Colleen, who was feeling much better; the smile had returned to her angelic face.

Twenty-one consecutive days of work produced a forty-minute film with a French and English soundtrack. Michel was exhausted and grateful for the opportunity. I still feel my gratitude to a fellow Canadian, a generous and self-effacing human being. Michel Audi had added himself to the countless human beings exerting themselves as best they knew how to help correct the injustice of colonialism and instituted racism. Thank you, Michel.

George Best and the ARSC group of Ottawa arranged for the premier screening. My brother Claude, his wife Bev, and my parents came to Ottawa for the screening. I acknowledged their presence and their valuable and continued moral support. The guests applauded, and with the Q & A session, I was sensing that more people would volunteer to expand our pro-liberation activities.

I had realized the unimaginable. The visual had accomplished the objective set out so many months ago. Again, I realized: don't quit, and if you can't do, develop connections with those who can. Both Colleen and I needed a rest so besides the cottage, we had access to a very peaceful retreat at another place, owned by a First Nations friend, Harold Green. He was the owner of Green Lake, named for him, which offered quiet, water, and civilized camping. I spoke with Harold about my activities, and we compared notes from apartheid South Africa to the conditions he saw on Canadian reserves. On every possible occasion, I dropped in to visit with Harold at his lake west of Carleton Place. Harold was an accomplished musician, wood carver, canoe builder in wood and aluminum, and a full black belt in martial arts. This summer gave me a chance to build up my strength, as the next phase was to be a demanding one.

The next step was to take the film across Canada, so the month of June was devoted to phone calls and letters to universities offering, through the student councils, to speak for a fee to students and faculty. The University of Manitoba helped coordinate the Western tour out to BC, while Waterloo, McMaster, University of Toronto, and Western also responded. The end of August signalled the beginning of a cross-country tour in Winnipeg.

In late June, I had a regular medical check-up in Toronto with my friend Dr. Lenzler. He came into the room and his huge hands buried my fingers. "Mr. Roy," he said, "I know you have brought back great samples for my lab." I responded, "I hope not, but in a few days you will know." His presence allowed me to react with unguarded emotion as he asked questions on the ongoing conflict in Angola. He wanted to know if progress was being made against this fascism and racism unknown to the outside world. I told him of my latest trip and the documentary film and general positive interest in the NGO community for supporting the liberation struggle.

His encouragement was more relevant to my spirits than his medical analysis. There would be test results in three days. I called Rev. Legge at the United Church, and he responded with an invitation for the next day.

June 21, 1972, I met with Legge in his office at 1200 hours. When I arrived, Garth gave me a warm welcome and told me he had arranged for a fifteen-minute presentation to the United Church board executive meeting in this building. It was a simple presentation, a few statistics, as the Church knew about Portuguese repression through its missions, and why I was doing this. The last ten minutes was Q & A, always a good occasion for the timely questions and what can be done.

I delivered the message with passion, conviction, and seriousness, and there was warm applause and acknowledgement by the Chair. Dr. Legge had dared to expose the executive board to some clear choices for the Church's mission. We returned to his office and he said he was particularly pleased with the impact on the board.

He added, "Jacques, the Church has voted a $5,000 grant for your work. Congratulations."

This was a big surprise—an acknowledgement of the successful work to date, and a contingency fund for the future. Garth introduced *United Church Observer* editor Mr. Bob Plant. I showed him photographs from Angola and spoke of the need to identify the struggle as a serious threat to world peace, the next Vietnam. Bob jumped at this view; he needed the nuts and bolts. This was easy. I showed this semi-cynical man the role of coffee and oil and the Canadian connection: part of Angola's oil exports were refined at Point Tupper, in violation of UN sanctions. Imported coffee beans for General Foods products came from Angola.

Our message: cease and desist or face a national boycott.

We spoke at length to his favourite question, "What is your motivation?"

And, as usual, I gave him my background and pointed out the contradiction of democracy in America and America's imperial disregard of human rights, while elected national governments that the USA does not approve of are removed through the covert operations of the CIA. Then the USA installs, finances, and props up a dictator like the Congo's Mobutu. America has no respect for the Third World, while American citizens have an excellent standard of living and are willingly co-opted by their privileges. The greedy military machine wants to control the oil, diamonds, and economic development, while cheating the rightful owners of their nation's wealth and by extension keeping the mainly illiterate peasants in poverty. A fair wage on the plantation would require an immediate increase of 400 percent in the price of raw coffee beans in order for the Angolans to have a decent life. This won't happen unless the economic rules are changed to reflect national aspirations. Bob Plant respected the challenge that I had set out to conquer and said he would help when he could with editorials or stories.

The interview over, he wished me luck. He had a new attitude to

Angola, one of hope. He produced a press release that told the Angola story and described what needed to be done as a sign that we understood the needs. The United Church of Canada had taken a very strong position in accordance with the United Nations' wishes.

A return visit to Lenzler's office confirmed the worst. The liver scan showed a twenty-percent increase in size due to amoebic dysentery and other parasites, so a complete rest was required along with medication and a special "bland C" diet. This meant everything needed to be boiled, no fat, and *"lots of rest"*-Lenzler's emphasis. I returned to Ottawa and started to rest. When my energy level increased, I tackled the tasks of preparing for the lecture tour.

The costliest part of preparing for the upcoming tour was to transfer the Super 8 film to 35mm, about $2,000. And the most difficult part was to rest, getting healthy and keeping the home front happy.

August 26 signalled the first of many lectures in Western Canada at universities, churches, and service clubs. The Q&A was the best part, because the questioners showed the weaknesses in the presentation and provided a kind of measurement of willingness to contribute. Getting to

"What can we do?" was the sign of success. Interviews on local radio stations, for school and local papers, and a few minutes with students wanting information for a term paper, made up each busy day.

The student councils were good organizers and found suitable free lodging while arranging the extra meetings with progressive teachers, students, and graduate students. Winnipeg's two universities and St. Boniface were very receptive, making cash donations in support of the education appeal that I was conducting

As with every public forum, the quantity of information was overwhelming, and when I delivered a measured dose, the effect was somewhat confused. The Q & A sessions dissipated the confusion and led to the "What can we do?" conclusion. At the University of Regina, I met my old friend Professor Gerry Sperling, alias Americo Vespucci, at the political science department and, following the public lecture, spent an evening at his home meeting with a group of very progressive Canadians. Dr. Penman offered his medical material sourcing skills to the MPLA, including personnel, and promised to come to do an onsite evaluation at his own expense. His enthusiasm followed my schedule to Saskatoon where the Mahoods, professors and medical friends, put me up in their home. Generous and engaging, this very political family gave me an insight as to how the province of Saskatchewan could support material aid to MPLA.

In Regina, my old friend the Bogey man, a well-respected civil servant, was working on his career and still wished that his dad had given him a parking lot in Toronto instead of an LLB in Regina. We met briefly, and I thanked him for believing in me way back in 1967 in Montreal, and told him that despite all of the jumping through hoops and endless distractions, I had kept the faith. My friends had also kept theirs.

The Calgary and Edmonton committees organized tight day and evening schedules. Here the questions had a "Red-baiting" quality, not progressive but defensive, as if the information I was presenting somehow challenged their integrity. Credible information might be an insult to one's assumptions about world events; it was an uncomfortable truth that, as consumers of Gulf Oil and Maxwell House coffee, they were participating unwittingly in the colonial war. Defusing these potential confrontations required patience and skill, without glossing over the essence that anti- colonial wars needed to be supported, according to the United Nations Resolution A/7200/Add 3., 17 October 1968.

Explaining US foreign policy for Africa with a military parallel to the Vietnamization of the Indochina conflict attracted labels of "communist"; there was real difficulty distinguishing anti-colonial from communist. The fear associated with the communist label made the US policy more palatable, and so this most outrageous lie told to North Americans would be unchallenged, "consumed"; the lecture series opened the monologue of fact to permit political dialogue.

In Vancouver old friends came to the lectures at SFU and UBC. Most had completed their degree and were planning to enter postgraduate studies; Paul K. had applied to Foreign Affairs, and Larry was a high- school teacher. My good friend Linda H. had been promoted to professor in the English department, with a happy personal life. We talked for a few hours following one lecture and met again at a reunion for friends of Angola.

By November 30, it was time to return to Ottawa. Colleen had

regained her strength and let rip her wit, on cue, when an opportunity arose. Her new outlook made our shared life precious again.

A politically progressive group of persons in Ottawa were publishing a newsletter called the Southern Africa Information Group— SAIG—and through member Sue Godt, I met a young man whose personality and humour resembled my own. Sue's brother Evan was a very quick study and a good worker, and in a few weeks proved his willingness to help keep the research on Angola on track as well as overseeing the coffee boycott, which was still on the drawing board.

There were some good responses in the newspapers:

Winnipeg Free Press Nov 20—"Oil and Coffee from Slave Labour: Boycott?"

Vancouver Sun Dec 14—"Names Coffee Brands and Possible Boycott"

Winnipeg Free Press Dec 22—"Bay Pulls South African Articles from Store Shelves"

Prairie Dog Press Dec 29—"Facts, Promoted Support to MPLA; Exposing UN Sanctions Busting," and "Who Helped Portugal."

NGO groups from across Canada wrote for fact sheets and prints of the film. Eastern Canada, in particular Quebec, had to be mobilized, as the Western tour had demonstrated a lack of awareness, which could be overcome if the information were presented in an organized way. The lecture tour could be used as a springboard for a coffee boycott, a fundraiser, and the visit to Canada of Dr. Neto and his shadow cabinet. With continued planning and measured results, Canada, a friend of the MPLA, could host a counterattack on US policy, which continued to go unchallenged in the media. Inviting the future President of Angola to address the Canadian Parliament would counter the US policy of finding another Mobutu for Angola. Neto was an African leader who cherished true independence, and the neo-colonial states of Zaire, Kenya, and Zambia were not acceptable models.

We would speak straight to the public to unmask the media's complicity with US policy; if challenged, we would publish our information: the statistics, witness accounts, and Canadian voting record at the UN.

"Liberate to Build" poster.

Meanwhile, Rivard pulled together the Quebec NGOs, and following a long two days of meetings, an agreement was arrived at to begin the coffee boycott. Within seven days, a plan of action, media material, and budget would be presented by the Boycott Committee, a joint venture with the Ottawa-based NGOs. My responsibilities were to approach and negotiate with importers of Angolan coffee: General Foods, makers of Maxwell House, Nestlé's Canada, and Standard Brands from Montreal. Our big break in this came from the co-operation of John Penner, union representative at Standard Brands, who provided the visual proof of use of Angolan coffee. He produced the empty coffee bags used in the General Foods coffee line, clearly stencilled "Product of Angola."

With this inside information, I carried out a cold call on Group Vice-President J.F. O'Neil at the Standard Brands offices on Sherbrooke

Street West in Montreal. I conducted it like a sales call and I "sold my story" by using the United Church Press release, wrapped in short, passionate sentences of concern and open-ended questions. "Do you know of the Angola coffee boycott in Europe?" and "Are you aware that your product has a hidden war tax?" He was "genuinely concerned" at the facts I presented and the implication of being identified with the slave-like conditions on the Angola plantations, and further, with the funding of the colonial war. This was bad PR, very bad PR.

We agreed to meet again soon, to allow for the process of recognizing the Standard Brands purchases of Angolan coffee and the search for other sources. This meeting also set a standard of honesty as the only credible basis for negotiation to assure a face-saving resolution of our differences. As I got up to leave, we shook hands as we addressed the possible consequences of failure to negotiate an end to the purchase of Angola coffee.

Standard Brands tried to dump responsibility onto the broker who handled their purchasing and the Tea and Coffee Association, but with Penner on our side, they could not ignore our facts. Meanwhile, in Toronto, Oxfam Canada's Michael E. Ryan and Mike Flynn from the Catholic NGO Development and Peace were engaging General Foods President Robert Hurlbut and Nestlé's President McCarthy in a newspaper dialogue in order to flush out their position.

My old friend Garth Legge got into the fray, first with Rev. Van der Veen's saying that the Dutch Boycott had been broken, and with General Foods as to the legitimacy of a consumer driven-boycott. The implication was that the boycott would hurt the Africans we all want to help. Rivard chaired the meeting regarding the conclusions of my discussions with Standard Brands. Conclusion—we proceed with planning and publicizing the boycott.

Till January, while dialogue continued with the coffee companies, we were producing literature, posters—shocking posters—, documented conditions of forced labour, of military enforcement using strategic hamlets, the NATO military link, and the United Nations /Canadian positions.

The NGOs prepared regional committees throughout Quebec, organizing visits and film showings in Montreal, Sherbrooke, Quebec City, Abitibi, Rimouski, Joliette, and St. Hyacinthe.

May 10 was launch day in Montreal, with follow-up by established committees, documents, and film.

Following a week of good work, I returned to Ottawa for a holiday with the Trooper, who had overcome the downhill slide of depression. This Christmas was a great get-together with Colleen's family. The holidays were pressure-free.

Back to reality in the new year:

January 19, 1973, letter to General Foods President Hurlbut from Mike Ryan, Oxfam Ontario Director: "I hope that you will share our concern for the people of Angola, . . . [and you] will discontinue purchase of coffee from Angola."

February 6, *McGill Daily* reprints an article from *Vancouver Sun* submitted by McGill student Ms. Demanins: "It is a situation which should be publicized in the *Daily*, since other papers are not going to do it." The daughter of a Montreal judge, Demanins had a highly developed sense of justice.

February 7, letter from Holland's *Angola Comite* stating that 1973 Dutch coffee imports dropped from thirty percent to 5.7 percent, with a three percent drop in all products of the (giant) food chain Alert Heijn.

February 15, Nestlé's response from President McCarthy: "Our purchases are made through dealers . . . depending on price and quality, we occasionally use small quantities in some of our brands . . . [this boycott is] injecting into trade a political element which it is very desirable to avoid.

"[W]e are not fully familiarized with the sociological and political circumstances of Angola, we understand that conditions have been improving over the last decade . . . suggestions that our company supports the general mistreatment of the people the peoples of any country is completely false. . . . Let us make it very clear that we do share your concerns for the mistreatment of any peoples for political ends."

February 19, 1973—Standard Brands V.P. J.F. O'Neil: "The use of Angolan coffee is not at all restricted to the three companies which you suggested in your letter, nor is it in any way confined to use as a filler in production of instant coffees. Rather, the situation which you challenge is industry-wide in scope and in fairness to all concerned would be more effectively dealt with by the Tea and Coffee Association of Canada."

On the political front, Canada's senior Trade Commissioner in Johannesburg, Roger Parlour, ". . . has announced that the Canadian Government has appointed Michael Chapman as Honourary Commercial Representative in Luanda. Mr. Parlor spoke highly of the potential trade between Angola and Canada, and pointed out that Canada is currently importing $35 million in oil and coffee with an export to Angola of 1 million dollars." Report from *Portuguese Africa* Feb 23, 1973.

February 28—Letter from Tea and Coffee Association, signed by McCarthy of Nestlé, to Reverend Garth Legge: "Angola robusta beans are in demand because of their quality and the dependability of supply. Reduction in Canada's purchases of coffee beans probably [would] adversely affect the whole Angolan economy to the detriment of the people of that country."

September 1973—A.H. reintroduced Angola beans. After intense public and political pressure—50 percent recorded as opposed to Angola imports—on October 12, Alert Heijn renounces its imports of Angola coffee. Switzerland, home of Nestlé, has a boycott committee, as does Great Britain.

The Ontario boycott promotion would be carried out under the Southern Africa Information Group—SAIG—label, as the material support had to be a separate entity from the social assistance provided by ARSC.

There followed more public speaking engagements with an increased emphasis on: ". . . actions that are pending due to failure to get a written accord from coffee merchandisers; the national coffee boycott is ready to go."

At the University of Windsor, a panel discussion made up of Joe Carlson, a white lawyer expelled from South Africa, U of T economics Professor Robert Mathews, and myself. We are in agreement: The future of all of Southern Africa is at stake.

As chief negotiator with the coffee companies, my articulation of this final position: "If these negotiations are unsuccessful, a boycott will be called for" was reported by the *Windsor Star*, which covered the public meeting.

The *Montreal Star* reported the beginning of the boycott in its Feb 22 edition.

Theme of the boycott: Coffee for Canada, Blood for Angola.

We had documents from the UN, the federal government, and Canadian churches, and support from the YM-YWCA, Portuguese Democratic Associations of Montreal and Toronto, and trade unions and workers in the S&B plant in LaSalle.

The Quebec information campaign from SUCO, Development and Peace, Rallie, and Oxfam had ten regional committees ready with write-in campaigns, public education in schools and churches, media supporting the boycott, and the material aid required to help the MPLA expand its objectives—independence for Angola.

Coffee boycott poster

The poster showed seven Portuguese generals and the president of Portugal saying, in speech balloons:

Angolan forced to work on plantation.

It's normal, each thing in its place.

Angola is our colony.

Angolans pick the coffee.

Our soldiers maintain order.

 NATO supplies the arms.

The companies make their profit and America has its coffee.

Have your coffee, don't worry about the rest.

Headlines about the education campaign and speaking engagements in Sherbrooke: "Poverty in Southern Africa, Wealth in the West" 19th March '73—*Sherbrooke Tribune*.

In Quebec City, the Université de Laval public forum produced a headline: "*Qu'est-ce qu'il a donc ce café qui nous vient de l'Angola?*" "What is it about this coffee from Angola?"

Le Soleil of March 21 was caught off-guard regarding the conditions on coffee plantations, the connections with Canadian consumers, the war of repression, and government links through NATO.

The article was supported by other sources such as *Monde Diplomatic* in August of 1972: "The Government of Lisbon has flung open its doors of foreign capital investment to 'favour the good use' of the overseas territories to the maintenance of the status quo." There was an economic analysis showing foreign ownership of oil, diamonds, and coffee.

In conclusion, *le Soleil* said, "No one can say, but the process of liberation is well underway, and probably irreversible."

In Saskatoon, the local SAIG reported a one-thousand-dollar donation from the Presbyterian Church, while the Anglican Magazine, *Anglican Churchman*, produced a full two-page spread on the Mozambique massacres. The *Catholic Register* published an interview on the coffee campaign. The day after this article appeared, a Portuguese delegation visited Development and Peace Group (an NGO run by the Catholic Church) in Toronto and asked them to retract their support for the boycott.

Later, a letter came to Mike Flynn from no less than the president of General Foods, trying to persuade the Catholics not to get involved. From Drummondville, the headline in *La Parole* of April 25 was: "*Angola, Terre de feu et de sang*"—"Angola Land of Fire and Blood." It attacked with: "*Colonie, ce mot fait encore peur mais il occupe une realité intransigeante confort soporique que le monde occidental connait depuis . . . la dictature. Débarrasser pour Hitler, . . . Duplessis . . . Le Portugal joue en fait le rôle de bootlegger.*"—"Colony, this word still scares, though it occupies a stubborn reality, the soporific comfort the West has known since getting rid of the dictatorships of Hitler . . . Duplessis . . . Portugal plays the role of bootlegger."

Rev. Murray McInnis conducted a public campaign against Gulf Canada by attending annual shareholders' meetings and raising awareness of the war tax dollars from oil exports. *Vancouver Sun* May 10, 1973—The

B.C. Conference of Canada ". . . asked its delegates to boycott coffee and petroleum products from Portugal's colonies. Tom Brown, formerly an agriculturalist in Angola, told the meeting Gulf Oil is a mainstay of the economy of the Portuguese regime and provides fuel for its army which subjugates the native Angolans."

Evan, meanwhile, continued to monitor Canadian imports of Angolan beans, and our tentative boycott message is reflected in a net drop. Speaking engagements continued and my high profile attracted RCMP surveillance from the lot where I parked my vehicle across the street from 510 Besserer. Always courteous, I greeted them every morning, and finally one day at lunchtime a knock at the apartment door announced visitors, two huge men, who identified themselves as RCMP and asked to speak to me. Without hesitation, I invited them in. They followed me to the kitchen where we sat and discussed my passionate promotion of support for the freedom fighters in Southern Africa.

The twenty-minute Q and A answered all their questions, but they remained suspicious of my personal motivations. I made it clear that our efforts to help the poor people in Africa—get the shovel— were motivated by Christian love of our fellows; the churches, the Canadian government, and the United Nations were sanctioning this noble gesture. They left and returned to write up the interview in their car, which was parked illegally in a private lot across the way from 510 Besserer.

More discussions with the likes of Clyde Sanger, Ottawa correspondent for *The Guardian* and member of the South African Information Group, Dr. John O'Manique, and Father McDougall of

St. Pat's polarized my thoughts about the legality of our actions, which were being interpreted by the RCMP as subversive and dangerous. Educating the RCMP was not a priority, but protecting myself from possible assault by white supremacists or by riot police during anti-Vietnam war protests restricted my actions.

Conservative MP Claude Wagner asked questions in Parliament as to the Canadian position on Angola. External Affairs Minister Mitchell Sharp's answer reflected positive support for the United Nations' demands for the immediate granting of independence to Angola.

A fair and just comment, but the infiltration of the SAIG by an RCMP officer suggested other ideas. On many occasions, the topic of weapons, guns for the freedom fighters, was brought up by this gung-ho individual who was passing himself off as a student, and always available for office duty.

My position was very clear at all times. Public opinion will win this war, as no politician would dare express support for colonialism or racism in South Africa. Our rhetoric was strong in support of armed struggle and in efforts to undermine economic and political support for the Tugas presence in Africa; NATO arms paid for with Canadian tax dollars.

The politicization of public opinion in response to our projects escalated defiance, CEOs were clearly identified with lies, distortions, and the last resort: everybody else is doing it. Picture the president of Gulf Oil, sitting at a United Church executive meeting and witnessing his religious partners learning that his oil imports are paying for the killing of Africans in the name of money. This must have been very uncomfortable and even more humiliating when the Church voted to support the education program of the ARSC.

As Vietnam continued to invade the television news, there was a "piling on" effect, as viewers connected the images of another liberation conflict. In-depth analysis would reveal long-range plans for a liberation war that would create one or two more Vietnams, which could destroy the military machine that gave six percent of the world population sixty-six percent of the wealth.

On May 10, the four Quebec NGOs held a press conference, and the education of Quebec citizens was underway. These dedicated men and women, on behalf of their respective organizations, clearly indicated that this campaign was not about underdevelopment, but about centuries of exploitation.

Le Devoir of May 11—"Efforts to support the Third World were neutralized by the purchase for example of Angolan coffee. International co-operation must pass through an objective analysis and the struggle against exploitation and injustice. It starts here."

Headline in the *Montreal Star* of May 10—"Canada Accused of Aiding Portugal in African Colony." The movie showed what the Angolans were doing while the four NGOs pointed to the Canadian government's failure to implement the UN resolutions. They mentioned the coffee brands by name, a tactic that had been successful in Holland, and then pointed to the use of mercenaries in Angola. Along with the documentation of conditions in Angola, we were delivering the message that we intended to match our deeds with the United Nations' requests.

In Ottawa, Rev. Jack Birch, Pastor of St. James United Church in the Glebe, ". . . made it plain that the money (raised) was meant for relief goods and not guns. Colonialism is out, Canadians need to drop their reserve about helping rebels."—*Ottawa Journal*, May 28, 1973.

During the quiet summer months, I continued to monitor and encourage the National Campaign supporters, knowing that the lull would test their resolve. The September renewal would be a strategic point in the final push to shut down the import of Angolan coffee.

On October 8, *Newsweek* carried an interview with Reverend Berenger and a photograph showing the decapitating of an African being held by two soldiers while a third wields a machete.

A grizzly photograph from a coffee plantation in Angola

The Reverend spoke of the African My Lai: "By their account, soldiers destroyed a village called Wiriyamu in late 1972 and murdered and mutilated some 400 black farmers."—*Newsweek*, July 30. "The missionaries have gone to a higher court. 'We want the Pope to know the truth of what is happening in Mozambique,' says Father Berenger, 'and to announce the truth publicly.' The Organization of African Unity will studythe Vatican's Concordat with Portugal, with a view to demanding that the Organization of African Unity—OAU— and its 41 member states break off relations with the Vatican unless the Pope denounces the Lisbon government publicly. That course of action has already been urged by

Canon Burgess Carr, the Harvard trained Liberian who speaks for some

50 million non-Catholics, the All African Conference of Churches. 'Catholics . . . being regarded here as the Dutch Reformed Church is in South Africa,' said the black Episcopal priest."

On October 14, I decided to test the last phase of the boycott with a run-through at the local GEM plaza on Merivale Road in Ottawa. From the trunk of my car, I used a small Coleman stove to boil water and make non-Angolan coffee. Shoppers stopped and accepted a free coffee and the information handout. Campaigning in public was relatively safe in Ottawa, but in Toronto it was a different matter.

Our message was received courteously and wishes of good luck were extended. *The Ottawa Journal*, October 15, 1973.

More headlines:

"We Kill for the Coffee"—*Progrès /Echo*, Rimouski, Dec 12, 1973 "Portugal Kills—Canada Buys"—*Poundmaker*, University of

Alberta, Sept 1-16

"National Boycott Starts on Products from Angola"—McMaster

Silhouette, Sept 12, 1973

CBC Radio's *This Country in the Morning* with Peter Gzowski also did a feature.

This nationwide push to educate Canadians on the politics of colonialism via a consumer goods boycott spawned other groups, which took on South African wines, oranges, the banning of athletes from international competition, and discussions on how to further isolate, through the British Commonwealth, the "leper" from South Africa.

During a visit to the CUSO offices in Ottawa, a young man named Jean Pelletier approached me and wanted to discuss the scope of my work for the MPLA. As second in command of the French CUSO, called SUCO, Jean wanted to know how his organization was helping and why it seemed so far ahead of his understanding on the issues.

He had read the education manifesto explaining the coffee boycott and shared reflections both personal and political with his father, Gerard Pelletier, a cabinet minister in Prime Minister Trudeau's government, and gave full approval of our tactics. It was only a thirty-minute discussion, but this encounter, sanctioning approval, led to another meeting to put a program on paper designed to address the needs of the liberation movement.

This second face-to-face produced the title of Coordinator for

Projects in Southern Africa, with a sizable budget to push the agenda, a salary, and a secretariat. My right-hand man, Evan, was to be my eyes and political feeler into office politics, a definite weakness of mine.

Two other conditions of employment were my exclusion from meetings with senior SUCO reps and a separate project fund for civilian assistance to the liberated regions. This accord was signed in Ottawa on November 16, 1973.

I was very happy with this agreement, as my dedication had been recognized, evaluated, and rewarded. This meant that the political labels of terrorist and subversive would not stick, and that my movements would not be monitored. The cabinet connection would help gauge the political limits; but the real test was the Canadian government's response to an invitation for Dr. Neto and his shadow cabinet to come to Canada and expose Canadians to the facts of life in minority-controlled Southern Africa.[4]

---

4   From Commons Debate page 1719: Claude Wagner: "Does the minister intend to welcome in person and officially Dr. Neto, president of the Popular Movement for the Liberation of Angola, who apparently will be in our country in the next few hours?" M. Sharp, Sec of State for External Affairs: "No, Mr. Speaker." Mr Wagner: "Mr. Speaker, I have a supplementary question. As the minister refuses to meet Dr. Neto, could he not initiate a movement centred essentially among nations of the same size as Canada, to alert NATO or other organizations so that justice can be done to the inhabitants of the territories concerned?" Mr. Sharp: "Mr. Neto will be received by officials of my department . . ."

The coffee boycott was having the desired effect of putting a face to the beneficiaries of slave labour on the coffee plantations and their attempts to minimize their role. Sales of Maxwell House and other tainted brands were down, as coffee imports decreased. The Church network in particular had the moral clout and the will to apply it. One reaction was a letter from General Foods President Hurlbut on November 21 to the director of the Catholic Organization for Peace and Development, Mike Flynn, which challenged our facts. It presented arguments by an Ottawa professor, Dr. Jost, *". . . an extremely sharp contrast"* between the Angola portrayed in some published reports and the one he had observed in person.

The clincher in this letter was, "In the case of General Foods, it is almost a year since we purchased, simply because they are in such demand as to command a substantially higher-than-normal price."

The paternalistic attitude from Hurlbut continued when he wrote, "While I would deny no one the right of dissent, I seriously question the impact a coffee boycott would have in righting the injustices of the world. Such a boycott was undertaken in Holland in 1971 and abandoned in the realization that only a worldwide embargo—if such were possible—would have an economic impact." This was simply untrue; the Dutch had stopped, and the world boycott was an ongoing effort. In conclusion Hurlbut said, "Without in any way taking sides regarding the political situation in Angola, we would like to cite certain factors which illustrate the complexity of the situation and how difficult it is to evaluate from a Canadian standpoint."

Here was what we knew as fact:

As of December 31, 1972, *Novaport* reported: "Due to a lack of buyers, the coffee warehouses are getting fuller all the time . . . increasing to a possible 11.5 million sacks of coffee by the end of the harvest of 1972–73 . . . an equivalent to a full year's production."

From the *Provincia* of Angola of January 4, 1973: ". . . by selling 15,000 tons to an importer in the USA . . . negotiated with various Angolan exporters and the Coffee Institute authorized the sale at below the minimum FOB price normally for export."

In early December, the reduction in imports of coffee from Angola, as reported by Statistics Canada, gave our pressure groups the moral high ground, and the boycott was terminated with a proviso that if the imports were to return to a number greater than the latest figure, we would reinstitute the boycott as had been done in Holland.

Rivard and the NGO partners in Montreal could smell the next step. Rivard said, *"Imagine que Neto et sa gang venir au Canada pour expliquer le MPLA, c'est l'enfer."* "Can you imagine bringing Dr. Neto and 'his gang' to Canada, it would be blowout."

Rivard and I spent the next few days at his century home in Lacolle, southeast of Montreal. We really appreciated each other, and our thoughts and views on Southern Africa enabled us to work as partners.

We concluded our mid-December get-together with a pledge that I would do everything within my power to have the MPLA leadership come to Canada in 1974.

In August of 1973, Dr. Neto had suggested, via a telegram, that my return trip to Dar be put off till the New Year. So as part of the next strategy, a January second departure date for Dar was fixed.

Christmas with Colleen, this time with my family in North Bay, was a good holiday. Colleen and I continued to struggle with our personal lives, better at some times than at others, and spent New Year's Eve and Day at the 510 Besserer apartment.

New Year's night we sat and watched *Front Page Challenge*. I had appeared and had stumped the panel in a previously recorded session. This marked another giant step in the evolution of our vision; without compromise, it was becoming acceptable in the mainstream media. Panellist Gordon Sinclair had been to Angola during the 1930s; this in itself was a news story. We spoke off-camera of his observations. He had seen the horrible treatment of Angolans. Portuguese settlers were king, and all others were slave or the equivalent; not independent, not free.

Another year had passed, and the African Relief Services Committee issued a project summary for the year ending December 31, 1973.

Seeds and tools for UNTA	$ 20,000.
Hand tools from Ottawa, Glebe Church	$ 4,000.
UNTA agricultural fund	$ 10,000.
Blanket drive, London, Ontario	$ 1,900.
Portable homes, British Columbia, 3,000 units	$ 6,500.
Medical drugs	$ 14,000.
Quebec City project	$ 7,000.
Complete 16mm film studio, accessories	$ 20,000.

The political front of our efforts could be summed up as follows: As the heads of Commonwealth governments met in August of 1973, Prime Minister Trudeau joined with the other leaders ". . . to recognize officially the legitimacy of the African Liberation Movements. The leaders committed themselves to provide the United Nations- sanctioned movements with all the 'humanitarian aid' they need in their struggle for self determination."

So on January 2, I caressed my friend Colleen and said another goodbye. This time she had the assurance that my travels were not in war zones. My stops were London, Geneva, and finally Dar to meet with President Neto.

CHAPTER TEN

The ability to deliver the best services, skills, information, technical know-how, andpersonnel in the most difficult of circumstances . . .

The London stopover was to meet with the coffee boycott committee and further encourage them to broaden the scope of their support and use the new structure to gather material support for the civilian population. A small core of dedicated Brits carried out the coffee campaign and provided personnel support to the liberation movements. They were doers.

In Paris, the medical team was still at work collecting and sending blood to Brazzaville via the overnight plane. I told them of the Canadian search we had undertaken to find a surgeon for the MPLA hospital in Cabinda. French food and wine along with great political friends made the long hours of the coffee boycott and speaking engagements recede into the distance. In Geneva, the IUEF had suffered a serious setback, as one of their trusted employees had turned out to be a South Africa agent with the BOSS, and he disappeared along with the documents outlining how to recruit young South Africans and detailing the relationship with the ANC. This seriously damaged trust of this group among the movements and put the lives of ANC cadres into mortal danger.

The return to Dar and the MPLA turned out to be very pleasant. I found my old friends Petroff, Loy, Mrs. Boavida, and Dr. Neto, who wanted to know how the work in Canada was advancing, the strategy, public response to the boycott, and Canadian government's view of the public's reaction to the boycotts.

It was all good news, as the coffee boycott has been declared a success, and a politically educated national organization was in place. I had also brought a copy of the film *Angola Liberation and Development,* with bothFrench and English sound tracks.

Neto immediately summoned Loy to prepare an evening to show the film to the MPLA *Camarades* and friends of the MPLA. This was a historical get-together of longtime friends in the same struggle, from different backgrounds and races, but never confusing the enemy—imperialism.

The heat combined with fatigue put quite a strain on my health during the first seven days following my arrival. I slept fourteen-hour days, and sometime around day eight the veil of fog covering my brain lifted and normal thought processes returned.

Showtime was at the MPLA compound near the Dar harbour. The French version was used, as it closely resembled the Portuguese spoken by the MPLA. The comrades really enjoyed the film, even though it was particularly hard on Mrs. Boavida, as the footage showed the last days of her husband's life. Dr. Neto gave the thumbs up as he expressed on behalf of the MPLA a job well done on telling the MPLA story. The colours of the jungle, the Angolan faces full of hope, the new life in the liberated areas with sewing machines and plantations—in fact a functioning village—were all effective images.

I spent some time with Kabuloo, who had just returned from a training course in Algeria. We had a full Chinese meal and discussed the overall strategy of the MPLA as well as the role of international support groups such as the African Relief Services Committee.

Over the next few weeks, Dr. Neto arranged meetings for the sole purpose of exchanging information and the experiences of the past two years. In particular was the increase in NATO weapons, American strategy, South Africa and Portugal's military pact, and the presence of South African officers in Angola to carry out upgrades of Portuguese soldiers. Southern Africa seemed at a standstill, and now the guerrilla warfare needed to be brought into the larger cities. Greater military risks for the MPLA, ANC, and SWAPO were necessary to tie down more troops and raise enemy death tolls, accompanied by an international political campaign to expose the dog and pony show of the Portuguese military; that is, that without the continued support of Europe, Canada, the USA, Brazil, and the long list of benefactors of this colonial war, Angola, Mozambique, and Guinea Bissau would be independent nations.

Instead, young men from Portugal and South Africa were risking their lives under obligatory military service and killing innocent civilians and guerrillas. For what? To defend outdated racist minority regimes? To benefit multinational companies in their quest for the dollar, rand, or escudo? To add to the confusion of apartheid with its multilevel definitions of a colour-driven society?

And these men, filled with so much propaganda and hatred, continued to live in this quagmire of racist intellectual stupidity. Why, and at what price?

The only way out of this endless war was through a negotiated peace, elections, and government based on majority rule.

Imagine getting Mandela with the apartheid leaders, Botha, de Klerk, Milan, to study the necessary step leading to majority rule? There was no other possibility if one wanted to avoid the incalculable dimensions of a nationwide bloodbath.

I loved Dr. Neto's approach. His calm insights had been worked out in the many hard years in jail. He was the leader capable of dealing with the most powerful. One could understand very well that negotiations with Neto, Cabral, or Machel required an intellectual strength that the Portuguese could not muster. Portugal was Europe's most backward country. What a house of cards.

America could negotiate but did not want to come out in the open. They preferred backroom manoeuvres, but in all negotiations it is the face-to-face process that counts, and the Portuguese for all the coffee in Angola—throw in all the grapes in Portugal—could not negotiate or be trusted to negotiate the independence of Portugal's "Overseas Provinces." For the Americans, the political-military structure represented the definition of imperialism. They were the Imperialists:

the colony, Portugal, having colonies of its own, Angola, Mozambique, and Guinea Bissau. With the US getting its ass kicked in Southeast Asia and now facing five potential wars of national liberation in Africa, finding surrogates like

Savimbi and Holden Roberto was all the more urgent.

Enter Kissinger and the multinationals with better definitions for nationals: "gooks" in Vietnam, now maybe baby-eaters, terrorists, and the new one who must be a communist who wants to play dominoes.

It was accepted wisdom among the liberation movements that a concerted worldwide education program was necessary to identify the real war machine and economic exploiters, the Americans, the empire-holders, known as imperialists.

What concerned Dr. Neto in the short term was the ideology pushed by certain members in Nyerere's cabinet and in particular the university student body. This was an ideology of racism—black racism. It was a dead end for the liberation movements and a dangerous precedent, in that only the Americans and South Africans would benefit, while the movements would suffer its consequences. I remember this discussion with Neto very well. He agreed to take on this ideological question on behalf of Nyerere, who was being bullied by this new ideology.

On February 7, 1974, Dr. Neto, president of the MPLA, presented a lecture at the University of Dar es Salaam entitled, "Who is the enemy . . . What is our objective?"

Dr. Neto had wanted to address this issue for a long time, as in the open attack on white liberation movements' freedom, fighters such as Turok from the ANC, FRELIMO, and the MPLA had placed undue pressure and falsehood on the fight that needed to be fought. Dr. Neto was capable and showed his political savvy by offering to take on this issue: To deliver a knockout punch to the racists and those who spread confusion, weakening the common front. Here is a précis of the original text:

Who is the enemy . . . What is our objective?

It is with the greatest pleasure that I am speaking before this university [students and lecturers], who show a desire for a profound understanding of our continent and of the different factors affecting its development.

I should like briefly to outline the fruit of my personal experience, the fruit of reflection on the national liberation struggle on our continent. This experience is simply an expression of a need experienced in Africa over the past five centuries, the need for each and every one of us to feel free.

It is also a broader expression of the common desire of men in this world to regard themselves as free, as capable of releasing themselves from the shackles of a society in which they weaken and die as human beings.

In my opinion, the national liberation struggle in Africa cannot be dissociated from the present context in which it is taking place; it cannot be isolated from the world. The imposition of fascism on the Chilean people or an atomic explosion in the Pacific are all phenomena of this same life that we are living and in which we are seeking ways to a happy existence for man in this world. This universal fact is however rendered particular in Africa through current political, economic, and cultural concepts.

The historical bonds between our peoples and other peoples in the world are becoming ever closer, since there can be no other trend on earth. Isolation is impossible and is contrary to the idea of technical, cultural and political progress. The problem facing us Africans now is how to transform unjust relations with other countries and people in the world.

In Africa we are making every effort to put a final end to paleocolonialism, which barely exists today in the territories dominated by Portugal, contrary to the general belief, since they are in fact dominated by a vast imperialist partnership which is unjustly protecting the selfish interests of men, economic organizations, and groups of countries. The so-called white minority racist regimes are merely a consequence and a special form of paleocolonialism in which links with the metropole have become slack and less distinct in favour of a white minority dictatorship.

This visible, clear, and open form of colonialism does not prevent the existence on our continent of another more subtle form of domination which goes by the name of neo- colonialism, in which he who exploits is no longer identified by the name colonizer, but acts in the same way at various levels.

However, internal forms of subjugation caused by fragmentation into small ethnic or linguistic groupings, by the development of privileged classes endowed with their own dynamism, are also forms of oppression linked with the visible forms known as colonialism, old or new, and racism. They easily ally themselves with imperialism and facilitate its penetration and influence.

Colonial and racist domination and oppression are exercised in different ways and at different levels. They do not take place in a uniform way on our continent, they do not always use the same agents, and they do not act on the same social stratum or on the same type of political or economic organization.

For this reason, everyone, whether colonizer or colonized, feels it in a different way. This phenomenon, in this day and age, is anachronistic, and it is desirable to replace it with other ways of relating, and we Africans are not yet very clear or very much in agreement on these new kinds of relations. . . .

Action against colonialism is closely linked with and part of something else of an apparently internal nature but which is in fact as universal as the first, which is the need for social transformations, so that man may be truly free in every country and every continent.

The national liberation struggle in our era is therefore influenced not only by the historical factors determining colonialism, neo-colonialism, or racist regimes, but also by its own prospect, its objectives, and on the way each person sees the world and life.

This is why the importance of the national liberation movements is *much greater than is generally admitted* [J. Roy's emphasis], because through their activity they are transforming themselves into accelerators of history, of the development of the society within which they are acting and also outside it, imparting fresh dynamism to social processes to transcend the present stage, even in politically independent countries.

The different types of colonization in Africa have endowed us Africans with different ways of seeing the problem of Liberation, and it is natural that it should be thus, since our consciousness cannot draw upon material to form our possibilities of knowing the world. Sometimes we differ in our concepts and hence in the practical implementation of combat programs, and the line taken in action for liberation does not always fulfill the twofold need to concentrate both on transforming the relations between peoples and intrinsically transforming the life of the nation.

Hence the need to see the problem clearly and to provide answers to the following specific questions:

- Who is the enemy and what is the enemy?

- What is our objective?

It is obvious that the answers to these questions do not depend simply on the desire to be free. They also depend on knowledge and on a concept of the world and lived experience.

This means that they cannot be dissociated from acquired political ideas, from ideological positions which generally result from the origins of each and every one of us.

I should nevertheless like to clarify the ideas I have just put forward and shall put forward later, basing myself on my own experience.

Angola is a vast country which today has a very low population density and which has been colonized by the Portuguese since 1482. This is the generally accepted idea. However, as far as colonization is concerned, Portugal did not succeed in dominating all of our territory on its first contact. It took centuries before it was able to impose its political and economic rule over the whole people.

And I wish again to emphasize that neither is it true that Angola is dominated only by Portugal. The world is sufficiently enlightened on this point to know that the political and economic interests of several world powers are involved in Angola; Portugal's administration has not prevented the presence of its partners, a presence which has been there for centuries. [Note: Portugal and Britain have a history of co-operation of 900 years. This was a highly celebrated occasion. JR]

For example, Great Britain, the country with the largest volume of capital investments in Angola, and the United States of America, with growing economic interests and longing to control our country's strategic position as well as other countries of Europe, America, and Asia, are competing for the domination of our people and the exploitation of the wealth that belongs to us.

To think that Angola, Mozambique, Guinea, and other colonies are dominated by small and backward Portugal today is to be as mistaken as to think that French society is now in the feudal era, for example.

Small and backward Portugal is not the chief factor of colonization. Without the capital of other countries, without growing investments and technical cooperation and without the complicity at various levels, radical transformation would already have taken place many years ago.

Therefore, if we can say that Portugal is the manager of politico-economic deals, we will see that it is not our principal enemy but merely our direct enemy. At the time, it is the weakest link in the whole chain established for the domination of the peoples. If we look at Portugal itself, at the internal picture it presents: a society which is still striving to transcend an obsolete form of oligarchic government, incapable of abandoning the use of violence against its people for the benefit of just a few families with a peasant class struggling in the most dire poverty in Europe, and where every citizen feels himself a prisoner in his own country. The Portuguese themselves are right when they say that their country is today one of the greatest disgraces of Europe and the world.

We can now give an answer to the question: Who is the enemy and what is his nature?

The enemy of Africa is often confused with the white man. Skin colour is still a factor used by many to determine the enemy. There are historical and social reasons and lived facts which consolidate this idea on our continent.

It is absolutely understandable that a worker in the South African mines who is segregated and coerced and whose last drop of sweat is wrung from him should feel that the white man he sees before him, for whom he produces wealth, is the principal enemy. It is for him that he builds cities and well-paved roads, maintains hygienic and salubrious conditions which he himself does not have. . . .

All the more so in that the society created by the colonialists, to come back to Angola, created various racial defence mechanisms which were made to serve colonialism. The same poor wretched and oppressed peasant who is exploited in his own country is the object of special attention when he establishes himself in one of "its" colonies. He is not only imbued with a lot of jingoism, but he also starts to enjoy economic privileges which he could never have before; thus he becomes a part of the system. He starts to get a taste for colonialism and becomes a watchdog of the interests of the fascist oligarchy.

We can therefore say today that the phenomenon of colonial or neo-colonial oppression in our continent cannot be seen in terms of the colour of individuals.

An ideological understanding of this problem also makes it easier to solve it, once the objectives of the liberation struggle are defined.

In special conditions there are cases where the racial problem is overcome. This is what happens in war.

There are conscious Portuguese who desert to join the nationalist ranks in one way or another.

Our experience of clandestine struggle showed that there can be such a racial cooperation in the struggle against the system. The Angolan experience has already shown that pure anti-racism cannot permit the full development of the liberation struggle. For centuries, our society has had to establish roots, to multiply and to live for generations on our territory. This white population dominates the urban centres, giving rise to the fact of people who are racially mixed, making our society interlinked in its racial component.

Everyone in a country who wants to participate in whatever way in the liberation struggle should be able to do so. The preoccupation in Africa of making the liberation struggle of blacks against whites is not only superficial, but we can say that it is reactionary and that this view has no future at the very time when we see more contact between blacks and whites on the continent in the era of African history.

The expanded relations with socialist countries which are against colonialism (in its old form) . . . have brought to Africa a noteworthy number of Europeans, Americans [read North Americans; JR], and Asians more than there have ever been in any era of African history.

Therefore, to pose the problem as one of black against white is to *falsify* the question and *deflect* us from our objective.

What do we want?

An independent life as a nation, a life in which economic relations are just—both between countries and within the country, a revival of cultural values which are still valid.

The idea of Pan-Africanism, the concept of negritude started at a certain point to falsify the black problem. I cannot fail to express my full political identification with the struggle of the black peoples of America where they are, and to admire the vitality of descendents of Africa who today are still oppressed and segregated in American society, especially in the United States. . . .

The social advancement of the black American has been noteworthy, to the extent that today the black American distinguishes himself in Africa not only by his comportment but also by his intellectual and technical level.

Only rarely do the physical characteristics of black Americans allow any doubt as to their country of origin. Thus, the phenomenon of miscegenation has produced a new kind of man.

There is therefore no physical identity and there are

strong cultural differences, as there could not fail to be.

Therefore, without confusing origins with political compartments, America is America and Africa is Africa.

America has its own life, just as Angola and Mozambique have their own life. Although we have to identify with each other as black men in defending our values, I cannot conceal my sometimes ill-founded concern at the way some of our brothers from the other side of the Atlantic have a messianic desire to find Moses for a return to Africa. For many this theory is certainly out of date.

But I return to the question of knowing, *who is our enemy?*

I do not wish to ignore at this moment the pressure that is exerted on the liberation movement to maintain so-called *black purity*. The case of America, where the racial struggle is the most apparent to the blacks, is often cited. What I am saying should not be taken as criticism of our brave black American brothers, who know better than anyone how to orient their struggle, how to envisage the transformation of American society so that man will be free there.

But allow me to reject any idea on the transformation of the national liberation struggle into a racial struggle. I would say that in Angola the struggle *also* assumes a racial aspect, since discrimination is a fact. The black man is exploited there. But it is fundamentally a struggle against the colonial system and its chief ally, imperialism.

I also reject the idea of black liberation, since the unity of Africa is one of the principles universally accepted by the OAU, and knowing that in Africa there are Arab peoples, some areas which are not black.

And as I have said, for us they are the enemies.

A people's struggle for political power, for economic independence, for the restoration of cultural life, to end alienation, for relations with all peoples on a basis of equality and fraternity—these are the objectives of our struggles. These objectives are set by defining who is the enemy, by defining who are the people and what is the character of our struggle . . . affecting not only the foundations of the colonial system but also the foundations of our own society as a nation and as a people.

So let us be realistic, the national liberation struggle in Africa does not have very sound bases in the international arena and it is not political or ideological affinities that count nor the objectives themselves, for in most cases other interests dominate relations between the liberation forces in the world.

Some would like to see the liberation movements take the direction of a class struggle, as in Europe. Others would like to see it racist, Don Quixote tilting at a windmill with a white skin. Others would like to see it tribalized, federalized according to their idea of a country which they do not know. Others, idealists, would like to see us heading along the path to political compromise with the enemy. These efforts to transform the liberation movements into satellites of parties in power, subject to unacceptable paternalism, are caused by the fact that most of the liberation movements conducting an armed struggle have to do so from outside their countries.

Exile has its effects.

The worst thing the Portuguese did to us, was to oblige us to wage a liberation struggle from abroad.

The audience applauded loudly and the delivery in a foreign language showed the will and passion by Dr. Neto to cut to the chase.

The enemy is imperialism.

The following day, Dr. Neto and I met at the downtown office to "next step" the Canada connection.

I thanked Neto for his eloquent speech and words of wisdom. This long-overdue presentation would help to straighten out the confusion of ideologies from out of Africa. He genuinely appreciated my comments. Next, Neto introduced Humbaraci, a Turk who worked as an advisor to the MPLA with expertise in military matters, who had a multitude of connections with European companies and governments. During the first minute of our threesome, Neto said, "I do not want to hear any personal feuds, only friendly discussions focused on the need of the war of liberation." The message was clear. Neto wanted to discuss the Canadian support for the armed struggle in depth, the MPLA position, the Canada connection with NATO, and the Trudeau Government's position—its nuts and bolts position—on the MPLA. Neto was a visionary, a long-range thinker, and he had an uncanny ability to focus on the next step.

Canada was next to the USA and opposed the USA on all Southern Africa issues, whether through the votes at the UN or the condemnation of apartheid or colonial Portugal.

How could we use the open airwaves, and the geographical breadth of Canada, to educate, to talk about American napalm in Africa and the developing scenario of American military intervention?

How could the long history of the United Church of Canada at the medical mission in Angola and its unanimous condemnation of colonialism by Collins, Knight, McInnis, and Gilchrist, to name a few, be added to the scales of justice?

The success of the national campaign against coffee imports, and all these other factors, pointed to a serious evaluation of what could be achieved with an invitation to go to Canada. Neto's eyes and gestures indicated that all of the work that had been done could be the springboard to get support, and to expose imperialism, to expose America, the enemy.

Neto also acknowledged that the international campaigns to support the Southern Africa Liberation movements required a further push of politicization so that world pressure on corporations and governments would force the United Nations and other world bodies to intervene, thereby ending the wars of attrition, the brutally repressive regimes in Rhodesia and South Africa. The release of political prisoners was essential to avoid an unstoppable bloodbath. Political prisoners could and did die in jail, so long as they were not well known like Mbeki or Mandela.

Neto had a busy week and therefore the four-hour conversation was terminated with an invitation to meet in Brazzaville, Congo, in two days. Humbaraci and I carried on over lunch discussing the need to get more small aircraft into the combat zones. The one DC–3 based in Brazzaville required parts. Colleen's father was in the aircraft business and, through Evan, arranged to send, as soon as payment was received, Humbaraci's list of parts within ten days. It was very clear that we could work together, as we both had little time for anything other than what would advance the MPLA agenda. I went off to the Luther house to make arrangements to go to Brazzaville with a twenty-four-hour stopover in Lusaka in order to make the Lusaka/Brazzaville connection.

I made the arrangements and arrived in Lusaka for the painful wait in an airport with a few chairs, no food, no water, and filthy toilets. I refused all invitations by the Zambia police to leave the airport and go into Lusaka.

The MPLA in Congo Brazzaville were there to get me through customs, and I have to admit that having a friendly government meant a smooth transaction; the paperwork for my entry consisted of a thumbs-up by Lara to a Congo official.

Speaking French gave me an opportunity to thank the assisting airport staff and the MPLA officials who took care of me. As this trip was part of my new job description, I asked the MPLA to put me up in a modest hotel, which turned out to be the Cosmos Hotel, a gift from the Soviet Union to the Congo Government. It was completely equipped from telephone to wash basin to doors. Everything was imported from the USSR.

Dr. Neto had informed the MPLA of my visit and its purpose. I needed to meet the other players, as the Cabinda front had been open since 1963. It was a strategic zone with Gulf Oil production of 65,000 bpd. Though part of Angola, a number of groups, in particular, the separatist Front for Liberation Enclave of Cabinda—FLEC—were attempting to break the historical link with the rest of Angola.

I took meals with Dr. Neto and his senior advisors, including Jose Eduardo Dos Santos, Lucio Lara, Iko Carreira, Kafuxi, Monimambu, Costa de Andrade, and many more.

Dos Santos, a graduate chemical engineer and a very sophisticated thinker who also happened to be a very pleasant person, was designated Neto's right hand man. Dos Santos is a remarkable man. Sent to the Soviet Union to study engineering, he first had to learn Russian and then compete with native speakers for classroom recognition. Lara was a Central Committee member and a founding member of the MPLA; Iko was an Angolan of Portuguese descent, a pilot, another thinker and strategist.

The same Monimambu, from the third region, along with Diendengue, lived away from this central location with his wife and was now responsible for the MPLA intelligence network within the CIA-backed group FNLA based in Mobutu's Zaire.

Kafuxi was the most familiar amongst the new friends as he was the *Voice of Angola*, the daily broadcast to Angola from the Congo. Every evening at 1900 and throughout Angola, the *Voice* gave the news of the day, commentary, and, most of all, recognition of an Angolan identity that had been denied for 500 years. The man had great wit and a blistering sense of humour and soon became a very good friend. Costa de Andrade was a powerful-looking man, one of Angola's poetry giants where the master giant was Dr. Neto. Angola's poets were numerous and biting in their word combinations and rhymes condemning Portugal and its colonial policies. Many, many Angolan poets were arrested under the arbitrary justice system and put into preventative detention as subversives against the state. At one lunch, Dr. Neto introduced me to a short man with little hair and a goatee, somewhat hunched over at five feet, eighty- five pounds, saying, "*Camarade* Jacques, meet Antonio Jacinto."

I extended my hand, and my brain kicked in. "But, Dr. Neto," I said, "I thought Antonio Jacinto was in jail." Dr. Neto added, "Well he was, and he is the same Antonio Jacinto." The remarkable poet, educator, and great Angolan had just been released. I stepped around to the other side of the table to give him a hug. The pain endured by the Angolan needed to be shared, and words in Portuguese, Lingala, Chokwe, Bundu, and Kibundu did a little to assuage the heartfelt anguish. Now he was back from the hellhole of the Portuguese jails to the work of building a nation.

Dr. Neto's driver, *Camarade* Catumbela, made the drive to and fro interesting. At twenty-six, he was very old, a veteran of the guerrilla war, with a great smile and a worldly view of politics, who truly appreciated the inclusion of non-Angolans in the MPLA war of national liberation. It was during these precious moments that I knew that getting involved with the MPLA was more than a gratifying political gesture, something that I could not measure, but felt at home with.

On February 15, 1974, Dr. Neto called me into a special meeting to share the decision taken by his inner cabinet about my future role with the MPLA. Dr. Neto said, *"Camarade Jacques Roy, vous avez fait preuve de toutes les qualités et par votre exemple que vous êtes, un révolutionaire, un internationaliste. Car vous menez votre vie en harmonie selon les besoins de la lutte.*

Dans mes fonctions comme Président du MPLA, je vous remets le document suivant. . ."—". . . you have shown all of the qualities and by your example that you are a revolutionary, an internationalist, and that you have conducted yourself in harmony and according to the needs of the war. In my capacity as president of the MPLA, I give you the following document. . ."

There was my photo on MPLA letterhead. Beneath it read: Jacques Roy, Director of African Relief Services

Committee, Ottawa, has been more than once to the liberated zones of Angola and has a close knowledge of the pressing needs for the civilian populations of Angola.

He is, pending the official establishment in Canada of a Permanent MPLA Representation, in charge of organizing and implementing various assistance projects for the civilian population under the MPLA administration.

Any assistance which can be given to him in the performance of his task would be appreciated.

Signed by Dr. Aghostino Neto, Président of the Movimento Popular de Libertation de Angola—MPLA.

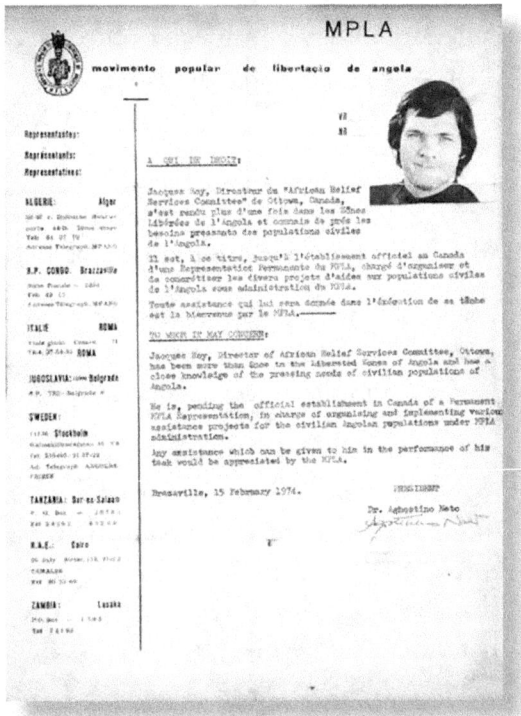

Jacques is appointed official MPLA representative to Canada. February 15, 1974

This honour left me speechless, humbled, and yet so very happy that I had finally been given some serious responsibility: entrusted to develop a foreign policy for Canada. A relationship with Canada, a middle power sitting next to the American elephant, would be invaluable in establishing for Angola a measure of independence from the competing spheres of influence of the superpowers.

Dr. Neto was very happy with the overall working relationship, and a few minutes later said that I should prepare a plan of action for the visit of the MPLA cabinet to Canada. It was official.

Over the next two days, I prepared an agenda, political objectives, and a material support plan for a cross-country tour that would begin April 25, 1974, in Ottawa, the agenda including Parliament, the support committees, and the political heavyweights who were willing to step up and be identified with the wars of liberation. For many it would be a big, big step.

The first stop was Ottawa, Trudeau's office, then Montreal and Quebec City, Sherbrooke, Toronto, meetings with church groups, meetings with the sympathetic NDP governments in Winnipeg, Regina, and Vancouver.

Financing raised by the NGO community would include air tickets, hotel, and ground transportation for six people

Security was to be handled by the Government in an unofficial way. This was a particular concern, as the Portuguese secret police—PIDE—had offered a $1 million dollar reward for the assassination of Dr. Neto.

Overnight, Dr. Neto studied the proposal, and the next morning over breakfast announced that the tour was on. I was beside myself; this not only represented a lot of work, but a great opportunity for Canadians who had been so supportive in the past to meet the future leader of Angola and his shadow cabinet.

I was under no illusions about the magnitude of the task. To bring the head of an active liberation movement to North America was unheard of.

Impossible? I, with others, would make it possible.

A few more days were required to study future projects like the hospital and transportation, training and logistics. A new film was needed and an agricultural specialist with equipment was also required.

After a solemn goodbye to my new MPLA friends, I was off to the Brazzaville airport with Lara and Catumbela.

This mission was at an end and a new one beginning, the start of a cycle of hard work and service.

Now, back to Paris and Montreal to start the next phase.

CHAPTER ELEVEN

Create opportunities to engage in dialogue . . .

April 1974

oday, April 21, I received a phone call from Loy in London, England, telling me of the arrival of Jose Eduardo dos Santos the next day. Security was stringent; each member of the delegation would arrive separately, except for Neto.

Dos Santos would arrive at 21:00 in Ottawa, and I went to meet him. The plane arrived, but somehow we missed each other, and I returned to the Sandy Hill apartment empty-handed, upset, and feeling helpless.

Jose called at 23:30 from the airport; he had been put on a different flight. After taking a few deep breaths to calm me down, I was sure that I would feel better once I saw him.

I drove up to the arrival doors, and there stood Jose with his unique shapka—a Russian fur hat—with flaps down and carrying a small handbag. As I pulled up, he identified me and his wide smile showed the gold front tooth and a small face peering out of the large fur hat.

We greeted each other warmly in the cold Ottawa air. Jose felt cold, but explained that his student days in Moscow were a lot more difficult. Jose was tired; as a veteran of the MPLA, he worked beyond his limits. Tonight, we were celebrating the start of a political tour, a first for Canada, and an opportunity for Canadians to connect directly with MPLA leaders. The airport authorities had received instructions from External Affairs, and entry requirements were waived. Loy was arriving the next day, and Dr. Neto along with the others arriving at 19:00 hours on April 23rd.

Colleen had prepared a meal for us. We settled into the stuffed barrel chairs in the small kitchen with a bottle of good wine, Jose told of the expectations, the latest military successes of FAPLA and the underground in Luanda and other large Angolan cities. A few hours later, we called it a day with a promise that a sleep-in was on the schedule for the next morning. The modest apartment living room became the sleeping quarters for this top MPLA cadre. A small mattress on the floor in a warm and friendly environment was most appreciated by Jose. To think that in a few years he would be the heir-apparent to the presidency of Angola.

By 0900, Jose was up and anxious to see the outline of the schedule. Today, April 23, the Secretary of State for External Affairs would speak to the question, "What measures has Canada recently taken in an effort to persuade Portugal to grant independence to the country of Guinea–Bissau and other African territories that Portugal claims as its own?" Answer: "The Canadian Government has expressed its concerns on numerous occasions that Portugal should grant self-determination to all its African territories. This view was conveyed directly to the Portuguese foreign minister during the December 1973 NATO Ministerial meeting in Brussels. The Canadian position was repeated during the recent sessions of the Committee on External Affairs."

Follow-up question: "What is the intention of the government to acknowledge, through recognition or other means, that the country of Guinea–Bissau has actively achieved independence from Portugal; and if not —?"

Mitchell Sharp (Secretary of State for External Affairs) responded: "Canadian practice is to grant recognition to sovereign states which have governments able to exercise control over the territory which they claim . . . who are able to discharge their international relations. The Canadian government is prepared recognize Guinea–Bissau when the Canadian Government sees that these criteria have been in fact met." Question by MP Rowland, April 23, 1974, House of Commons.

Jose now understood the political thrust of the support committees and the implications of this Canadian governmental support. Tomorrow, the question to Minister Sharp from Claude Wagner: "Does the Minister intend to welcome in person and officially Dr. Neto, president of the Popular Movement for the Liberation of Angola, who apparently will be in our country in the next few hours?"

We relaxed and toured Ottawa by car as Jose, who had travelled extensively, wanted to see and enjoy a different type of day. His demeanour and intelligence made our excursion a memorable day. By evening we returned home and prepared to go and pick up Loy. By 20:00, Loy was in sight, and his exit from Lansdowne International was uneventful.

Back at the Besserer apartment. Jose and Loy shared the floor in the living room, a level below hotel standard, but three-star accommodations considering the conditions in Liberated Angola. They just laughed at my embarrassment about the sleeping arrangements.

The following day, Mitchell Sharp addressed the question of the regarding Neto: "No, Mr. Speaker."

To a supplementary question, Sharp responded, "Mr. Neto will be received by officials of my department. I gave an answer yesterday about our attitude toward Portuguese colonial policy." Commons Debate, April 24, 1974.

We had accomplished the first phase of the political game: getting the attention of the Canadian government. Next, financial aid for the liberation movements.

April 23rd at 19:00, Dr. Neto, Eugenia, Rocha, and Mingas disembarked and were greeted by our reception committee and journalists. Neto said, "We are very happy to be in Canada, a good friend of the MPLA. We are looking forward to explaining our objectives and visiting with our Canadian friends and government officials."

Off to the Lord Elgin Hotel in downtown Ottawa. A few hours later, Neto called a meeting to see the final program and expressed his need to meet Canadian government officials, to which I replied, *"Monsieur le*

Président, vous serez reçu par les hautes instances du gouvernement en tant que Président du MPLA. Votre présence est attendu. "Mr. President, you will be received by the highest officials of the federal government. Your presence has been expected."

It was now midnight, and the full schedule for April 24 required a good rest beforehand. The NGO community was our warm-up for the heavy politics that awaited us on Parliament Hill starting on Thursday the 25th. A public meeting was chaired by Professor John O'Manique from St. Pat's College. Dr. Neto's theme this first evening was dealing with the colonial and imperial thrust into Africa by the USA. It is now very clear for all to see, but at the time the evidence for American support of the Southern Africa minority regimes was scarce, and we needed a good information campaign to succeed in demonstrating how these deviations from democratic rule were impeding the natural evolution of self- determination. After the public meeting, a good night's rest was in store.

The MPLA delegation was in a safe place and RCMP security on duty. I went back to the apartment, but due to all of the buildup to the arrival, I could not sleep.

At 05:00, the telephone rang, and I knew something was in the works. It was a journalist calling to say that there had been a military coup in Portugal, and could Dr. Neto address this event. I asked what the situation was in the streets of Lisbon, and the reply was, "Calm, and at first glance, it seems to have been a bloodless coup by the military rank and file."

My first thought was to get to the Lord Elgin Hotel and awaken Neto, for he would certainly want to hear this momentous news. This would play havoc with plans for the next steps, as it seemed progressive elements in the military had had enough of the colonial wars and had taken to the streets with a non-negotiable position of peace and democracy. The walk to the Lord Elgin was like a ritual procession of one as I carried the great news and tried to imagine the impact it would have on all we had planned and hoped for.

I had learned long ago that a long walk puts things in perspective. I made my way to Dr. Neto's floor and greeted the security guards and informed them of the overnight events in Portugal and the possible implications for our Angolan guests. They seemed quite surprised by the news but did not understand the political implications. So, with a deep breath, I knocked on Neto's door. He opened the door and invited me to sit in the living area.

Dr. Neto said he was very tired, and added, "I hope you have good news to justify calling this early."

In my best French, I said, *"Camarade Président, Il y a eu un coup militaire pacifique à Lisbon, et le Portugal est sous le Commandement des Forces Armées."* "There has been a peaceful military coup in Lisbon, and Portugal is under command of the armed forces."

Neto's face remained stoic. He stared at me and turned his head as if to listen more carefully without saying a word.

He seemed to have difficulty believing what I was saying.

"Est-ce vrai?" "Is it the truth?"

"Mr. le Président, c'est vrai."

He got up and came over to hug me, and now the mood turned upbeat. *"Eugenia, as Forces Armade fazer un golp militar em Lisboa,"* Neto told his still-sleeping wife. She responded by repeating what he had said as a question as she made her way to the couch in the living room, interrupted by a huge hug from her husband. Neto added, *"Jacques Roy, c'est l'histoire quise déroule,"* ". . . history is unfolding."

I sat around for fifteen minutes to allow the Netos to get dressed and decide what to do with this great news. Neto got his little black book out and called Mario Soares in Lisbon. The lines were jammed, but with a little pressure, he got the operator to understand the urgency of his need to speak to the head of the Socialist Party, an old friend of the MPLA president.

The call finally went through and the conversation not only confirmed the news, but also the hoped-for implications. It was time to wake up the other members of the delegation, and within three minutes all were in Neto's living room. As Neto related his conversation with Soares, Jose, Loy, Mingas, and Rocha broke into delighted exclamations and revolutionary hugs for everyone. All those hard years of war, pain, exhaustion, and the careful work of creating a new society were now bearing fruit.

Could it be that the war would soon be over, or was this a ploy to attempt decolonization to a neo-colonial state with a black figurehead, as in so many African countries?

I went downstairs and obtained the late editions and the early edition of the April 25th *Ottawa Citizen* and returned to Neto's room. Coffee had arrived, and the newspapers became the focus of the thoughts and emotions of these men and woman, as their imaginations caught the hope and happiness of independence, so close but still elusive.

I called Rivard to tell him of the unfolding events, and he just could not believe the timing. We would arrive on Friday in Montreal to continue the trip, but some modifications were in store. Meetings were held with government officials in their offices on Thursday the 25th. The most important meeting was with the Standing Committee on External Affairs and National Defence. Dr. Neto was in great oratory form and his delivery, in French, was eloquent.

"Our government is seeking aid amongst different countries and this is what we would like from Canada:

"Political and materiel support. From a moral view, there is no doubt that throughout the world and in particular in Canada, there exists a sentiment in our favour. We need political support. The UN resolutions . . . in Oslo in '72 and '73 show that this approach by itself is not effective. But to go from the resolution to action is much better— UN decisions to recognize the liberation movements as the legitimate representatives of their peoples. We would like to see the UN decision applied in Canada. This is very important, as it gives us a voice in the world. In fact, our visit here today is another step. A few hours ago, we had a meeting at the Ministry of Foreign Affairs, and the top officials spoke to the same problems. These are important steps, very positive and are greatly appreciated."

A member of the committee raised the question, "How can we be certain that our assistance will not be used in a military fashion?" Neto replied, "We are very frank, realistic that all that we do in our country is to win independence. If we have school, it is to prepare our future. If we treat our sick, it is to prepare them for the struggle, political or military. If we recuperate our mutilated persons, it is to serve our country. In all of our actions, it is an action for independence . . . this aid will reconstruct our country."

As Dr. Neto got up to leave the committee room, I caught his eye and his expression indicated that this face-to-face meeting had been very good. We were off to meet Minister of Communications Gerard Pelletier and his officials. The political note here was that Prime Minister Trudeau would hear the results of this meeting. He, Pelletier, and Marchand were the three wise men that former PM Pearson had brought to Ottawa. This ministry also was responsible for special political matters and the MPLA fitted this category. My "boss" at SUCO certainly knew how to organize a high-impact meeting with his father.

Whenever Neto spoke, he always made it very clear that he was speaking for all.

Neto called me over and asked that I set up a meeting with the Prime Minister's office. I called Ivan Head's office and arrangements were made for Neto and Head to meet. Head was the right person in the right place at the right time. He was Trudeau's special assistant with special responsibility for foreign policy and foreign relations. He would go on to be president of the International Development Research Centre from 1978 to 1991, and afterwards was the founding director of the University of British Columbia's Liu Institute for Global Issues. He would give Dr. Neto an understanding hearing.

After their get-together, Neto returned to the Lord Elgin and told me that he was very happy with the planning and results for the day. He was very grateful for the meeting with Head.

What had they discussed?

What was Neto wanting from Canada that Canada could deliver?

Neto said that the MPLA would ask Canada for real favours very soon. Mr. Head agreed that he would wait for the request

That same evening, a press conference was held on Parliament Hill. Questions ranged from the military coup in Portugal to Neto's satisfaction with the political events and meetings of the day.

April 26th, off to Montreal where the *Angola Comite* had arranged a full schedule in Montreal, Quebec City, and Sherbrooke. The Montreal setup was now in full crisis mode due to the events in Portugal, and Neto spent time on the phone with his political collaborators. This day had a focus of, "How to help the MPLA." Rivard from Oxfam and the other executive directors were brought into one room along with the MPLA delegates to review and to finance the projects that I had prepared during my last trip, projects for the civilian population that could be easily supported by the NGOs and would allow the fundraisers to have a public education component. Sitting around a large wooden table, each group tabled a series of these projects, and, one by one, Neto addressed their validity and importance, and the respective NGOs took a financial portion of the overall cost. MPLA had a need for a farm tractor in the Cabinda region and a trainer, costing $65,000. SUCO took the cost of training, Oxfam the cost of the tractor, and Rallies Tiers Monde the cost of the seeds and fuel for one year. There were many projects with a total value of more than $550,000 over the next two years.

The political sophistication of certain members was shallow. One project was the purchase of 3,000 watches, which the MPLA wanted for its teachers. One gentleman asked Dr. Neto, "I thought Africans could tell time by the sun?"

My heart sank and as I looked around I could see Rivard shaking his head and remaining silent.

Neto immediately recognized the naïve and inherently racist question and intervened.

"You are right, we can tell time by the sun, but we have a problem on cloudy and rainy days." The group broke into laughter. The young man accepted the explanation and voted to accept the project. (Every time I see Rivard, we recall this incident, shaking our heads again.) On the 26th, we headed to Quebec City, and an evening meeting of more than 400 persons was held. During these events, the steering committee continually adjusted the schedule. On this day, Jose Eduardo Dos Santos went to address the University of Sherbrooke and to give the required public support to the local committee headed up by a very dynamic Sister Judith Bergeron.

A major concern since the coup was the increased security risk for Neto. We had brought two of René Lévesque's bodyguards for the Quebec–Montreal part of the tour, as we had identified former MPLA personnel who had been expelled by the party for fraud or other charges as possible sources of trouble.

Early Saturday morning, April 27th, we returned to Montreal for a photographic exposition at the Pierre Dupuis High School. It was a cultural evening including the committees from the Portuguese, Vietnamese, Palestinian, Haitian, and Chilean communities as well as the Teachers' Federation (CEQ) and the African Students in Montreal.

Toronto meeting at OSIE.

Left to Right; Jose Eduardo dos Santos, Pedro van Dúnem, EugeniaNeto, Dr. Neto

Music, poetry, and messages of support for the MPLA and all of the liberation movements around the world made this evening for the more than 500 people attending a memorable and historical event.

The events in Portugal continued to impact the schedule. Neto would come to Toronto, but the rest of the trip would be led by Dos Santos. On Sunday morning, we held the final brunch and Neto's farewell speech and the salutations from the Angola/Quebec Committee.

"Dear friends, we ask for your help. It is when the beast is injured that we must kill it [a direct reference to the events in Portugal] before the beast lashes out, so I ask you to help us even more . . . I say, till we meet again."

Rivard arranged for the delegation to visit city hall in Montreal to be received by the mayor, and the traditional signing of the guest book. Rivard knew his way around and had organized a police escort with sirens, non-stop to the airport, normally an honour reserved for a head of state.

Neto was taken aback by this reception. He was now a world leader; he needed to be recognized as such.

Next stop was Toronto, and the local committee was very organized. By late afternoon, the delegates were in their hotel rooms and resting before the Toronto events.

A public meeting at OISE had standing room only, and Neto did not disappoint. It was now day three after the coup, and it was becoming clearer what the Portuguese military coup were planning. Independence for the African territories was still a secondary matter. The first strategy was to drag their feet, which meant finding an alternative to the MPLA.

Neto was at his best. Guests for the evening were John Saul, Judith Marshall, and Murray McInnis, the former missionary in Angola. The media were only lukewarm towards the MPLA, but the churches and NGOs were grateful for the visit and backed it up with tangible support for material aid projects.

Mingas spoke excellent English and therefore was a media spokesperson. An articulate man, a doctor of economics, this six-foot-tall man charmed and flowed with information and hope. Loy and Dos Santos dealt with NGO concerns and projects. Neto did the TV morning shows and the individual interviews. The calls with Portugal continued, and Neto needed to be in Europe to steer the political discussions and to ensure that the principles of independence for the "overseas territories" that took so long to implement were not to be cast away.

With the remaining delegates we went to Winnipeg, Regina, and Vancouver. The NDP governments were very welcoming, and the Saskatchewan portion proved the best, as Dos Santos obtained a commitment to have Dr. Penman visit Angola's war zones and then use his research to funnel more medical equipment to the MPLA. The MPLA were elated by the reception. After ten days, projects amounted to

$700,000 and the promise to get more as the development of events would allow better flow of goods, services, and personnel to and within Angola. The trip was now coming to an end, none too soon, as I was exhausted. Dealing in French, English, Portuguese, and the numerous Canadian accents had made my brain tired.

From Vancouver, the MPLA delegates returned to London, England and to Congo Brazzaville.

I flew to Ottawa and to the silence of the Besserer apartment.

Colleen was understanding and happy with her life. Through all these events, my friend Evan kept the Ottawa office up and going. Everyone did their part.

The final financial budget showed a balanced sheet on the expenses, while the projects were beyond our expectations. It was May 5th and time for a holiday. Ten days later, Rivard called and wanted to follow up the documentation. He had organized a photo album of the Quebec section and a film documentation of the trip. We also dealt with the approved projects, in particular the technical training of auto mechanics in Cabinda and the hospital as proposed by Dr. Penman.

My brother André responded on June 14th with an approval to come to the Congo and join up with the MPLA. He would come from Botswana, where he was ending a two-year CUSO contract as transportation specialist. He had established a technical-training, driver- training, and transportation centre in the Gaberone. This was great news, as Andy operated very well with his African students and administrators.

His presence ensured continuity for the African support group when I stepped away for other business.

To return to Angola and start putting the Canadian involvement of personnel into action was the next urgent step. The rest period lasted till August; another trip to Congo Brazzaville was in the works.

A letter arrived from Canada Council announcing that I had been awarded a $4,000 bursary to make a film in Angola. The results of the MPLA trip had allowed me to evaluate the work of Jean Pierre Masse (JP), and, given my existing workload, it might not be a bad idea to let him do the filming while I oversaw the project on-site. I had to think about this, as I knew the reality of Angola and the MPLA. JP needed to be flexible, culturally and emotionally. I spent more time with Jean Pierre in Montreal and encouraged him to read as well as to condition his body for some serious walking. He agreed to get a little more serious, as he had met the MPLA delegates and understood. In time, he proved that he did get the message that a war situation makes one a little unstable, till one changes one's frame of mind.

Masse wanted to go to Morocco with his wife on a holiday and then proceed to Congo Brazzaville.

In a no-nonsense telephone conversation, I warned him that under no circumstance should he try to enter Congo B without my permission and presence. The method of entry by the MPLA had a security element to it and even if he used my name, it would not enough to get him in. MPLA knew who I was, but to begin explaining that JP was a friend . . . not possible.

In early August, Colleen's parents, Colleen, and I went on a serious canoe trip in the Chapleau region of Northern Ontario. Coleen's father, an excellent outdoors person, was truly in his element. We consulted with a local trapper who pointed out the beauty and pitfalls of the Woman River, which ended at the falls at Ivanhoe Lake. It was a great trip, including some twenty-two portages, some unbelievable fishing, scenery worthy of the Group of Seven, and a lesson in Canadian mining exploration (we found remnants of large, abandoned stoves in the forest). This quiet time was a very good break for my soul and body. Paddling from early morning for about six hours and then finding a suitable spot indicated by our trapper friend made the trip a movie that I replayed often during the somber days of Luanda or recuperating from malaria and dysentery.

Being in such a remote area gave me an opportunity to do some fishing. We ate fresh pike and pickerel, while Coleen's father made a fresh batch of bannock enough for the evening meal, breakfast, and lunch in the ever-moving canoe. Large rock outcrops and warm lake conditions were ideal for diving and swimming. The campsites were on high ground but the 20:00 hour cooling of the day meant blackflies. They interrupted our meal and our social gathering around the fire. I enjoyed the friendship and trust of Colleen and her folks for some twelve days. On arrival at the end of the last hard day of paddling, history had passed us by. Richard Nixon had resigned over the Watergate affair and it had not affected our lives in the least.

In late August, while consoling my mother, who was in Buckingham to bury her father, I received a call from Jean Pierre claiming he was in Congo B; he was in jail and under arrest for national security breach and possible espionage charges. I laughed at his predicament and told him he would stay in jail till I arrived, which was within the next fifteen days. I was, however, very angry at his folly. Unfinished MPLA business remained to be done.

Was this a precursor to more bad behaviour? I learned before my departure that my friend Jean Pelletier at SUCO had resigned, and this made me very weary. The narrow-minded elements of SUCO, who had tried to equate the independence struggle in Angola with the politics of Quebec, did not approve of my views. Now they were trying to find a way to get rid of me.

CHAPTER TWELVE

Not just a doer . . . but . . . a thinker, choosing in advance what sort of values wewant.

October 1975

D r. Neto sent out a press release officially announcing the date of Angolan independence, the formation of a new republic under the political wing of the MPLA, on November 11. This was the official declaration of independence and another task that further linked my life with the Angolans. With my friend Evan, we planned the November 11 Independence Day Celebrations for Ottawa, Toronto, Montreal, and Quebec City. News from Angola up to the final date was alarming; the CIA-backed group FNLA attacked from the north, and the colonial settlers, backed by UNITA, from the east, combined with the apartheid army trying to reach Luanda from the south, making the MPLA's task very difficult.

Dr. Neto's declaration of independence was good enough for me to plan celebrations as public education exercises, but in reality the flux of Angola's status along with distortion in the press indicated that another "war was required" to straighten out the mess. The MPLA had bargained forcefully and in good faith, with a positive outlook that would need to be vindicated, after "War no. 2." The Americans would make the MPLA government pay for not following their "rules of engagement."

MPLA had already assured Gulf Oil from Calgary, later named Chevron, that the Cabinda operations, and the oil industry as a whole, would not be nationalized and that a joint venture arrangement was the only equitable approach.

The MPLA knew through its technical connections with Humbaraci that there was plenty of oil off the coast of Angola and it was only a question of time before the full impact of the discovery well would be coming on line.

I later learned, in the summer of 1998 during a high-school reunion, that a boyhood neighbor, Jeff Chase, one of the senior managers for the Chevron Operations in Cabinda, knew that one could deal with the MPLA. His only complaint was the fact that visas were not being issued in a way that was compatible with the running of the business; that if an employee was to stay for three months, then an equivalent visa should apply, as the traditional renewal of monthly visas required the employee to leave the country and wait for the renewal document. Over all, the MPLA knew that the oil industry was necessary for the military side of the power game and therefore would not put in jeopardy the dollars and business credibility that had been announced and planned for in the MPLA platform. Again, the US tried to distort the reality in order to justify the continued support for the zealots of the UNITA and the FNLA.

At the events we organized, I read the prepared text in Ottawa and Montreal, but the Quebec portion was sabotaged by African students who refused to let me speak. They introduced me as Dr. Neto's chauffeur and put on an evening of "How great is African independence; Africans with so many sacrifices will attain nationhood," while they, the emerging elite, were enjoying a comfortable life away from the struggle and the danger.

Following celebrations for the independence of Angola, I returned to an empty apartment; Colleen had left. She knew that I would continue working for the liberation movement and could see her needs would not be met. She just moved on.

Since I enjoy working physically, it was time to get into a project that gave me an outlet as well as a way of shifting my mindset. The other reality was that Angola was now an independent country, heading for a long civil war since the United States, South Africa, Zaire, and Israel were not going to accept MPLA as the government. The United Nations, as well as the Organization for African Unity—OAU—supported the Luanda-based national government.

Since I had suffered from hunger many times during the war of liberation, I focused on food production and volunteered in a co-operative at Manseau just east of Montreal that was producing tomatoes and cucumbers. Since the huge demand for fresh local produce was inadequately met by a low rate of production, this was a compelling field for me.

During the winter of 1975-76, I manufactured greenhouses that would be installed in the spring. News from Angola was very grim. Continual power cuts and water shortages were caused by the terrorists groups of the FNLA and UNITA. Following my first food production season, it was time to evaluate my options. It had been a good year on the farm, and my strength had returned and my mental equilibrium was much better.

I continued to promote Angola and granted an interview to CBC radio, on a programme called *This Country in the Morning*. My old friend Professor Dr. John O'Manique was now at Carleton University's Patterson School of International Studies and invited me to speak at a meeting with faculty over lunch; a two-hour presentation with Q and A.

This was followed by a lecture at the University of Waterloo. It was my third time at UOW. This last presentation would be memorable. On entering the student cafeteria leading to the podium I was struck by the impact of US propaganda, illustrated by posters spelling out in large letters:

DOWN WITH JACQUES ROY,

AGENT OF SOVIET IMPERALISM

LONG LIVE UNITA !

This was reprinted from the *People's Canada Daily News* on December 29, 1976.

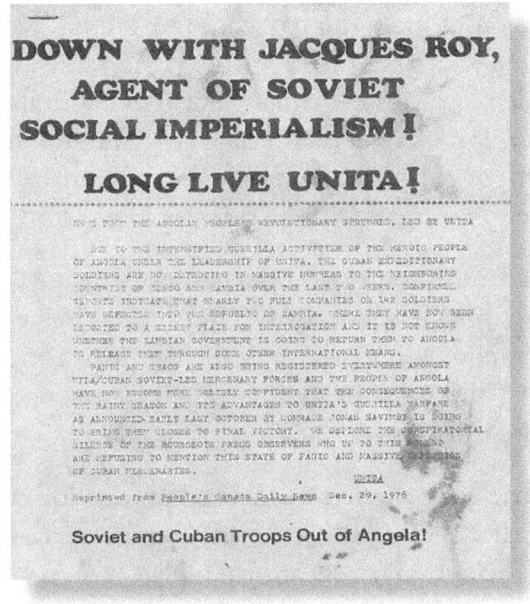

Pro UNITA posters found at the University of Waterloo.

This Maoist group, funded by the CIA, tried very hard to shake my arguments. Tenacious and spread throughout the room, their plan was to disrupt the presentation. It was a slugfest, a lot of name-calling; my position was that, not only were they liars and funded by imperialism, they were part of the media deception allowing the neo-colonial oppressors to create confusion and dissension—the reason Angola was in such a mess.

Getting away from the farm was great for my morale, but returning to the farm made my dilemma more evident; it was always a downer.

Using organic techniques, which I learned from textbooks as well as from Mr. Nadeau, a seventy-five-year-old retired dairy farmer I had hired, we were able to produce flowers, tomatoes, leaf lettuce, and cucumbers. However, at that time, the consuming public made no distinction between pesticide-infested food and local, organically grown produce.

The cost of heating the greenhouses with oil was prohibitive. I learned that the Dutch had a hay burner, an automatic device that actually burned hay. A normal square bale produced the equivalent heat of one gallon of fuel. The hay could be old hay, which has lost its nutritional value while maintaining its calorie value. This deteriorated hay was a burden to the local farmers. For $30,000, I had a one-million BTU (200 kilocalorie) boiler that produced no pollution, met European standards, and got rid of waste hay for the local farmers, who would otherwise have to burn it off in the open.

I installed the impressive boiler, water pump, and accessories. This heated my house, also providing domestic hot water and to the greenhouses, by circulating hot water through a two-inch cast iron pipe and transferring the heat through large heat exchangers. My cost per annum dropped from $15,000 to less than $1,000.

The payback of two years made food production costs much easier to manage. A parallel 200,000 BTU unit that burned used transmission oil completed the automated heating supply.

I met the director of the Adult Education program at the University of Sherbrooke, Dr. Peter Bernath, who granted me an interview for the teaching of English as a second language—ESL. Seconded to the Teaching Hospital for Sherbrooke, CHUS, the mature students from the medical faculty were my students. It was great teaching such bright people who loved to learn and who each had a great sense of humour. These classes relieved the isolation of my greenhouse operation.

Every lecture was full of laughter and generous contributions of humanity and stories, all in English, of course. The best story I can recall: Two medical students are on their way to Dallas for a convention. During the flight, the pilot announces to the captive audience that he has just learned who shot JR. Some passengers are very upset while others are saying, "I told you so." The range of emotions seemed so odd for these medical doctors, who were hearing it all out of context. All they knew was that the author of a murder had been revealed; unlike their fellow passengers, they had no knowledge of the television series that generated the story. As well as being very poor in the English language, their bafflement was reinforced by their isolation from American popular culture. They stared at each other, at a loss.

After a lot of hard work, reading newspapers, and some exchanges with delegates at the convention, the origin of the murder of JR in a television series called *Dallas* came to light.

When they returned to class, they were asked about the Dallas convention. Since English was the only medium in the classroom, the improbable story was told. One of the doctors, a natural storyteller and comedian, had the group laughing incredulously for thirty minutes over the cultural gap faced by so many French-speaking citizens outside of Quebec.

In October 1976, Dr. Neto invited me to join the independence celebrations in Luanda. I gladly accepted and made my way via Lisbon, arriving in Luanda with no MPLA personnel to get me through customs and into the country. I was the last person through customs, and without a visa, the officers put me in a small room with a window till they could sort out my identity. I used my MPLA identification paper, the one signed by Dr. Neto, but since it was old, it did not pass the test. As I waited to get clearance, the head of protocol *Camarada* Scorcio walked by the window where I was sitting and immediately stopped to greet me and inquire why I was in detention. He understood that this old piece of paper could be suspect for the young soldiers. He asked for the soldier to come into the room and proceeded to explain the legal document of the MPLA. Scorcio further explained that during the war of liberation, many countries had helped the MPLA, and many documents were in circulation; however, an MPLA document signed by Dr. Neto, the president, needed to be looked at in a different light. Scorcio explained to the young man that sometimes "old papers are better than new ones." The soldier apologized and gave me a big hug. Another learning experience: remember the high illiteracy rate; he could not read the French and English document, and more superior officers were unavailable, so he was protecting his country from foreign invaders and mercenaries.

All is well, and I am off to Hotel Panorama, situated on the finger-shaped island called *ilha* advancing some fifteen kilometres into the Atlantic, forming a southern seawall for Luanda Harbour.

A chauffeur is assigned and I begin to search for my friends.

My house is now occupied by refugees, and there is no sign of *Camarade* Morais, who was given the responsibility for the house. My comfort level soon turns to gloom. Kafuxi, Diendengue, Morais—my old buddies—are now targets for assassination and highly protected. I leave messages, but to no avail. The security is overwhelming. After one week of no success, I decide to sit at the door of the Secretary of State for Energy, Comrade Kaboolu, and wait for six hours before seeing him. Overwhelmed by the workload, he gives me a half-hour briefing, and we conclude that it is not a good time to be in Angola.

I meet with Scorcio, Paulo Jorge, Diendengue, Kafuxi, Kabuloo, Lara, Carreira, and Pacavera. There is an air of resilience, a pause allowing the new independent state of Angola to breathe lightly and begin preparations for the next war. Tension in Luanda and the sporadic gunfire create an uneasiness below the surface, a feeling that the lid of peace could blow off the relative calm.

MPLA had assigned a driver so that I could meet and be secure in my runaround meetings. One evening the driver suggested that we should take in a movie. As in colonial times, your entry ticket was to an assigned seat. I followed his lead, and within five minutes, two Angolans appeared with tickets to the seats that we were in. The driver would not agree to move, and a commotion started up. I said to the driver, "Let's get out of here," since I knew that this could set up an argument, fully appreciating that we were wrong and outnumbered. So I grabbed his hand and pulled him towards the exit and returned to the hotel. Another incident occurred when the driver decided while waiting for my meeting to end, that he would run a few errands, without notification. When I arrived at the street level, the driver was away, so I walked back to the hotel, situated on the Luanda Island a distance of five kilometres from the meeting site. The driver finally realized that I had found my way home and explained his actions while realizing that he had jeopardized my safety. He was removed from the driver pool.

I had to accept this real new Angola, and of course this meant that I would not see Dr. Neto, a very sad realization that my time was up. Someday when the power structure is in a peaceful mode, I could contribute to the rebuilding of my adopted home—Angola.

There was no way to predict how long this would take, or the military cost, collateral damage, and the human cost that would be borne by the Angolan people.

Having spent two weeks developing a full understanding of the dark situation and long-impending war, I am heartbroken and return to my tomatoes and flower production in Canada.

CHAPTER THIRTEEN

The three-legged stool of understanding is held up by history, languages and mathematics. . .if you lack any one of them you are just another ignorant peasant with dung on your boots.

—Robert Heinlein

I continue to listen to my shortwave radio, and the news, mainly from the BBC and France Inter, is not good. The South African army is now involved, and the first steps to divide the country in half are underway. If their plan works, Angola will have a West and East Angola. There will be real problems in pulling this off. The USA loves apartheid and minority rule and pushes the FNLA and UNITA to join their military adventure, and an "anticommunist" front is created. America's General Curtis LeMay proposes to blast a canal with limited nuclear weapons in order to isolate the communists in Angola and therefore protect the apartheid government. Since 1975, the ANC army, Spear of the Nation, have been building their army in bases provided by the Angolan government.

On April 10, 1977, CIA operative John Stockwell resigned from the agency. In his book, *In Search of Enemies*, the CIA point man writes, "Under the leadership of the CIA director we lied to Congress and to the 40 Committee which supervised the CIA's Angola program." He goes into some detail: "We entered into joint activities with South Africa. And we actively propagandized the American public, with cruel results— Americans, misguided by our agents' propaganda, went to fight in Angola in suicidal circumstances. One died, leaving a widow and four children behind. Our secrecy was designed to keep the American public and press from knowing what we were doing—we fully expected an outcry should they find out."

Savimbi meets secretly with Botha while, in Lusaka, the Angolan government is attempting to negotiate a cease fire to be followed by elections.

Angola is the key to the sub-Saharan continent. It has a strong army and is rich in resources. The politics of the MPLA are very different from the Zambian and Tanzanian regimes, forced to live under constant threat of aerial bombing, book bombs' attacking key figures, and the economic stranglehold on landlocked Zambia, which needed to import food through Rhodesia and its UDI government. Humiliating independent Africa was a very common strategy of the minority governments. They constantly repeated that if it were not for the Europeans, Africa would starve.

In September of 1979, while watching the CBS news, I learn that my friend Dr. Neto had died of cancer. I was very sad.

My great friend was no longer; for the next two months, I grieved. The founder of the Angolan Nation, a man who had given me a role to play in the independence of his country, who treated me as a friend, was silenced.

Angola lost a great man, leaving sadness and a rudderless nation.

The MPLA had to find another "big man." This could happen only through political development. I remembered a young Angolan from the 1974 visit to Canada, a certain Jose Eduardo Dos Santos. Having travelled with him during the Canada tour, I knew he had all the potential to be a great leader. Time would tell.

American business entered the propaganda war when "Forum for a Healthier American Society" (Vol. III, No.1, January 1981) appeared as a centre document in *Newsweek* magazine, sponsored by Smith Kline.

In particular, we must stop treating South Africa as a moral leper and look on her as a necessary ally . . . We must, through the efforts of American business, labour and church leaders, and through quiet diplomacy encourage South Africa to alter her policies with respect to human rights. But we must not make absolute adherence to our standards a prior condition for alliance.

This was discouraging, and a challenge. When US corporations become mouthpieces of American foreign policy, their lies and deception cause great distortion to democratic ideals.

My friend Evan visited me in my self-imposed exile on the farm. He continued with his work as a first-class printer, volunteering his time to the anti-apartheid movement in Ottawa and to the NDP. When the party had a printing job to do, Evan was the man to go to. During one of his visits, he mentioned that he had spoken to Colleen. She was well, and suggested that, since we were living apart, a formal legal divorce should take place.

On the train to Toronto to visit a friend, I stopped in Montreal for a job interview with Oxfam Quebec. The retiring Oxfam Director, my old friend Pierre Rivard, had proposed me to the hiring committee but within a half hour it became clear that I was not the guy, so I made my way to the VIA Rail station and took my seat.

The conductor, while checking the tickets, asked if everything was all right. My fellow passenger said she found it cold. He carried on his ticket collection and when his boss asked, "Is everything okay?" he replied, "Except that woman who is bitching" (in French, *chialer*).

I jumped up and took him to task. "She responded politely to your question about her comfort. Your response was aggressive and uncalled for." The dressing-down worked, and my fellow passenger appreciated my stance. She introduced herself as Joan Donnelly, executive secretary to the president of Domtar, a major Canadian paper company. Her French was very good, and we were off to the bar car, on her tab.

Joan and I kept in touch and soon she announced that she was engaged to Brian Riordon, a Montreal lawyer. I explained my marital reality to him. He was very astute, and his good heart jumped in, "I will take care of it, pro bono."

Joan introduced me to a group of Montreal friends who rented a cottage at Blueberry point on Lake Massawippi. I met many interesting people. My role was to make sure I brought tomatoes. In fact, I was known as *Jacques la tomate* or Tomato Jacques. It was always a great outing.

On September 16, 1983, the Superior Court of Quebec ruled, and an official divorce was granted. We shared a wonderful meal. Colleen seemed in good spirits and much happier, and so we parted.

Then one weekend in the summer of 1984, two Toronto businessmen, Ken and Gerry, came to visit Blueberry Point and wanted to visit my greenhouse operation. The conversation soon turned to a business opportunity they were looking into and they needed someone with my technical skill and drive.

In September of 1984, I drove to Uxbridge and met the potential owners, who asked for a cost estimate to re-energize their 600-acre recreation park. Within seven days, it was clear that this was an opportunity not to be passed up, offering a partnership in Pleasure Valley. The program would be picnic area and slo-pitch tournaments in the summer and in the winter season, cross-country skiing. Many ideas were floated, including horseback riding, a sugar shack program for the schools, as well as a serious Monday to Friday school program geared to high school athletic programs. Many of these programs needed to be suited to the French school curriculum, another great opportunity.

I returned to Bromptonville and put the fifteen-acre greenhouse operation up for sale; over the next four weeks I had no offers. One person wanted to rent. My hand was forced, and the renter moved in.

He paid the first month and never made another payment. It would take another year to move this parasite out and with the mess he left behind, there was nothing to do but leave it as is. I left the farmhouse without closing the front door, a total loss.

I moved to Uxbridge and prepared for the winter season of cross-country skiing.

The daily routine of up at six am and at the valley by 7:30 soon reminded me of the farm, all work and little play. During the spring months, we introduced maple sugar visits for schools, and my bilingual skills opened up new markets. I soon regained my physical condition through bush clearing and long days on cross-country skis.

As the years rolled by, I never lost touch with my passion for the independence movements in southern Africa.

CHAPTER FOURTEEN

American Help in the Apartheid Wars

In June 1985, in Jamba, a small town in the heartland of Angola and a base for Savimbi of the UNITA secessionist army funded by China and the CIA, a secret meeting was underway. A young Republican, Jack Abramoff, an ultra-orthodox Jew, represented the International Freedom Foundation, codenamed Pacman, along with members of Oliver North's North American right, Nicaraguan contras. Their host was none other than Jonas Savimbi. Abramoff, paid by New York right-wing Lewis Lehrman, was there to covertly advance US policies. He offered political and military guidance to Savimbi and proposed to convince the CIA to covertly channel weapons to Savimbi's war.

In 1995, South Africa's Truth Commission revealed that the International Freedom Foundation—IFF—was run out of Johannesburg, though officially headquartered in Washington

In early 1986, President Ronald Reagan took a very big step and received UNITA founder Jonas Savimbi at the White House and proclaimed that Savimbi was Angola's Abraham Lincoln. This meeting was the work of the ultraconservative Political Action Group, whose membership included Jack Abramhoff.

In 1995, South Africa's Truth Commission revealed that the International Freedom Fund had been used to give the South Africans a channel into the American establishment, funnelling $1.5 million per annum to smooth over problems and keep up a smear campaign against Mandela.

But the most damning proof of the USA's support for apartheid was revealed in a January 24, 2006 *Mail and Guardian* article by Craig Williamson, one-time apartheid spy and book bomb specialist, that the South African military had funded an elaborate military intelligence operation code-named Operation Babushka. This was not just to undermine the ANC, it was also designed to support Savimbi.

From his high perch, lobbyist Jack Abramoff, member of the K street Washington gang and Republican insider, was convicted as a felon in 2006, during the George W. Bush administration.

It was a clear indication that the USA would continue to be bold, arrogant, and overwhelming. In order to Africanize the war, the Americans needed to channel arms and personnel through Zaire so that South Africa could be perceived as a non-player in the battles for Angola.

"The decision has been made and the process is in motion," reported the *Daily Dispatch* of February 26, 1986, quoting Chester Crocker, a US official expert in disinformation and Washington's hatchet man, who preferred to insult and denigrate Angolan officials instead of hearing the message. This attitude could only foster contempt at a diplomatic solution when experts such as Angola's Foreign Minister M'Binda went toe to toe and asked the most obvious of questions regarding independence.

The Angolans could only shake their heads at the miscues and inability of the US to conduct meaningful dialogue, while Angolan officials were left measuring their arrogance, contempt, and false appraisal of the Angolan reality.

"Wishful thinking" was the operative American phrase.

Knowing Minister M'Binda very well, I could imagine his demeanour would disarm the arrogance quickly and grind out a true position for dialogue on matters of substance. Diplomatic double-speak would be denounced and dialogue become a monologue, an American monologue, as the MPLA would listen for days, weeks, and months if necessary till the Americans and UNITA surrogates ran out of words.

The discussions leading to the Lusaka Accords was a classic example of an objective dialogue with focus; other inputs were discarded without response.

Agreement to have elections was accepted. MPLA got the most votes, while President Dos Santos defeated Savimbi for the post of president.

Here is what the *Globe and Mail* of Toronto had to say in its editorial of November 4, 1992:

. . . 800 international observers had declared the voting mostly free and fair, Mr. Savimbi cried fraud, gathered up his fighters and returned to the bush . . . Democracy, it seems, has lost its luster for UNITA's "great leader" . . . Mr Savimbi must take the blame for this turn of events.

Simultaneous negotiations took place between the ANC and the apartheid government to seek the release of Mandela and to set a date for elections leading to majority rule and independence.

Of course the presence of Cuban troops brought in by the Angolan government to defend the southern Angolan front and the subsequent military action at Cuito Cuanavale were invaluable in protecting Angolan sovereignty. The South African army, for all its bravado, was defeated, and only a political settlement that included the Cuban forces needed to be negotiated. The Cubans leave, and there is independence for Namibia and Zimbabwe, and elections in Azania.

After two years at Pleasure Valley, it was time to move on. I volunteered my services to the Canadian Executive Services Organization—CESO. My first assignment was at the Half Moon Club in Montego Bay. The project was energy conservation and technical training.

Over the winter of 1986/87, I volunteered in the CESO office and carried out more projects in Jamaica and with the First Nations in Ontario.

In the fall of '86, I met a woman who had lived on a kibbutz in Israel, spoke excellent French, and was sympathetic to my passion for Angola. Soon Ann and I were a couple and agreed to a future together.

In January 1988, CARE Canada contacted me and asked that I set up a meeting with the Angolan ambassador at the UN. CARE Canada, USA, and Europe were having difficulty getting into Angola. Angola had sent my old friend *Camarade* Pacavira to direct the Angolan diplomatic operations at the UN. The meeting in February went off very well, and CARE got the green light.

On December 7, 1988, a daughter we named Danielle was born, a great joy. I found this family setting so very good for my soul.

Daughter Danielle age 3.

Since Angola was not calling, I started up a construction company, which was very successful. I enjoyed fatherhood and built my schedule around Danielle's needs.

On January 26, 1989, we took possession of an 1860 home in Whitby, and over the next four weeks just put in the labour necessary to ensure a pleasant environment for all.

I made sure that Danielle learned French, learned how to skate and enjoy the outdoors, and learned how to travel by making many trips to Florida to visit my parents. We shared the annual event of the Royal Winter Fair.

There was plenty of work in the construction industry, but it eventually collapsed. Time to move on again.

In the fall of 1989, I obtained a teaching post in French as a Second Language—FSL—at Seneca College and Durham College. This adult education opportunity was very good for my spirits; I was contributing to a more inclusive world.

Over the years, I had been aware of the Rotary club and its ideals. However, the politics of apartheid and the continued exclusion of non-whites made me very uncomfortable. Once Mandela was out of jail, Rotary needed to be open to non-whites, just as the clubs around the world were forced to reckon with the presence and contribution of women. After some prodding, I accepted and in January 1992 became a full and active member of Rotary in Whitby, Ontario.

I loved the four-way test, especially the first question: "Is it the truth?" That did it for me; I joined Rotary.

However, I soon learned that the old boys' network was very active. Non-whites and French Canadians were tolerated. I could handle the near-second-class membership in certain clubs. I certainly did not speak to my passion. I was known under my construction name of Jacques of All Trades. I visited other clubs and soon found a number of very dedicated members who accepted women and other minorities.

In 1997, Angola opened its embassy in Ottawa. I was not invited to join, which really got me upset. The new Angolan ambassador at the UN, replacing Pacavira in July of 1991, was M'Binda. I called him to express my concerns. Over the weekend, he attempted to get the Chargé d'Affaires at the Ottawa embassy to understand, but he, too, was refused, despite a recent letter from President Dos Santos encouraging me to continue. I sent a copy of this 1997 letter and copy of the original letter dating back to February 1974.

I was ignored and excluded.

Meanwhile, Canadian airplane manufacturer Bombardier invited me to a meeting to discuss how I could help them arrange a business connection in Angola. Retired General Gordon Rea was the point man.

January 7: The Wednesday morning meeting required that I spend the night in Ottawa. I started on the four-hour road trip at seven

p.m. As I headed down Highway 401, the weather forecasters announced the grimmest of news: "Heavy freezing rain, stay off the road."

Getting to Ottawa was important and so for the next eight hours, at a snail's pace, witnessing the flashes from exploding transformers and stopping often to add de-icing fluid, I made it to the Market Place Hotel.

On time for the 8:30 meeting, Mr. Rowbottom, General Rae, the head of overseas sales, and I sat down to discuss their needs. By 12:00, the weather conditions forced city officials to close all downtown buildings and by 1:00 p.m., I was back in my hotel room. This comfortable "prison" would hold me until Friday night and a visit with the top Angolan official. Result: no co-operation. I had survived the worst ice storm but failed to shift my involvement with the Angolan government. The return trip to Whitby on Saturday was a sombre affair.

By the summer of 1998, I'd had enough of the separation from Angola. I purchased a ticket and prepared for Luanda.

The home front was now coming apart. Danielle's mother no longer thought that my "raison d'être" was acceptable. I spoke with Danielle on a few occasions during the car trips to her summer camp, explaining that her papa had other things that he needed to do. And so in late August, 1998, I drove her to camp and told her that I loved her very much and I would be leaving. I would return, but I was leaving to follow my dream.

The trip to Luanda was abbreviated by a five-day stop in Lisbon. I wanted to see the site that I knew through books: the most notorious place, the jail that held political prisoners, where Neto and many other African leaders had been detained; the International Police Defence of the State—PIDE—had a reputation for torturing and executing "enemies of Portugal," as those who aspired to freedom were defined. The jail was situated in the heart of Lisbon on the road leading to the castle that protected the government of the day during invasions by the Spaniards.

Portugal was the host country for the world exposition, and I visited the site many times. Angola had a very impressive pavilion. The ongoing war was a major topic of discussion.

I walked a lot and worked my mind, planning the tactics of this journey.

I focused on the question, how can the war be stopped? How can Canada play a vital role?

How can the spirit of Lester B. Pearson, Nobel Peace Prize winner, effective international leader, be applied to Angola?

Pearson had created CUSO, which gave me the opportunity of a lifetime. It was time to apply Canadian generosity to Angola.

Angola was the turning point for all of Southern Africa. The steps to independence of Namibia, South Africa, and Zimbabwe start with Angola's being free.

It is Angola's turn to have peace. What are the obstacles to peace?

Who finances the terrorists and who benefits from the war?

Buried in the details of the Lusaka Accords: a ceasefire, the disarming of UNITA, the integration into the armed forces, and the supervision by the Blue Helmets of the UN. Their mandate was ending on August 31, 1998. What then?

The more information I included in the question of what is to be done, the better my spirits became.

Rotary had taken up the mantle to eradicate polio, and if I arrived as a member visiting the local club, willing to participate in the vaccination campaign, I would create a great opportunity to meet Angolans as well as other nationalities.

On the plane to Luanda, I changed into my shorts and tee-shirt. I knew that this would upset the officials, since this type of clothing is considered to belong at the beach, but my comfort was more important.

Arriving at Luanda, again with no visa but carrying my "old piece of paper," I was stopped again. I went on the offensive, stating that "I was coming as a guest of *Camarade* Paulo" (Jorge, Secretary for External Relations for MPLA). His name certainly got their attention. I was allowed into the concourse but could not leave the airport till someone from Paulo Jorge's department came to get me.

I was soon whisked away to Hotel Tropico, a famous site, since many of the mercenaries and other undesirables who had come to help UNITA had stayed here.

I quickly learned that UNITA members of Parliament and other high officials resided at this hotel. No guns were allowed into the hotel but I could feel the tension of the ongoing confrontation between the government and UNITA. Under the Lusaka Accords, UNITA had been given senior postings, including ambassadorships to seven countries. Canada was one of the seven postings where UNITA ambassadors were to represent the government at the highest level.

The next day, a senior MPLA person came to visit and provided a bodyguard with a vehicle.

This long-awaited return to Angola was a dream come true. It had been twenty-one years since my abortive attempt to make contact in 1976.

Soon Paulo Jorge wanted to see me. As I made my way by car to

MPLA HQ, the sight of so many war victims, some in wheelchairs, others on crutches, shook me, the effects of land mines so evident. A vibrant city congested with traffic, Luanda had been overwhelmed by internal refugees who had fled the upcountry terrorism of UNITA. Built for 300,000 people, the beautiful city now held more than three million persons and the war effort meant that upkeep and growth of services were non-existent. Raw sewage and pools of stagnant water gave water-borne diseases a place to flourish.

Paulo Jorge greeted me warmly. In mutual respect and in the need to hear how our lives had changed since our last get-together, we talked for more than five hours. We explored potential goals as well as who could help us achieve them. The next day, the chauffeur drove up to Villa Alice so I could see my old home. On our way, we passed statues of soldiers that I had known. The largest hospital was called Americo Boavida and the bookstore Anibal de Mello, while the military had honoured one of their own, *Camarade* Jika, in naming the main military base and training centre. I was deeply moved. The driver kept asking if I was okay; my silent observation spoke volumes. These men I had known were part of history. All heroes, they had died in service of the struggle for independence. These reminders of my friends and comrades made me very sad and very proud.

My visit to the *mauselau* (mausoleum) dedicated to the Founding

Father of the Nation, Dr. Neto, would wait for another day.

My first planned meeting, with Dr. Albino Malungo, Minister of *Reinsertion National* (National Reintegration), gave an inside view of the problems—and I mean problems. As a result of the American-imposed war, there were food shortages, refugees, some 90,000 land mine victims, increasing by forty persons a month, a breakdown of spirits in the population; a huge mess. Angola had more land mines—13,000,000—in its soil than people.

Where do you start?

Some fifteen minutes into the meeting, he excused himself to make a call and returned to say that someone wanted to speak to me. He handed the phone and the French voice said, "*Bienvenue en Angola, ici le Camarade Petroff,*" and I replied "*C'est pas vrai!*" It's not true! "*Camarade Petroff, quelle plaisir.*" "What a pleasure to hear your voice."

He was very courteous and happy that I was in Luanda and told me that as soon as he found a spot in his busy schedule I must come to see him.

Busy is a very pale description of his responsibilities, since General Petroff was the Minister of the Interior responsible for state security forces, intelligence, and the police forces. *Camarade* Malungo had given me an insight as to what had to be done. Land mines and their removal were a top priority. No, I said under my breath, that's not true. Everything is a priority.

More meetings followed.

What role for Canada? Why is Canada not playing a larger role?

Canada still had a political presence with a designation of "Honorary Councillor," the very same status that was extended to the Portuguese colonial regime for so many years. Having been one of the first nations to recognize the Angolan government in 1975, it sure had been slow to support a legitimate and world-accepted democratic Parliament.

Since I knew the HC, it was no surprise that his way would be to discourage any support for the government. I will later give an example of this inaction-oriented Canadian official.

MPLA officials and the government could not understand the logic behind the faint public expression of support for the emerging government, since Canadians through the NGOs had been so upfront in supporting the anti-colonial struggle.

Paulo Jorge was setting up meetings with other government ministers and planning an audience with President Dos Santos.

It was time for me to open the Rotary connection; I was able to meet the past president of the local club. She and her husband picked me up at the hotel and made sure that I was well taken care of. They had not the slightest knowledge of my past and were certainly inquisitive, so I told them, "I can understand Portuguese but cannot speak it." This gave me an excuse for being silent during the meeting.

The majority of club members were former colonials who used the local sailing club as a meeting place. Upon entering the very nice room, I met Dutch-, Portuguese-, German-, and English-speaking Rotarians. The meeting was conducted in Portuguese, and I remained seated and silent till the subject of the upcoming eradication of polio project came up.

I acknowledged that I would participate; all I needed was a ride to the distribution point. The vaccine had been delivered by container and needed to be broken out into regional allocations and distributed via truck route and small plane. I was very uncomfortable with the mindset, and most of all, the colonial language and contempt that filtered through the language. Anti-MPLA sentiments were expressed, and UNITA was deemed to be invincible.

However there was one interesting member whom I recognized as a fellow guest at Hotel Tropico. He was not just another member of Rotary, but also the Admiral of the UN Blue Helmets peacekeepers in Angola, dressed in white. Here was someone I really wanted to talk with. It was just a matter of timing, since we shared the same roof.

A fellow Rotarian had invited a guest. Dressed to the nines, this thirtyish black Angolan, attending his first meeting, was surveying the room and sizing up the membership, very polite and nodding his understanding. When the meeting broke up, I went over to meet this new guy. Well spoken in English, he offered his hand and introduced himself as Luke, and, following polite greetings, I asked where he worked. He answered, "I am a pilot for Sunangol." Sunangol is the state-run oil company. Translated, this meant, "I am a member of MPLA," so I asked him immediately for a ride back to the hotel and he agreed. We walked to his Land Rover, and as he opened the passenger door, a handgun fell to the ground. He immediately looked around to see if any others had seen it. The coast was clear.

As we drove back to the hotel, I told him who I was and that I was a guest of the MPLA through the offices of Paulo Jorge. He said, "Man, you kidding me." I responded with a no. "Well, then let's go the local bar and talk some more." We needed to be in a safe place. Luke started to talk, and his questions were very precise. It soon became a dialogue as we got over our mutual surprise.

Luke dropped me off near the hotel and promised to come back tomorrow. He would call first and set up an outside meeting place, since we could not be seen together in the hotel setting. It was three a.m., but I was too stimulated to be sleepy.

On my way to breakfast the next morning, the admiral stepped into the same elevator and, as we rode to the top, greeted me as a fellow Rotary member and invited me to join his table. This was one invitation I was sure to accept. We gathered our buffet-style meal and were soon joined by soldiers from the UN Peacekeepers; following the introductions, the business of the UN took over.

Their conversations were littered with anti-government slurs, anti-Angolan slurs, meaning that the "P" word (Portuguese version of the "N" word) was used like lemon on fresh-cooked fish.

The mentality of this gang of soldiers was pure neo-colonialism. They were better than the locals, who would never be as smart or hardworking as the Portuguese. It was Portuguese know-how and racial superiority that had built Angola (sic). The "fuses" of my patience and humanity were popping in my head. I had heard this so many times before, but hearing it now, repeated by people with more serious influence, was very difficult. Not only had I discovered an ideological gold mine, the UN was not doing its jobs. The demilitarization of UNITA was taking much more time than it should. UN-appointed soldiers continued to allow UNITA mobility and secret arms caches. It was only a question of time before the reality of their action would be exposed.

Since the breakfast soldiers had not inquired what I was doing in Luanda, I needed to insert that I was involved with the admiral in the polio eradication program through Rotary. Boy, was this a good story; and having the admiral agree established my credentials beyond anything I could have hoped for. The admiral offered me a permanent seat at his table. What luck!

Luke called late that morning and met me up the street at a local coffee bar. He said that he would show me Luanda. Soon, we arrived in a slum area and a visit to one of his girls, meaning an informer, part of a system of monitoring the city through a number of women posing as hookers. He got a licence number and description of the intruder. Nobody except the locals went to these areas. If a stranger came here, it was to subvert Luanda peace and create panic through explosions and acts of sabotage. The Zambizanga slum had no running water, slow public transportation, stagnant water pools, beaten red earth paths, extreme poverty, apparent hopelessness, and the strength of the Angolan struggle. The war inflicted by the American surrogates UNITA, using slave labour to extract diamonds to finance the civil war—all the elements added up to genocide.

Luke wanted to show me another of his tasks, so we drove to the beautiful beaches of the *ilha*—the island. We entered a restaurant, and the warm greetings accorded to Luke were soon passed on. I was a friend, no name or origin declared. A table was reserved, and the food and wine arrived as well as many passing greeters. Some of the greetings were in Portuguese and others in local languages. It was more than just greetings, it was a summary of overnight events and a new "things to do" list.

After the meal, we walked over to the palm tree area and to a woman sitting there. They exchanged greetings and her verbal report started. There had been unusual activity and visitors to the island. Could this be part of a landing of mercenaries and saboteurs?

Since she was working for the security branch of the government, she required money. Her eyes, like so many Angolan women in the guise of street hookers, provided an excellent security network. They acted like hookers, but their price was beyond reach.

They were there to see, not act. Luke was the go-between and the conduit for money.

Government officials had bought up the Luanda service stations and closed most of them down. The few that remained open provided free fuel to security vehicles and controlled the quantity of fuel provided to any other vehicles; no large quantities in extra containers permitted.

Luke dropped me off a few blocks from the hotel. I was very tired and stimulated. I could see security matters were very much under control.

Following my second meeting with Dr. Malungo on August 31, I made my way to the lobby and my waiting ride back to the hotel. Today I would get a lift with the head of Angola's NGO community, Ms. Palmira Tjipilika—a very impressive woman, full of charm, who had the difficult job of sorting out and assigning outside help within a fragmented territory. Acts of terrorism were random throughout the country, so security for the NGO community was always a consideration.

It was four p.m. and time for the radio news. "This broadcast has been interrupted by the following communiqué from the Supreme Court of Angola," said the announcer.

"In a historic decision this afternoon, the Supreme Court of Angola has suspended immediately all activities of UNITA. The party has been suspended and all government officials occupying posts designated by the Lusaka Accords are also suspended."

Ms. Tjipilika and I looked at each other in utter disbelief. She pulled over to the curb so we could chat.

Was this the end of UNITA? More questions and checked emotions, UNITA had never co-operated, so the excitement could only be related to the possibility that this strategy the government had followed would hasten the end of the war.

The moment of decision had arrived, and soon another bulletin announced the arguments presented by government lawyers laying out UNITA's continued lack of respect and non-adherence to the

Lusaka Accords; the continued sabotage throughout the country; the assassination of innocent civilians; the continued mining of roads and gardens demonstrated the illegal activities of UNITA contrary to the spirit of the Lusaka Accords.

Music resumed following the update, and I got out at the hotel.

The immediate effect of the Supreme Court decision meant that the UNITA cadre living at Hotel Tropico were now without money or work. Every morning following breakfast they stood on the sidewalk outside the hotel lobby, and since travel was forbidden and bank accounts frozen, life was no longer good.

The Luanda UNITA group elected to expel Savimbi from the party and they reconstituted UNITA–*Renovada*—Renovated UNITA. Numerous meetings with government officials led to the resumption of their activities.

Over the next two weeks, meetings with different ministries were positive, and all expected the war to go on. The question was always, "How can we stop this war?"

The meeting with *Camarade* Petroff proved most informative. He had his finger on the pulse of security matters and expressed his frustration over the destruction of his country by a group of thugs, a group who thought apartheid was a good deal for Angola. Petroff and many others had to wait through hopelessness with no end of the war in sight.

It became clearer and clearer to me that Canada could have a pivotal role in the conflict. It was like an equation in algebra that won't resolve without the variable k, which is unknown, but essential. Canada could supply that k factor without objection.

Luke showed up and said, "Today I will show you the scope of our military strength and capability." We were going into the main military base, and as we approached the guarded gates, soldiers appeared and stood at attention as they recognized the green Rover and its driver. The barricade lifted before a full stop and we meandered over a crooked road inside the base. Large mounds of sand and hangers shielded the MIG jets and helicopters.

We swung over to the offices area and got out.

"*Camarade* Jacques, I need to go to my office, so come with me."

We went to the second floor, and the numerous windows gave a great view of the base. Luke asked me to sit in a room till he returned. As I stood overlooking the hanger floor while admiring the aviation hardware, the door behind me opened and this huge man entered. I absolutely froze. "*Non e possible*"—"Not possible," I said. Towering over me was a man whose face I recognized immediately.

This was the son of Americo Boavida. I was stunned by his resemblance to his dad. He walked over to me and we embraced. This was Munduman, the little boy I had known in Dar, now also a pilot for Sunangol. My emotions could not be contained and the tears of joy flowed. At six feet two inches, this duplicate of my friend, his dad, held me tight and within thirty seconds, Luke entered the room. He had known about my relationship with the Boavida family and he had given me a great surprise. Munduman added that his mother would dearly love to see me; he would get back to me with a date.

More meetings with government officials; the results were the same, Angola has lots to do but only if it has peace. I visited Mrs. Boavida in her Cezario Verde home for four hours. She was so pleased when I gave her a copy of the last interview that Americo had given. She offered to call Mrs. Neto and I spoke with her briefly. Given the frantic activities created by the Supreme Court decision as well as the shortness of notice, it was not possible to see her. Mrs. Neto invited me to her home during my next visit.

I called my old friend Pacavira, now governor of Kwanza North, a province that was heavily damaged by terrorists and under constant threat of more military assaults. "*Camarade* Jacques, you must come and see me. I will send a car to pick you up." Two days later, we were ready for the 180 kilometer trip. Two armed guards and a journalist from the local Angola Press News Agency also travelled with us.

The first hour went smoothly, and then we hit the dirt road. Full of holes created by land mines, some six feet deep, it was like being in a cement mixer, body constantly thrown around, dust and mental insecurity. We came through Catete, the village where Dr. Neto was born. All bridges and roadside structures had been destroyed by UNITA. What a mess.

We made it to another paved road surface, and as we climbed the hill and rounded the curve at the top, there stood a large Russian tank overlooking the area. My heart sank. This was really serious, but my nervousness was soon calmed as the village of N'Dalatando, residence of Governor Pacavira, was in sight. He was very happy to see us, and a simple Angolan meal was awaiting our arrival. I suspect that not too many visitors get here by road. Government officials fly in.

It was now 3:00 p.m. I was tired and hungry, it had been a non-stop trip, and I was very happy to have arrived safely.

For the next four days, we saw the massive destruction by UNITA. The infrastructure, water pumps, buildings, churches, and office buildings lay in ruins.

Long discussions continued to haunt the future of the crown jewel of Portuguese colonialism. Independent and still at war, I could feel the energy and spirit being evaporated from the Angolan soul.

The return trip to Luanda was uneventful.

I had seen enough and heard more than I expected. It was time to draw up a plan of action, but first I needed an official designation to allow me to begin pushing the buttons of Canada's government.

Paulo Jorge arranged a meeting with President dos Santos, and as we waited in the antechamber, we were informed that our meeting had been overridden by the urgency of the situation. The American ambassador needed to speak with President Dos Santos, since the recent suspension of UNITA had shifted the balance of power. So we got back in our car and returned to Hotel Tropico.

On September 22, 1998, Dr. Malungo appointed me to represent his Ministry in matters related to land mines and land-mine injuries.

In December 1997, the convention of forty countries on banning production, distribution and usage of mines had begun.

In March of 1999, the convention, now signed by 122 nations, became a treaty under international law.

Armed with this new appointment by the minister of *Reintegration Social*—Social Reintegration, I came back to Canada and stopped in Ottawa to give a copy of my official document to the highest officer in the Embassy of Angola, but he refused to see me. So I went on to Whitby.

While I was in Luanda, I missed Danielle terribly, but all my attempts to reach her were frustrated by my partner, who seemed to be trying to create a rift. I called the Whitby police and asked them to go to the house and stay until my call came. Within thirty minutes, I was speaking to Danielle. This challenging event was a warning sign of things to come.

Home life was no longer, since Ann had instigated legal separation and within twenty-four hours of my return, papers were served on me and I needed to defend my daughter and myself.

Well, my old friend and lawyer Mr. Tesluk was there when I needed him. I showed him the papers and he said in a reassuring voice, "Give me the papers and do not think about this. Take care of your daughter and stay well, I will fix this." And he did. His pro bono efforts were payback for the care that I had shown towards his three teenagers when they worked at Pleasure Valley.

As the first step of my plan of action on Angola, I arranged a meeting with local MP Judy Longfield, an old friend, and sought through her office a meeting with Bill Graham, Chair of the Standing Committee on Foreign Affairs. Judy accepted and arranged the meeting.

Bill Graham and Jacques Roy concluding that Canada must do a study on blood diamonds, Nov. 1998. Sep. 21, 2001, the U.N. adopts The Flowler Report. It is a unanimous decision for the Angola government.

Mr. Bill Graham, a well-known MP and confidante to PM Chrétien, received me within three days at his Toronto office.

He greeted me very warmly and I presented my letter of accreditation from Angola in regards to the land mines issue.

We sat down, and I briefed Graham on the situation in Angola and the unbelievable hardship that the war was causing Angola and all of southern Africa.

He was very sympathetic and asked the great question: What can Canada do?

"Mr. Graham, Angola needs more anti-aircraft guns or a study of the role of diamonds." Better known as blood diamonds, the flow of stolen Angolan diamonds from areas controlled by UNITA and the funds for terrorism in Angola needed to be tracked.

Canadian diamond expert Ian Smillie, research coordinator for Partnership Africa Canada, had devoted much of his efforts to the question of blood diamonds. This time a higher level of investigation was required.

Without hesitation, Graham picked up the phone and called Canada's ambassador at the UN and discussed the idea of this study. Ambassador Robert Fowler, who was also the PM's personal representative for the African continent, agreed to the idea.

On January 1, 1999, Canada took up its seat for a two-year mandate on the Security Council.

This was the legal break we were looking for. I was very proud of Canada.

My home was now being sold. I found an apartment close to Danielle's school, and the legal rupture was complete.

In January of 2000, I decided to write my story, and for the next six months, six days a week, I poured my heart out through the keyboard onto the computer screen. The basis of my writings was the many notes and diaries that I had kept. Putting my life on paper was very difficult, especially when I had to relive the details of the death of Boavida, Quidado, Neto. I was understanding the depth of my life in another culture. So emotional, it was often overwhelming.

On many occasions, I just went for a long walk.

I also gave interviews to *L' Express*, Toronto's French newspaper, to the *Whitby Free Press,* and the *Oshawa Times*. This latter, a full-page interview, caught the attention of a group of businesswomen in the Oshawa Centre who got in touch with me, wanting to help. They proposed that a blood drive in the centre hall of the mall would be ideal; it would take place on the Saturday before Mothers' Day. Local city officials, the MP, and the MPP showed up to support the effort. Despite my valiant effort to have the local Rotary Club participate and be the official recipient of the funds, which would be turned over to the Red Cross for use in Angola, I was turned down. The $3,000 we raised was given to the Red Cross, but not designated for Angola. A local Red Cross official also ensured that the group photo excluded this Angolan representative at the event.

In early 1999, Ambassador Fowler visited Angola with a team of experts. Soon they were observing an emerging pattern in the flow as former UNITA soldiers who had left the party and the continuing war came forward with details of the diamond smuggling. Through many interviews and street communications, African countries such as Zaïre, Côte d'Ivoire, and Sierra Leon were identified as transit points for the diamonds packaged in cigarette packs and delivered to Antwerp for the final cutting and polishing for mass distribution and consumption.

In April 2000, the Fowler Report was completed, and in December 2000, the UN accepted the report as is. More time would be required to set up the sanctions against UNITA.

CHAPTER FIFTEEN

*Friendship is the only cement that will ever hold the world together;
there must be not a balance of power, but a community of power; not
organized rivalries, but an organized peace.*

—Woodrow Wilson

In June 2000, I came to the end of the first draft of my biography.

In order to publish, I needed to find Colleen and have her sign off as accepting that she would appear. Gathering my courage, I called her parents' home in Ottawa. The initial reaction by her father was disbelief, since it had been more than twenty years since the last contact. He was very gracious and said that Colleen was staying with them, as she had a new job in Ottawa, and he would pass on the message to call.

A few days later, Colleen did call. Her sweet voice sounded solid, mature, in charge of her life. This was a change.

She agreed to see me and accept a copy of the manuscript. As a professional editor, I knew that the content required a massive revamping, but her view was important.

So, on July 15, I drove up to Colleen's parents residence in Ottawa, where she and her mom were sitting on the front porch. Colleen came to the car to greet me, and I gave her flowers. She wore a long, colourful skirt, had very short hair, and her presentation and body language made it clear that Colleen was a confident woman. I was impressed.

After a great meal, Colleen and I headed out for a nightcap. Over the next two hours, we shared some of our life experiences. Not only was she great-looking and very sweet, she was also single, I noticed.

I continued to promote Angola through my Rotary connections, and my Montreal and Quebec lectures allowed a stop and a visit with Colleen. One month after our first get-together, Colleen asked that I stop to see her. She had finally unpacked her things after her Montreal stay and had found some letters and photos that could be of interest for the book.

She had read the manuscript and agreed to let her name and role become public. In an eight by ten envelope, she presented me with a treasure of numerous letters. I was very heartened by the fact that she still had these in her possession. What a find.

Colleen and I agreed to spend Christmas together with her family and New Year's in North Bay with my mom and my brother Claude's family.

Valentine's Day in Whitby was magnified by Colleen's presence. I had prepared a wonderful meal and the appropriate champagne. This would be a great occasion to ask her to marry me and start a new life. On bended knee, I popped the question and proffered the ring. She agreed to marry one more time. This time it was for the correct reason: love.

At the end of February, I moved in with Colleen and soon found work as a painter.

We set August 18, 2001, as our wedding date and it would be in the backyard behind Colleen's apartment on Crichton Street overlooking the Rideau Canal. The celebrations would be the next day at the Ecology Museum in Hull, amid an exhibition of artwork by New Brunswick artist Marie Hélène Allain. A religious nun, Marie Hélène had developed a theme called "A Stone for You." What a setting.

The events of Sept 11, 2001 and the condemnation of terrorism was now serious news.

The Fowler Report, accepted in December 2000, declared on September 21, ten days after the towers came down, that "UNITA is a terrorist group," and imposed travel restrictions and froze financial assets. Headlining the list of sixty-nine new terrorists was Jonas Malheiro Savimbi, *favourite son of the United Church of Canada* (My emphasis).

After more than a quarter century, MPLA had been vindicated. The Angolans would soon breathe freely. Former UNITA soldiers, now within the Angolan Armed forces—FAA—track Savimbi, and the bearded one is killed on February 22, 2002.

I later learned that Canadian mining exploration company Southern Era were working with the head of UNITA and during one of their secret rendezvous, gave Savimbi two large pistols with ivory handles. With these weapons, Savimbi would shoot the second-last shot of the civilwar.

April 4, the Angolan government decreed a national holiday called *Dia National de Reconciliation*—National Reconciliation Day.

In 1995, Rotary International established the Polio Eradication Champion Award. Since its inception, the winners include former US President Clinton, former UK Prime Minister John Major, UN Secretary Kofi Annan, Egypt's First Lady, Mrs. Suzanne Mubarak, Nigeria's President Olusegun Obasanjo, and Angola's President Jose Eduardo dos Santos.

Angola sent its first Ambassador, Miguel N'Zau Puna, who arrived with his councilor Edgar Gaspar Martins, younger brother of Ismael Martin, now Angola's Ambassador at the UN, a long-time friend of mine dating back to the first war.

Meeting Edgar was very good, uplifting to my spirits. Perhaps his presence and the arrival of an official ambassador will see an integration of my services with the Angolan government.

An official contract was signed on April 2, 2002, with a start date of May first. My title was advisor with responsibilities in commercial and economic matters between Canada and Angola.

I immediately got to work on the economic dossier, and since the Board of Trade in Toronto is where business is carried out, I arranged for the Minister of Finance from Ontario, the Honourable Jim Flaherty, to meet with Ambassador Puna in Ottawa.

During the meeting, Finance Minister Flaherty, Rotarian and former counsel general for Ghana in Toronto, told Ambassador Puna about the importance of Toronto and suggested that Jacques Roy, who is well known in Canada, would be an excellent person for the task of representing Angola. Ambassador Puna agreed, and on June 1, 2002, I was accepted by the Board of Trade.

After April 2, 2002, the land mine dossier was pushed. I met with

M. Sebastien Carrier, who was the Angolan desk man on matters pertaining to the Ottawa Convention.

I was very polite, but each meeting ended with more frustration and misunderstanding as to the status of Angola within the Ottawa Convention.

I asked Sebastien, "What is it that you need to put in motion projects regarding Angola?"

His answer, "We need to have Angola sign the Convention and deposit the signed document with Canada's Ambassador Livermore."

"M. Carrier," I said, "President dos Santos of Angola has signed the document."

He answered, "I have not seen the signature." I could not believe that he did not know this.

I scrambled back home and found a copy of the announcement of the signature. President dos Santos had signed it on December 2, 1997, and somehow it had not been deposited at the Ottawa Convention.

I saw Ambassador Puna immediately, and explained the situation. He would make the necessary inquiries. The original document finally arrived, and so did the scramble to get Ambassador Livermore to see Ambassador Puna to turn over the document.

I was told that Livermore was overbooked and he would be leaving, after completing his five-year mandate, on Friday, July 2. This impossible date had to be made possible.

After coaxing and abject pleading, the coordinating secretary gave us a five-minute window. We needed to be there for 10:20 to meet him on his way back for coffee.

We followed the instructions, and on July 2, Ambassador Puna handed the signed document to Ambassador Livermore. Angola was now part of the Convention ideal and regulations.

Ottawa Convention. Karen Mollica; Ambassador N. Puna; Ambassador for Ottawa Convention, Ambassador Mr. David Livermore, and Jacques Roy. Photo by Jacques Roy.

Time to turn to projects and funding under the Ottawa Convention.

Since early 2002, I had been speaking with John Green, Director of the Prosthetic and Orthotic section at the Ottawa Children's Hospital, since part of their mandate was providing expertise to land mines victims.

John and I had met with Mr. Carrier and agreed to fund an exploratory mission to Angola with the objective of twinning the Ottawa Hospital with the Americo Boavida Hospital and to evaluate how a long- distance medical hook-up could be accomplished.

The mission was approved, and five days before our flight abruptly cancelled without explanation. I was furious; another mess, another interference by Foreign Affairs in a clear-cut mission. John and I provided the best possible duo to accomplish the agreed mission.

Later, I learned that the mission had been carried out by retired LT Colonel Roger St. John, from British Columbia.

On his return, a redacted document was given to the Angola Embassy. I read the "observations" and "conclusions" in utter disgust. He had obviously been steered to downgrade Angola's progress.

Who had set up his mission and what were their objectives? I needed to know who this Roger St. John was.

A little search on the 'Net, and bingo: there he was, a pro-American Canadian soldier and a member of Rotary. Using the Rotary contact, I sent an e-mail asking if he was coming to Ottawa soon. He was, and so, on November 13, we met for breakfast at his Hull hotel.

Cordial at first, I turned to direct questions. JR: Who set up your in-country schedule? St. J: Honorary Counsel, Allan Cain

JR: Did you not meet with General Petroff, head of the Land Mines and Unexploded Ordinance?

St. J: There was no meeting.

JR: Did you meet General Cruz, field commander of Mine Clearing?

St. J: I did not.

JR: Did you not think that these two men that I have mentioned, principal players in the government structure, were worthy of your attention?

St. J: I did not set up the meetings, or *inquire as to why I did not see these men.* (My emphasis. JR.)

JR: Where did you go in Angola?

St. J: I visited Dr. Foster at his hospital.

(Foster is a known sympathizer of Savimbi and critic of the

MPLA.)

JR: Did you meet with the Angola Red Cross? St. J: I did not.

St. John had suggested in his report that any Canadian going to Angola should check in with the State Department—as in the *US* State Department.

What the hell was that all about?

Is our Department of Foreign Affairs not good enough to brief our Canadians?

The humanitarian dimension of his report omitted completely the reality of the land mines victims. He also did not know that Angola had a Rotary Club. This was shocking, since he was the President Elect for 2003–2004 in Chilliwack, B.C.

St. John had also recommended that the Angolan programs dealing with land mine removal were not to be supported—only those associated with equivalent NGO, such as HALO, the German de-mining team, Médecins Sans Frontières, or the United Nations Development Program, UNDP.

St. John agreed that he was not well prepared for the mission and that he had failed to evaluate the strength of the Angolan infrastructure to deal with so many land mine injuries and their removal.

Our ninety-minute breakfast meeting had been very useful. To this day, I do not understand how St. John could possibly have been considered an adequate replacement for John Green and Jacques Roy. This terrible decision, loaded with political revenge, prevented Canada from carrying out its historic role.

Meanwhile, Ambassador Puna and his councillor, M. Martins, carried out a new diplomatic effort to correct this biased view of Angola.

In early 2003, the new ambassador to the Ottawa Convention, Ambassador Ross Hynes, accompanied by the Angolan desk person and land mine assistance program officer, went to Angola. His report was very positive and recognized that Angola was doing all it could and needed more support for its national infrastructure. It was a reprieve for Canada's tarnished image.

Courtesy visit with Canada's U.N. ambassador Robert Fowler to acknowledge the Fowler Report which the U.N. Security Council adopted. Jacques Roy, Ambassador Fowler, Ambassador N. Puna, Counsellor Edgar Martins.

Ambassador Puna requested a meeting with Ambassador Fowler, who was in Ottawa for a short time. This meeting was to show Ambassador Fowler Angola's appreciation for his work on the illegal funding of UNITA and that Angola deeply appreciated the service that he had provided. Canada had risen to the occasion.

Fowler signed copies of his report for Ambassador Puna, M. Martins, and myself.

A copy was signed and dedicated to President Dos Santos and sent on to Luanda.

We received a grant from the Canada Council for the Arts to make a film out of the footage I had shot in Angola. In 2005, my friend Jean Pierre Lefebvre sorted out the raw video that had been taken in 1974. Without ever going to Angola, filmmaker JPL turned out a historic document. Revealing the poetry of Antonio Jacinto on film meant a lot to Angolans. Part of the living history of their nation was on film.

In 2006, Victoriaville-based Claude Paquette and his publishing house Contreforts published a biographical overview of my life entitled, *Tout près de l'oubli*.

It received excellent reviews in the Ottawa paper, *Le Droit*. The headline read: "The spy who opened the irons of Angola . . . a story worthy of the adventures of Indiana Jones and James Bond . . . revealing in detail personal experiences of a spy *une vie rocambolesque* translated, an incredible adventure whose story needs to be told." (Dominique La Haye, *Le Droit*.)

Angolan diplomat Edgar Martins wrote, "The book is *maravilhoso* [marvellous]."

A fellow Rotarian from the Hull Club, Jean Guy St. Arnaud, reviewed the book and wrote, "Jacques Roy is a great Rotarian. Most Rotarians prepare the parade . . . many are in the parade Quidado has

directed the parade."

Mrs. Neto wrote, "   during the war, I heard your name many

times without appreciating your real contribution to the struggle of the Angola people. During the events of April 25, 1974, my husband and I were in your country. The support committee for the MPLA and to President Neto was *formidable*. You received him as if he was Head of State.

"Signed, High Esteem, Maria Eugenia Neto"

On April 26, opposition leader Bill Graham responded to receiving a copy of *Tout près de l'oubli* with the following: "… I took good note of the benevolent proposal to the Liberal Party of Canada and myself. . . thank you."

On August 22, 2006, Angolan diplomat Rogerio Santos and MPLA representative in Canada asked if I would provide a Powerpoint to celebrate the fiftieth anniversary celebrations marking the founding of MPLA.

My friend Jim Austin from Eganville and I pulled together photos and other documents, and on December 9th, I did a running commentary that showed what Canada and Angola had shared since 1968. Addressing Angolans living in Canada on such a day was truly inspiring. I had grown an Angolan heart.

Garth Legge, the United Church of Canada "cheerleader," was given a copy of the manuscript in October of 2000. Legge had previously given me a letter of recommendation and lauded my work. After the reading, he sent me a letter including:

"Our church . . . [which] went to work among the Ovimbundu of Central Angola in the 1880s had been highly committed to the welfare of the Ovimbundu."

Here is what is *not* said:

UNITA were educated by the United Church of Canada, and practiced, in his own words, "tribalism."

In 1974, the UCC wanted to give money to all of the liberation movements in Angola. I told Legge not do that; MPLA is the only legal movement and your links with UNITA are suspect. He accepted my advice.

When Neto was in Toronto, UCC did not want to be seen with MPLA.

Legge accepted my evaluation of one of their missionaries and had her removed. (See May 1975 visit to Huambo.)

He continued: "I was glad to stick my neck out as a friend, but you will understand my position. Now that I have seen your book,

I cannot allow my personal statement to be published and I know that you will continueto take comfort from it personally. You will adhere to my request. Meanwhile, I know that you will respect my request not to publish my statement as I have said above."

His letter was such a copout; he showed how unprincipled he was. Legge was so keen to support my work for the Angolan civilians, but he baulked at the obvious political implications, at least in public. He knew we had been correct in our assessment that independence free of tribalism required both armed struggle and repeated negotiation with the colonizer. The alternative would have been a repeat of Zaire, Zambia, and now Kenya, all racked with tribal conflict.

Sid Gilchrist admitted after thirty-five years of observing colonial bad behaviour, "I should have spoken out clearly against the denial of human rights to Africans. It is much more difficult, however, to convince oneself that we should have waited so long to declare to the world the enormity of the evils of colonialism." (Sid Gilchrist, *Angola Awake*, Ryerson Press, 1968.)

That is all behind us now. I continue to work on behalf of my adopted country, through membership in the Board of Trade in Toronto, fostering investment in Angola's rapidly expanding economy. Fuelled by income from oil, which has reached an output of 1.9 million barrels per day, the economy is growing at twenty percent per year. The biggest brake on development is a lack of cement. I devote myself to explaining to Canadian investors that peace has established a stable political setting, and government policies and programs support economic development.

Other projects I am involved with are seeking to meet agricultural needs by setting up large-scale dairy facilities and by developing agrimineral sites in Angola, as well as providing technical training for the mining and forestry industries. On the NGO side, the land mine victims program is still front and centre. I do not expect to run out of things to do any time soon.

Afterword

LIGA DOS VETERANOS DE GUERRA
DE LIBERTAÇÃO DE ANGOLA

Cartão de Membro N.º 00A

Nome: JACQUES ROY
Natural: CANADIAN / CANADIANNE
Data de Incorporação: / /
Categoria: MEMBRO BENEMERITO
Validade: 8 / 07 / 2013
Luanda, aos 8 / 07 / 08

O TITULAR — O SECRETÁRIO GERAL

...O Veterano de Guerra é o pilar do sacrifício da Independência e da Libertação...

Cabe ás Autoridades Militares, Policiais e Civis o dever de honrá-lo e protegé-lo.

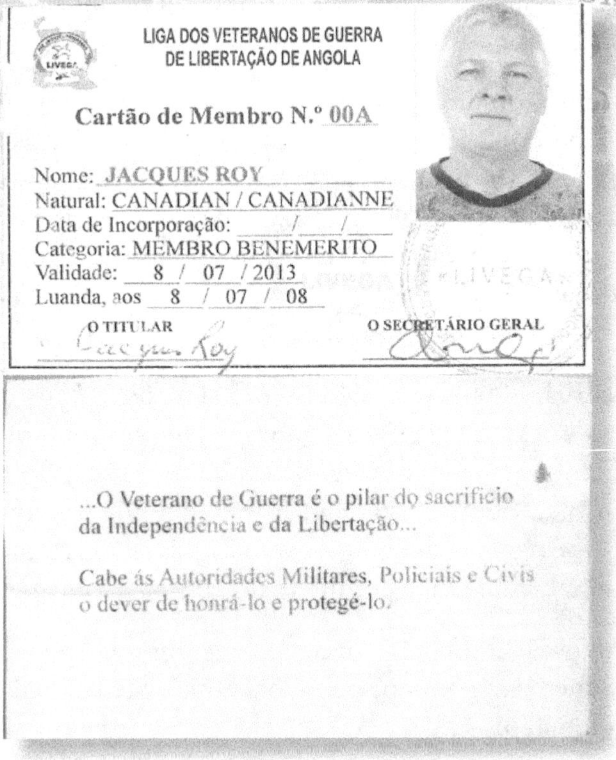

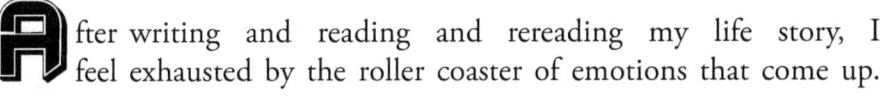

Angolan Veterans card. Front: "League of Veterans who liberated Angola". Back: "Veteran of war is a pillar of sacrifice for Independence and Liberation. If falls to Military Authorities, Police and Civilians who must honour and protect."

After writing and reading and rereading my life story, I feel exhausted by the roller coaster of emotions that come up.

It seems astonishing that a kid from Northern Ontario should find he has dedicated his life to the liberation of a colonized people across the world. I do not think I can fully explain it.

At the time, I was so focused and so determined to make a contribution, so impressed by the dedication and sacrifice of the men and women of the liberation movements, I didn't really think much about how extraordinary it was for a white kid from Kirkland Lake to be deep in-country with Angolan guerrillas, at risk of death or capture by Portuguese soldiers, or posing as a Canadian tourist while gathering intelligence for the ANC in South Africa, at a time when detection could have meant our lives.

All I know for sure is that, having participated in two independence movements, with a view to the independence of a whole region, five countries, and learning to live as so few of us individualists in the west ever have to, without any control or choice about what comes next, has shown me a way of being human, in the supportive company of other committed humans, that I don't believe I would have discovered if I had not made those fateful choices so long ago.

In February 2008, Vice Minister for Foreign Affairs invited me to Angola. Two weeks turned into 4 months and witnessing the election. An overwhelming victory for the MPLA after so many years. They now had proven their political skill and it was time to continue the serious rebuilding of Angola. I did a lot of walking since my friends Luiza and Vicente had taken me in, a gesture that *really appreciated* .

But it was in August that the Veterans of Angola –LIVEGA– officially inducted me into this select of people who resisted the Colonial and neo-colonial presence.

My old friend General Monimambu, now Ambassador Monimambu was my witness in the serene ceremony conducted by LIVEGA Secretary General, General Quina.

General Quina now Secretary General of Angolan Veterans LIVEGA,holding Armalite, NATO issued weapon that he captured in 1964.

Inducted into LIVEGA. Ambassador Monimambu, myself, and SecretaryGeneral, General Quina

The personal satisfaction of having achieved this level was humbling.

In September 2009, the Minister of Culture, Ms. da Silva invited me to participate in a conference on the life of Founding President Dr. Neto. I prepared a speech that touched the 12 years of knowing the wonderful man but the long lasting imprint he had on my life. His wonderful poem says it all.

'Create' from *Sacred Hope* by Dr. A Neto

Create

Create love

Create love with dry eyes

My health became a serious issue. I collapsed into a coma as I entered the hall. I spent the next 5 days in a great hospital suffering from no mobility, and great pain. The return to Canada was in a wheel chair and 4 weeks later was diagnosed to suffer from PMR. In December 2011, an invitation to celebrate the 55th anniversary of the MPLA in Luanda wasdeclined due to ongoing health issues. With more rest and healing time, the acupuncture from the fingers of Dr. Tran in Ottawa will enable a return to normal activity.

Signed in Ottawa February 2012, Jacques R. Roy

Appendix

Angola Historical Summary

•   In 1483, Portugal established a base at the Congo River, home of the Kongo State where the Ndongo and Lunda lived.

•   In 1575, Portugal established a base for the slave trade in Cabinda. The long coastline allowed another colonial power, the Dutch, to occupy Luanda from 1641 to 1648.

•   Portugal retook Luanda in 1648 and had little success in recovering lost territories. Full control does not come till the twentieth century.

•   Starting in the 1880s Canadian missionaries established a mission in the Bailundo area.

•   Portugal uses its colonial occupation to provide soldiers to the fascist cause during World War II. Angolans show up as cannon fodder on the battlefields in Egypt. The Salazar family, friendly with Spain's dictator Franco and Italy's Mussolini, are very happy with the war efforts of Germany and, given their ideologicalsimilarities, support and consolidate oppression all the way into Africa.

•   In 1951, Portugal gives Angola the status of an Overseas Province. Numerous anti-colonial efforts are brutally repressed, and world opinion turns a blind eye to the slave trade and the products of slave labour.

•   However, in 1956, the first Angolan doctor, Agostinho Neto, sonof a Methodist missionary, has been very outspoken in the anti- colonial movement. He gathers community leaders under one political party and establishes the *Movimento Popular de Libertation de Angola*—MPLA, the Popular Movement for the Liberation of Angola. On December 10th, Dr. Agostinho Neto is named president.

- Under colonialism there is an illiteracy rate of ninety-nine percent, an infant mortality of sixty percent, and an average life expectancy of twenty-six years. This is completely unacceptable for the MPLA. It is time to resist, and, given how Zambia, the Congo, and Kenya have turned out following their independence,a different ideological structure needs to be created.

- The mobilizing of anti-colonial forces is viewed by Portugal as a threat justifying military action to protect their "overseas provinces."

- On February 4, 1961, Dr. Neto is arrested and detained in Luanda's most secure jail. Led by the MPLA, the military prisons are attacked, and Portuguese repression unleashed. All blackssuspected of aiding the resistance are executed on the spot.

- "Many reports have been told by observers of helpless Africans, remote from the site of the revolution, and completely unaware of what it was all about, buried by the hundreds in the ground by bulldozers, and thrown into the Quanza River until it stank sothat chains were placed across it to catch the rotting corpses. . . Eyewitnesses tell of the inconceivable atrocities practiced on these Bantu people who were rounded up and slaughtered without trial, without a chance to say a word in their own defense, and with an almost complete lack of the most rudimentary human compassion." (*Angola Awake*, Ryerson Press, 1968, p. 53.)

- 1962—Dr. Neto is told by the Portuguese governor of Angola as he is loaded on a military aircraft, that he will never see Luanda again. Exiled to Belgian Congo, Neto attempts unsuccessfully to get together with Holden Roberto. Upon independence of French Congo, as Congo Brazzaville, he reforms the MPLA with eighty survivors of the Portuguese massacre.

- MPLA opens Uige and Cabinda military fronts.

- In 1964, the presence of Mobutu as dictator in Zaire, a puppet of the USA, helps to create the Revolutionary Government for Angola in Exile—GRAE. Its leader will be Holden Roberto, brother-in-law to Mobutu. His group will be guided by the CIA and will be renamed the *Front de Libertation National de Angola*—FNLA.

- Roberto is soon joined by Jonas Savimbi, an Angolan tribal leaderwho is a loose cannon and a psychopath. Roberto and Savimbi soon part company as Savimbi, who sees himself as a saviour of Angola, seeks out his own friends. His group is *Union National Independence Total de Liberation de Angola*—UNITA.

- His tribal and pro-colonial stance is not lost on the large influx ofsettlers, some 500,000 poor, illiterate peasants from Portugal, andthe Western businesses that have made profitable investments in Angola, attracted by plentiful resources and cheap labour (actually forced labour, but called "contract labour" for the apartheid mines and coffee plantations and other labour-intensive jobs).

- To teach "the pathetic, illiterate Angolan how to work [sic]," the Portuguese invents and introduces the *Mission de Civilization*— Mission to civilize. The Contract Labour Law is in effect and the anti-communist slogans appear.

- July 1, 1970—the three leaders, Dr. Neto, president of the MPLA (Angola), Amicar Cabral, secretary general of the PAIGC (GuineaBissau), and Marcelino dos Santo, vice-president of FRELIMO (Mozambique), are received by Pope Paul VI at the Holy See.

- Although no official photo is allowed, Portugal is furious at this meeting. Three "terrorists" (sic) will now be regarded as freedom fighters. They are legitimate spokespersons for their peoples onan international stage. There is no turning back.

- In early 1973, Canadian NGO SUCO takes seriously the needs ofthe liberation movement. SUCO Director Jean Pelletier, son of cabinet minister Gerald Pelletier, takes the lead and appoints Jacques Roy as liaison officer to the Liberation Movement.

- On April 25, 1974, the Portuguese military carry out the military coup, called the Coup of the Roses, and colonialism is officially over. The neo-colonial phase begins.

- Dr. Neto and his shadow cabinet, including Jose Eduardo dos Santos, heir apparent to Neto, are visiting Canada during this period. They are seeking Canadian assistance, are in contact with US officials, raising funds and awareness of the anti-colonial war. Neto appears before a Foreign Affairs Committee and later meets with Canadian Prime Minister Trudeau and his secretary, Ivan Head. This sets the stage for a future Canadian role in resolving the civil war. There is no contact with US officials.

- On January 15, 1975—Neto, Savimbi, and Roberto sign the Alvor agreement that sets November 11 as independence day.

- February 4, 1975—Dr.Neto returns to Luanda, fourteen years to the day since his exile. He has outlasted—outwilled—colonialism. More than one million Angolans are at the Luanda airport to see him fly in. The country celebrates; a national hero has returned.

- The stage is set for a long, bitter struggle, a country caught in the end of a cold war. MPLA is backed by the Soviet Union and the Organization of African Unity, minus the American puppets.

- FNLA is backed by the USA.

- UNITA is backed by the Angolan settlers, the USA, China, and apartheid South Africa.

- The FNLA from the north, UNITA from the centre, and, in collaboration with racist South Africa, from the south, join forcesin trying to extinguish the MPLA's hold on the capital, as the November deadline approaches.

- The MPLA survives and begins its defence of the country against the CIA, apartheid, and the blood diamonds that finance UNITAand the civil war.

- Spring of 1975—Kissinger, the 40 Committee and the CIA are putting together money and material for the "next Vietnam." John Stockwell is chosen to head the task force to run the war against the Angolan government. Soon he will understand the illegality and misinformation/disinformation of US strategy and learn a hard lesson. On April 1, 1978, he quits the Agency.

• November 11, 1975—MPLA declares independence and is recognized by the United Nations and most African States. The USA and South Africa join forces and refuse to recognize the newly acclaimed nation. They will support apartheid and minorityrule and facilitate military efforts against the MPLA-led government.

• In 1978, Publisher George J. McLeod of Toronto released the writings of CIA operative John Stockwell. *In Search of Enemies* isan unauthorized analysis by Stockwell of the US intervention in Angola and the senseless policy of propping up minority and illegal governments.

• In 1992, following the Lusaka Accords, elections are held and MPLA wins a fair election. Savimbi refuses to accept the result and goes back to the bush to continue his war of attrition. Senior members of UNITA split and take up positions with the Angola government.

• UN blue helmets are brought in to demilitarize UNITA andintegrate the UNITA fighters into the main army. The United Church of Canada continues to support UNITA.

• Savimbi, with the support of South African apartheid forces,establishes a southern front at Cuito Cuanavale. The Angolan government soldiers are overwhelmed, and introduce to the battle front Cuban troops that have been flown from Havana through Newfoundland Canada. This is Canada's contribution. This new military strategy defeats the apartheid/UNITA armies.

• Cuba, South Africa, and Angola negotiate and sign a peace settlement for Namibia.

• Cuba withdraws its troops.

• This sets up the release of ANC hero Nelson Mandela and elections for South Africa.

• The ANC have trained some 100,000 soldiers in military bases in Angola.

- The United Nations Blue Helmets are to disarm and help integrate UNITA soldiers. It is a fiasco, since Savimbi continues to massacre even his own soldiers.

- August 31, 1998—the Supreme Court of Angola suspends UNITA for failing to live up to the spirit and law of the Accords. UNITA is reconstituted, while Savimbi is expelled and further isolated.

- November 1998—Bill Graham, MP and Chair of Canada's Foreign Affairs Committee, is asked by Jacques Roy to involve Canada, to identify the flow of illegal diamonds from Angola that return as weapons for the illegal activities of UNITA. Graham starts the process. This is an historical step and a familiar role for Canada.

- January 1999—Canada takes up its seat on the Security Council and begins to look into the financing of the civil war through the illegal sale of "blood diamonds." Canada's United Nations Ambassador, Robert Fowler, heads to Angola and follows the trail of diamonds. They lead Fowler to Zaire, Cote d'Ivoire, Senegal, and the diamond bourses of Antwerp.

- Fowler reports to the UN Security Council in April 2000, and the Fowler Report is accepted unanimously in December of the same year. Canada is credited with identifying and drying up the funds for this twenty-six-year civil war.

- On September 21, ten days after two New York towers come down, Savimbi and sixty-seven other UNITA leaders are classified as terrorists, and severe sanctions are imposed that include freezing of bank accounts as well as travel restriction. UNITA has been officially banned.

- February 22, 2002—Savimbi is killed.

- April 4th is declared an official holiday called Peace and National Reconciliation.

- National reconstruction begins.

About the Author

Jacques Roy is the second-born in a French Canadian family from Kirkland Lake Ontario. His lifelong passion for justice and authentic independence for the former colonies of southern Africa, particularly his "adopted country," Angola, has kept him actively engaged in Canada and abroad.

An accomplished carpenter, furniture designer and fabricator, gardener, ESL/FSL teacher, energy consultant, journalist, professional speaker, and a Rotarian, Jacques still hopes the world will catch up to his whirlwind efforts. He continues to put into practice the words of his friend Dr. Neto, "Solve the problem."...

Jacques R. Roy received his diploma from the Northern Ontario Institute of Technology in 1965, he works as a plant engineer for Bell Telephone in Montreal in the same year.

Jacques went to Tanzania as a volunteer with CUSO, at the Institute of Technology. In Montreal, language training in Kiswahili, and African Affairs and Culture.

Arriving in Dar es Salaam on August 25, 1967, he began to teach.

Inducted into FAPLA on September 15, 1967, after meeting Dr. Neto, Head of the Angola Resistance MPLA. Dr. Neto needed radio communications for the war zones.

On October 1st, 1967, Dr. Neto received the plans and budget and forewarned against returning to the office, due to the threat of Assassination.

Jacque was nominated by the MAPLA's "Representative in Canada".

He was acknowledged as the MPLA's "representative in Canada" in November 1967 and established the National Organization African Relief Services Committee after moving to Burnaby, British Columbia.

A research team is established, to investigate foreign investment in Southern Africa and dispatched to the MPLA , Frelimo,Guinea B, ANC, Swapo, and Zanu, and established the result.

In December, a teaching position opened at Burnaby Central High School.

On September 1968, Jacques returned to Montreal to assist with Quebec NGO's plans for boycotts of Angolan coffee, and South African products oranges, wines and athletes.

Coffee boycott became successful within 30 days.

An ANC intelligence gathering mission started in November 1970, Colleen arrived in Zambia and this was the initial step in creating a cover, to enter South Africa.

On February 15th, Colleen and Jacques met the ZIT representative to end the teaching contract.

They got married and completed the first mission via Botswana and Rhodesia. The second expedition, the

"honeymoon" and the marriage continued in Kruger Park.

Colleen returned to Ottawa, while Jacques traveled to Angola to do a documentary film on the use of napalm, chemical defoliation and daily life.

Angola establishes an embassy in Ottawa and appoints Jacques R. Roy as a "council expert" advisor.

The independence of Angola is established on April 25 when the military overthrew the fascist. Jacque enters Luanda with his security guard and open an office at 149 Avenue de Liberation. And asked by Dr. Neto to go back to Canada to celebrate November 11th, Independence Day, in Ottawa, Montreal, and Toronto.

Testimonials

We . . . recognize and [are] most grateful for the support and contribution to the struggle for independence as you have adapted and served the objectives of our march towards independence.

A diplomat, an educator, a practical man, sensitive to the world view, an internationalist. Your efforts provided our 1974 visit to Canada as a very successful diplomatic mission.

Jacques is our friend and is welcome at all times in Angola.

Dr. Agostinho Neto, President of the newly independent Republic of Angola, 1975.

Jacques Roy—Canada has provided invaluable skills and knowledge to the A.N.C.

He knows our objectives and adapts extremely well to the changes of our struggle against Apartheid.

He is a trusted friend, an ally and compatriot.

Jacques has shown persistence, dedication and provided valuable results.

Chris Hani, Thabo Mbeki, Lusaka 1972

Mr. Roy . . . has a considerable amount of natural energy, initiative and drive. I know he has been putting his knowledge and interest in electronics to good use . . . wish him well—including success in securing any position for which he applies.

Michael Sinclair, CUSO Field Director, 1968

Jacques produced an excellent documentary on the struggle in Angola . . . unique experience and story told with a purpose . . .

So impressed that I loaned my Cinema House for a week in Old Montreal for a one-week showing of this historical document. Film was well received.

Rock Demers, film producer, Montreal, 1973, Governor General Award, 1998.

Jacques Roy knows our needs very well. He is mandated to implement these.

Dr. Albino Malungo, Minister, Angola, September, 1998.

Greatly appreciated your work, co-operation . . . in particular your understanding in regards to our problems and difficulties.

Paulo Jorge, Secretary External Relations, MPLA, 1972

Invited Jacques Roy and his film on Angola . . . class found the session most productive through his film . . . through his film they were able to get a grasp of propaganda on a global scale. A chance we seldom have. Mr. Roy's film is a fine example of this . . . value of his work for classes, public meetings alert us to the present and future conditions.

Professor Dennis Murphy, M.A., University of Loyola, Montreal, 1973

The film "Angola Liberation and Development by Jacques Roy brought a great . . . most promising . . . very pleased to help in its distribution.

Robert Forget, Directeur, Videographe, Montreal 1973

I enjoyed immensely meeting with you again . . . your dynamism is infectious and your dedication most laudable.

Yvan L. Head, Ottawa 1987, Former Secretary to Prime Minister Trudeau.

During his stay with us, Mr. Roy has exhibited intense and energetic commitment to the assessment of our needs in both energy conservation and organizational procedures.

He has imparted a great deal of knowledge and practical advice and recognize . . . lasting benefits.

R.I. Whitfield, Director of Operations, Half Moon Club Jamaica, 1986

Executive of the General Council was impressed with Roy's story and voted to give $5000 . . . to assist in the carrying out of an effective educational program in Canada. United Church of Canada, 1972

I have found Jacques to have a keen commitment to justice and independence . . . with a wealth of practical skills and connections which he mustered in aid of the Angolan people.

He has devoted over a period of 30 years much of his considerable energy despite enormous odds . . . to the welfare and emancipation of the Angolan [people] and their economic development.

Rev. Garth Legge, United Church of Canada, 1998

You have dedicated years of involvement to Angola. Your diplomatic relations combined with your security clearance from the Angola gov't as well as your duties as a Canadian Representative of social and demining programs for the Angolan gov't, have provided you with a very valuable core knowledge and a keen understanding of the issues facing Angola.

Therefore I am pleased to recommend you for a position on the Expert Panel with the Security Council Committee.

Jim Flaherty, MPP Whitby Ajax, July 5, 1999

Jacques Roy, aka Quidado, is a great Rotarian. Most Rotarians prepare the parade . . . many are in the parade . . . Quidado leads the parade.

Jean Guy St. Arnaud, Rotary member, Hull/Gatineau Quebec

I would like to thank you for your initiative in organizing a meeting of all the service clubs on this important issue. The need for a crisis shelter in Ajax-Pickering has existed for 5 years. Our compliments to Jacques Roy for chairing the meeting of October 19, 2000.

On Behalf of the Board of Directors **Jackie Gibbs**, President, The Ajax-Pickering Women's Center Inc.

Dear Jacques, I was sorry to learn that you have submitted your resignation to the club. Rotary Club of West Ottawa.

I will miss you. The club will miss you . . . in the meantime, keep writing and inspiring people.

Jack Troughton, President '74-75. Past Governor 7040, 94-95. PHF `79 Paul Harris Fellow+8, RBF.

WOW!! What a story . . . the section of you and Colleen in South Africa has the making of a TV show!

Jack Troughton, President '74-75. Past Governor 7040, 94-95. PHF '79 Paul Harris Fellow+8, RBF.

Dear Mr. Roy, On behalf of the staff and students of Sinclair Secondary School, I wish to thank you for your presentation and for sharing your experiences. It was a most interesting and and informative session. Again, many thanks for your time and effort.

Sincerely, **Kim McPhee** and STAR Students Mayor of Whitby

2008 Photos

Jacques with Luiza and Vicente, hosts for 2008 visit.

Throwing Jacques a 65th birthday.

Left to right; Professor Viera LIVEGA, Ambassador Kimbata, Jacques, General Quina retired, Secretary General of LIVEGA.

Angola youth participating in polio campaign. Photo by Jacques

Jacques reunites with General Sparticus Monimambu 30 years after interviewing him in Dar es Salaam. He is now Ambassador Filipe Monimambu. We had a great reunion with traditional Angolan food at his humble house some 40 kilometres from the capital of Luanda.

Angolans were captured, tagged and tied together on a raft and sent down the Kwanza River to be picked up by the Portuguese military. This is the origin of the expression "sold down the river". More than 5 million suffered this journey.

2009 Photos

Angolan Minister of Culture Rosa Cruz e Silva peruses *Tout près de l'oubli.*

Journal de Angola, September 26, 2009. "I delivered the news to Netoon April 25th".

2012 Photo

Jacques with Ambassador Agostinho Tavares da Silva Neto, February2012. Photo by Amanda Spears

Letter of endorsement by Agostinho Tavares Ambassador of the Republic of Angola in Canada—Ottawa

Mr. Jacques Roy's book, Don't Quit – Don't Cry, represents a powerful tool of reflection for people of all ages, peace, freedom, liberty and democracy lovers, in search for a better and righteous world for everyone, regardless of political, economic, social, cultural and religious status.

The struggle for liberty of the oppressed people and dominated by authoritarian and colonial regimes has no boundaries; thus, our friend and fellow Jacques Roy, while a young man, joined the movements for liberty in Africa, to support the Angolan nationalists, who were fighting for a just cause: the Angolan independence.

The book is a fair testimony of men of good will, who sacrificed their lives and of their own families, to fight, side by side, with other people around the world, to end the oppression, exploitation in order to conquer the legitimate right to life, well-being, liberty and independency.

Mr. Jacques Roy's great example should inspire the new generation, either in Angola or in Canada, in a way to contribute for the reconstruction of a better and harmonious society, leaving behind the selfishness and the imposition of factors that goes against democratic values.

I would like to take the opportunity to congratulate my fellow friend Mr. Jacques for his brilliant soul and to encourage him to maintain his humanitarian spirit and to pursue the liberty of all oppressed people around the world.

Best regards

Agostinho Tavares

Ambassador of the Republic of Angola in Canada—Ottawa